D0569924

Grandparents

Chicken Soup for the Soul: Grandparents
101 Stories of Love, Laughs and Lessons Across the Generations
Amy Newmark

Published by Chicken Soup for the Soul, LLC www.chickensoup.com
Copyright ©2019 by Chicken Soup for the Soul, LLC. All Rights Reserved.

The publisher gratefully acknowledges the many publishers and individuals who granted Chicken Soup for the Soul permission to reprint the cited material.

Front cover photos: woman and baby courtesy of iStockphoto.com/LattaPictures (©LattaPictures), man and boy playing guitar courtesy of iStockphoto.com/ baranozdemir (©baranozdemir), woman with graduate courtesy of iStockphoto.com/ IPGGutenbergUKLtd (©IPGGutenbergUKLtd) and man with girl on bike courtesy of iStockphoto.com/Paul Bradbury (©Paul Bradbury)
Back cover photo courtesy of iStockphoto.com/kali9 (©kali9)
Interior photo courtesy of iStockphoto.com/Nadezhda1906 (©Nadezhda1906)
Photo of Amy Newmark courtesy of Susan Morrow at SwickPix

Cover and Interior by Daniel Zaccari

Distributed to the booktrade by Simon & Schuster. SAN: 200-2442

Publisher's Cataloging-In-Publication Data
(Prepared by The Donohue Group, Inc.)

Names: Newmark, Amy, compiler.
Title: Chicken soup for the soul : grandparents : 101 stories of love,
    laughs and lessons across the generations / [compiled by] Amy Newmark.
Other Titles: Grandparents : 101 stories of love, laughs and lessons
    across the generations
Description: [Cos Cob, Connecticut] : Chicken Soup for the Soul, LLC,
    [2019]
Identifiers: ISBN 9781611599862 | ISBN 9781611592863 (ebook)
Subjects: LCSH: Grandparent and child--Literary collections. | Grandparent
    and child--Anecdotes. | Grandparents--Literary collections. |
    Grandparents--Anecdotes. | LCGFT: Anecdotes.
Classification: LCC HQ759.9 .C45 2019 (print) | LCC HQ759.9 (ebook) | DDC
    306.8745--dc23

Library of Congress Control Number: 2018965074

PRINTED IN THE UNITED STATES OF AMERICA
on acid∞free paper

25 24 23 22 21 20 19   01 02 03 04 05 06 07 08 09 10 11

Grandparents

101 Stories of Love, Laughs and Lessons Across the Generations

Amy Newmark

Chicken Soup for the Soul, LLC
Cos Cob, CT

Changing your world one story at a time®
www.chickensoup.com

Table of Contents

❶

~The Joy of Becoming a Grandparent~

❷

~Grand & Great Laughs~

3

~Treasured Moments & Memories~

4

~Through the Eyes of a Child~

5

~That Mutual Unconditional Love~

❻

~Gifts & Gratitude~

❼

~Play Dates~

❽

~Role Models~

❾

~Modern Grandparenting~

The Joy of Becoming a Grandparent

Who I Want to Be

Proper names are poetry in the raw.
Like all poetry they are untranslatable.
~W.H. Auden

We learned we were going to be grandparents via FaceTime during Thanksgiving dinner. The room erupted in laughter and happy tears. When the commotion died down, my eldest son asked, "So, Mom, what are the grandkids going to call you?"

What a good question! Through the years, I had considered what I wanted my grandmother name to be, always knowing that ultimately I would answer to whatever this first grandchild chose to call me. It was important to me that my name didn't cause confusion with the assorted grandmothers and great-grandmothers within the family, and many of the traditional names like Grandmama, Granny, and Grandmother were in use. Besides, those didn't feel right for me. I wanted something that felt like a name, not a title.

I thought that Lolli and Pop were possible contenders for my husband and me, but I was told "Not happening!" by the expectant parents, with all the siblings in agreement. YaYa and PaPa were shot down, as were Tootsie and Pop. Finally, they decided that Papa had merit. My husband had his name! I, however, was still nameless.

At Christmas, I still hadn't found a name that fit, so the kids decided to get more involved. Instead of asking what I wanted to be called, they asked what kind of grandmother I wanted to be.

Significant. I want to be significant in my grandchildren's lives. I want to bake cookies, tell bedtime stories, go to school programs, and rock them to sleep. When we are miles apart, I want these precious children of my children to know my heart as well as my voice. I want to be one of the "God blesses" in their prayers.

Adventurous. I dream of watching butterflies sipping nectar from a daylily while listening to a little voice describe the colors on its wings. What fun we will have running barefoot through the grass and sliding down hills on flattened cardboard boxes, imagining that we are on a runaway train or an airplane going to a far-off land. The living room will be a wonderful place to build castles and forts from blankets and cardboard boxes, acting out scenes from favorite books or our imaginations.

Sensitive. I want my grandchildren's emotions to be safe with me. I want to share belly laughs, whisper hopes and dreams, and chase monsters under the bed. I want to listen more and talk less, being there for my grandchildren.

Spiritual. I want to make memories of bedtime prayers and Bible stories, getting ready for church and making sure there is an offering to put in the plate. I want to talk about heaven while lying in the hammock, looking at clouds, and wondering together if the streets of gold are shiny or dull.

Youthful. There is no better way to look at the world than through a child's eyes. I want to watch an ant on the ground and make up stories about what he is doing and where he is going. I want to giggle while playing peek-a-boo and laugh every time a big splash is made in the bathtub full of bubbles. I want to be the grandmother who plays inside and outside, experiencing joy with each grandchild, according to his or her personality and interests.

After dreaming out loud about what kind of grandmother I wanted to be, my adult kids decided to put three names in a hat and randomly select my name. They made a big production out of it.

My name couldn't be more perfect. They call me Sassy.

— Sharon Carpenter —

Wrapped Around My Heart

*It is as grandmothers that our mothers
come into the fullness of their grace.*
~Christopher Morley

I always thought becoming a grandmother would be a nice experience, but it wasn't a huge priority on my bucket list. When my only child, David, and his girlfriend, Line, became engaged, both were in their early thirties. They weren't in any hurry to set a date, let alone have a baby, so I simply accepted that no new branch would be sprouting on our family tree. It didn't matter to me as long as they were happy.

One morning in early December, my husband and I awoke to knocking on our bedroom door, followed by my son's voice urging us to get up. He had an emergency key to our home and had let himself in.

Panicking, we tumbled out of bed and ran to the kitchen, terrified that something horrible had happened.

"What's wrong?" I croaked.

"Nothing," David assured me. "I wanted to give you an early Christmas present." He pushed a package toward me. "Open it," he grinned.

"But we agreed not to exchange gifts this year," I protested. "You just bought the house, and we..."

"Humor me and open it, Mom!" he insisted, beaming.

I did as he instructed and pulled out what I thought was a flash drive for my computer. Staring at it quizzically, I handed it to my husband, Don, who looked at it, and then surprised me by whooping with joy!

"Merry Christmas!" my son chortled happily, and I forced a smile. "Thank you so much!" I murmured, still puzzled. Though it was sweet of him to get us something, I was a little baffled by his choice.

"Uh — honey," Don murmured when he finally noticed my perplexed expression. "You have no idea what this is, do you?"

"Of course I know what it is!" I insisted.

"And you're not happy?" David asked, his face beginning to shadow with disappointment.

"Why wouldn't I be?" I replied. "It's a very thoughtful gift. Even though the one I have still has so much room for data on it, a back-up spare..."

Their loud laughter interrupted what I was about to say, and I stared at them both, becoming more and more confused.

"Sweetie, it's a pregnancy stick — and it's positive!" my husband chuckled.

I felt myself flushing at my ignorance. Sure, I knew they existed, but I had never actually seen one up close. My own pregnancy was confirmed much differently.

"Oh!" I breathed, and rushed up to hug and congratulate my son. I was glad I said all the right words, yet something was missing. Where was the delirious excitement I'd always observed in others when they received a similar announcement? I knew my reaction was lukewarm compared to that of most people. Even my normally laid-back husband was doing a victory dance across the kitchen floor as if he were somehow personally responsible for the news.

I was secretly thankful that Line had a previous commitment and could not be there for my lukewarm reaction. She would have been terribly hurt by it. Luckily, my son was still amused by my naiveté over the pregnancy stick, so my strange behavior went unnoticed.

I spent the next few months dutifully saying and doing what was expected of a grandmother-to-be. I worried when Line developed gestational diabetes and asked about her results with genuine concern after every checkup. I helped plan a baby shower. I watched and smiled appropriately when the ultrasound video confirmed they were having a little girl. I tossed names back and forth until we all settled on "Kara" as being the perfect one. I even enjoyed selecting adorable frilly outfits and intriguing little rattles and teething rings. Still, that doting-grandma microchip that should have been activated months earlier to make me babble with excitement remained dormant. I was pleased, but still not strutting with delight. My apathy distressed me.

Kara made her appearance two weeks early. I suspected she might. Line mentioned a mild backache several times that day. She chalked it off to working a little too diligently on the nursery, but I recognized the signs. I whispered to my son to keep an eye on her. I was sure it would happen soon.

That evening, we received the call, and after only three hours of labor, Kara's very first picture arrived via text. My husband stared at it blissfully while I wondered why hospitals didn't clean up newborns anymore.

We had to wait until visiting hours the next day to see her. While Don paced, car keys rattling annoyingly in his hand, I did housework. I was certainly anxious to see our new little arrival, but again not as eager as I should have been.

I'd confided my low-key emotions to a few close friends who assured me I'd change once my granddaughter was born. I truly hoped so. I already loved her, sight unseen, but it wasn't enough. I wanted to feel that overpowering elation — that urge to jump out of the car before we even parked so I could rush to the maternity ward and cuddle this newcomer. My granny meter, however, remained stuck on its tepid setting.

Instead, I trotted behind my husband, who was enthusiastic enough for both of us. I followed him to the elevator, and then down the sterile hall that led to Line's room.

David was holding Kara when we entered, eyes shining with pride as he cradled her close. Before I could speak, he placed her into my arms. I stared down at the tiny, sleeping bundle nestled inside the folds of her blanket.

I studied her perfect features and stroked the now-clean silky skin of her face. Long lashes rested against cheeks that looked as if they'd been gently tapped by rose-petal dust. Barely visible brows furrowed ever so slightly while her lips puckered in instinctive sucking motions.

I folded back the soft flannel to expose the hands resting on her chest, touching each finger gingerly so as not to disturb her. As I did so, she grasped my finger and opened her eyes.

They say babies can't focus or smile at that age, but no one can convince me that her gaze didn't meet mine, or that her mouth didn't curve into a smile before she sank back into a peaceful slumber.

My husband asked to hold her, and an alien possessiveness overtook me. A thick lump formed in my throat. Suddenly, every long-hibernating grandmother gene inside me awakened. All I wanted was to continue holding that precious child in my arms and never let go.

From then on, I reveled in every moment I spent with Kara, patiently rocking her through colic, changing diapers without revulsion while her own father gagged, feeding her from ridiculously designed bottles, and inhaling her sweet baby scent. As she became more aware, I began to see the world all over again through the awestruck eyes of a child.

Grandmotherly pride took its time in finding my heart, but I'm grateful it finally hit its mark, showing me how foolish I was to ever think I could easily live without that little baby who smiled her way into my life.

— Marya Morin —

The Power to Heal

Forgiveness does not change the past,
but it does enlarge the future.

~Paul Boese

My wife and I were getting ready to board a plane at our local airport. The gate attendants had just begun the boarding process when my phone rang. It was one of my estranged sons.

I looked down at my phone in disbelief. Answering his unexpected call, I was met with only static. *Oh, well,* I thought. *It must have been a butt dial.* Nevertheless, I texted him from my seat in the plane. "You just called me. I suspect that it was an accidental call. I hope you are well."

Several years earlier, in a life-changing cycling accident, I sustained a traumatic brain injury. Like so many others, my personality changed. And when it did, my sons backed away from a dad they no longer knew. The loss of my children was the biggest casualty of my injury. Over the years, I still texted my sons regularly just to let them know they were never far from my heart. My texts went unanswered for years. I was accustomed to it by then.

I never expected what happened next. "Dad, I did call you. We need to talk." His reply to my text left me staring at my phone feeling bewildered.

By this time, the flight attendants had announced that phones needed to be in airplane mode. We had a very short layover a few hours later. Through most of that first flight, I vacillated between being excited that my son had finally reached out to me, to being afraid that I was setting myself up for even more loss. It was a very long three-hour flight.

"I'll call him back when we get to our gate," I shared with my wife when we landed in Minneapolis. Unknown to either of us, the Minneapolis airport is the size of a small city. We got to the gate mere minutes before they swung the cabin doors shut on our next flight.

I called my son and heard the first words he'd said to me in a very long time. "My daughter was born six weeks ago. I am now a father, and you are a grandfather." My heart stopped. Not only did my son reach out to me, but he came with news I had never even considered. "We need to get together and talk," he said, his voice full of emotion.

We were again told to put our phones in airplane mode. In this life-changing moment, I paid no attention to the flight attendants. By this time, the pictures started showing up on my phone as my son texted me photo after photo of my new granddaughter. I sat by the window on our next flight in tears, looking at the pictures of a newborn baby girl over and over again.

Later that same week, when we were back home in New Hampshire, we got together at the invitation of my son. For a couple of hours, on what was perhaps the best day of my entire life, I held my granddaughter, met my son's family, and talked. That precious day was more than two years ago.

Over the past couple of years, our lives have changed in unimaginable ways. For most of that time, I watched my granddaughter one day a week. I watched her grow from a newborn into a beautiful baby. I watched her learn to crawl. I was there when she took her first steps, and I have been blessed to simply be part of her life. She calls me "Papa" now and smiles when she sees me, which melts my heart.

My daughter-in-law has said on many occasions that my granddaughter has healed other strained relationships. This tiny, wondrous human being has been a miracle child to me, and to others as well.

Earlier this year, my son's family grew again with the birth of our new grandson. My son recently purchased a home in our town, and not a week goes by that I don't see my grandchildren. For some, it's a pretty straight line from being a parent to becoming a grandparent. But for many people like me, there are twists and turns in the road. Somehow, against seemingly insurmountable odds, we have found our way — and it started with the birth of one precious granddaughter.

— David A. Grant —

The Pre-Announcement

Children are the rainbow of life.
Grandchildren are the pot of gold.
~Irish Blessing

Nowadays when grandbabies are in the making, the first announcement is often "We're trying" instead of "We're expecting." How are we prospective grandparents supposed to react to that?

I remember the phone call from California to our home in Massachusetts when my daughter, Star, and her husband, Joseph, announced that they were now "trying" for a baby. Oh, there was a lot of happy hollering from us. "Congratulations! Best of luck! How exciting!"

In the days that followed, I cruised through baby departments to nose the cotton softness of pinks and blues, eye the Beatrix Potter plates, and stroke lace-framed bonnets. In no time flat, good news would fly down the pike, or so I thought.

Always, my phone calls to Star began with, "Well? And?"

But several weeks passed, and then a number of months.

There's an unspoken agreement in the face of no results: Shut your mouth. It's a long road for couples anxious to reach Destination Babyland. Why add to their disappointment by bringing it up? Since my daughter's anxiety was just under the surface, I erased all baby talk from my conversations. I trained myself to expect nothing by banishing the subject from my daily thoughts. My frequent jaunts to baby departments ended.

"I don't belong here yet," I whispered to the footie pajamas during my farewell tour.

Then one day, Star called with the long-yearned-for news flash: "I'm pregnant!"

Oh, joy. The blissful shores of Grandma Land have been sighted. Yet I felt strangely numb. I had done such a dandy job of stifling myself that now I couldn't pop my cork.

"Are you sure?" I said calmly.

Also trained to expect nothing, my daughter's reaction mirrored my own disbelief.

"Mom, it doesn't feel real," she whispered.

We lowered our voices like convicts about to make a prison break. We needed signs that all systems were go.

I said, "Oh, give it time. Carrying a front-loaded watermelon will change all that."

"Mom, I wish I felt morning sickness or something, just so I could believe it."

I was the Wise Woman instructing the Little Grasshopper on the mystic ways of motherhood.

"Hey, don't wish for that. I puked seventeen times before 7:00 in the morning when I was pregnant with you. Food was the worst. One time, there was a billboard sign with a Big Mac, and your dad had to pull over on the freeway so I could throw up."

We exhaled and cautiously, slowly tiptoed into topics: maternity styles, nutritious eating, and "how the heck something that big comes out of you."

When we were about to hang up, we remained somewhat reserved. My daughter and I were so disciplined in locking the idea of pregnancy into a compartment that we couldn't jimmy it open. The unreality remained. Yet we reassured each other that the moment would arrive when utter and permanent joy would sink in.

For me, it happened on my way to the restroom. I was at Macy's when I passed through the baby section. Casually flipping through the infant racks, I was charmed by miniature fire trucks and dinosaurs, but it was the baby pink bunny suit that did me in.

Suddenly, I hunched over the tiny hangers with tears streaming down my face in a shoulder-bobbing, crying jag of joy. Other customers tiptoed around me as I clutched the matching bunny hat and blubbered, "Oh, my God! I finally belong here."

— Suzette Martinez Standring —

A Most Awesome Miracle

Just when you think you know all that love is...
along come the grandchildren.
~Author Unknown

One sunny, warm spring day a few years ago, one of my sons called me. "Hey, Mom. Can we come over for dinner on Sunday?"

Of course I said yes. Dinners with our three kids aren't something we do every week, but it's not uncommon. Still, they're usually more spur-of-the-moment than planned ahead.

"Got some news for you," he told me.

"What is it?"

"Tell you Sunday. Bye."

It was Thursday. He couldn't pique my curiosity and then make me wait three days for information. I called him back. He didn't answer. Instead, I got an immediate text telling me I had to wait until Sunday.

Over the next few days, my husband Rick and I offered ideas to each other about "the news." A new job? He and his long-time girlfriend were getting married? He couldn't be moving away, right? Our sons both lived about a half-hour drive away, and our daughter's college was only a couple hours west of us.

Those three days felt like ten. Finally, Michael and Sarah arrived on Sunday afternoon. Trevor, our older son, was already there. Our daughter, Nicole, came home for the weekend and stuck around for dinner and "the news."

Alerted by our Golden Retriever that a car had rolled up the driveway, Rick and I met them outside. Hugs were exchanged before we asked what was up. Michael said, "After dinner."

Oh. No. I shook my head at him. "I'm not feeding you until you spill it."

He breathed deeply and sighed. "Fine." In the foyer, he focused quietly on Sarah as she rummaged through her purse. We waited impatiently, joined by Trevor and Nicole. Finally, she removed a piece of paper and unfolded it. It was an 8 ½ x 11 sheet of crude, shadowy photos. I'd seen such images before, but they still took a moment to process.

It was a sonogram. Of a developing little human. And it was three months along.

Rick said, "When are you getting married?"

"Um, I don't know," Michael said. Sarah shook her head.

Rick let it drop after I stepped on his foot.

The pregnancy went smoothly, and the following October, Rick and I got *the* phone call. We headed for the hospital.

After an hour or so, a nurse came into the room bearing a handful of red and yellow wristbands. "Who gets the red ones?" she asked Michael.

"Me. And her and her." He pointed at Sarah's mom and me.

The nurse attached the appropriate band to each person in the room. I asked what they were for. "Yellow bands can be on the floor, but will have to leave the room soon. With a red band, you can stay for the delivery."

The privilege stunned me. I got that little pain behind my eyes—the one you get when tears are gathering, and you don't want them falling out. This was a joyous, wonderful occasion, and even happy tears weren't welcome.

At 4:30 a.m., after those of us with red bands had snoozed a bit while a nurse kept constant watch over mom and unborn babe, the doctor arrived, and things got serious. I warned the nurse my son didn't do well at the sight of blood.

"I'm staying at her head," he said. The nurse scooted a chair behind him, just in case.

Having had three Cesarean sections, I'd never been present for this kind of birthing. I wasn't about to turn away.

It was riveting. It was amazing. Our first grandchild, Michelle, came to us at six pounds, seven ounces, alert and interested in the world around her. She cried out only once as the nurse diapered her and settled her into an incubator. She moved her eyes to take in what she could of the room and the people in it. We all talked to her, and she seemed to recognize each separate voice, as if she remembered hearing it before.

I stayed until evening, taking my turn at holding Michelle, cooing to her, and rocking her. Other family members came and went. She slept peacefully through all of it, waking only for nourishment and diaper changes.

Eventually, I forced myself to leave. At home, I fell into bed and slept for nearly fourteen hours. I lay down smiling and awoke grinning. As I'd slept, the whole experience had played out for me in a dream, just like the real deal and in living color.

Michelle is two years old now. She's smart, friendly, happy and fun. She's sweet and beautiful. She's a precocious, little daredevil. She trusts blindly and often knows things the adults around her don't. For instance, when she flies, with no notice, from the sixth step up, she knows somebody will catch her! (So far, she's not wrong.)

I hope she knows we'll always be there to catch her, even if her jump — or fall — has nothing to do with height.

Our granddaughter spends a lot of time with family members on both sides. She has sleepovers with Rick and me frequently, and also with Nicole, who moved close to home after graduating (not for us, but for Michelle).

Maybe Rick and I will be graced with more grandchildren; maybe not. But for the rest of my life and beyond, I will be grateful for the gift Michelle's mom and dad granted me the day I watched my granddaughter take her first breath in this life.

I believe astounding wonders happen every day. Some we notice;

most we don't. But in the middle of the night a couple years ago, I had the great honor of witnessing an unforgettable, most awesome miracle.

—Julie Phayer—

Baby Lessons

Grandchildren fill a space in your heart
you never knew was empty.
~Author Unknown

An only child with no children, I didn't know anything about babies. If they didn't bark, wag their tails and poop in the back yard, I had no clue. Then my twenty-three-year-old step-daughter, Ann, decided to leave her husband. We invited her to live with us until she found a job and an apartment.

Ann was going to drive from Texas to our home in Virginia with her nine-month-old baby. But I was attending my father's family reunion in Chattanooga the next week, so I suggested she break up her trip by joining us there.

Poor Ann had to drive with the windows open in the August heat as her car's A/C was broken. And then she spent an extra two hours getting lost on the way to my parents' house. But when she finally arrived in a sweaty tank top and cutoffs, we met my grandchild and my parents' great-grandchild, an adorable little girl with big hazel eyes and wispy, light-brown curls. She wore only a diaper and tiny pierced earrings.

Kayla.

"Oh, Ann, she's beautiful." I hugged them both.

Ann handed Kayla to me. I balanced her against my shoulder. Whoa, she was heavier than I expected. Her little arms encircled my neck. My awkwardness didn't seem to bother her.

Daddy was enchanted. He'd always wanted grandchildren, but all he'd gotten from me were grand-dogs. He was recovering from a leg injury while we were there, and his doctor told him to stay off his feet as much as possible. Almost every time he sat in his recliner, he perched Kayla in his lap. I snapped pictures of them as he put red sunglasses on her. They were so big they almost swallowed her tiny face. Daddy laughed until his eyes teared.

The night before I was scheduled to fly home, my husband called. "You know, you could take Kayla on the plane with you. She's too young to need a ticket."

"Oh, my god, Ed. I can't handle a baby on a plane all by myself. I've never even babysat."

"You'll be fine."

"I don't think so. Besides, Ann wouldn't want to leave Kayla alone with me."

"That'd be better than her dealing with the twelve-hour drive — especially with no A/C."

To my surprise, Ann liked the idea. I swallowed hard.

My flight was scheduled for 6:00 p.m. Ann left early that morning, so she'd be in Virginia before we arrived. She left the stroller with me for the airport. She had piled about thirty diapers and eight bottles of milk on the counter.

"Am I gonna need all that stuff?" I asked my mother as we sat in the breezeway's swing with Kayla.

"I don't think so," she said.

I sighed and shook my head. "How on earth am I gonna do this?"

"Don't worry. I'll help you."

Baby lesson 101 — diaper changing. We placed Kayla on a towel spread on the bed. She kicked her legs as my mother unwrapped the diaper.

"Now, this looks easy. First disposable diaper I've ever seen," said my mother as she pulled apart the Velcro tabs. "Not like the old days. When you were a baby, we used cloth diapers and big pins."

I struggled to straighten the new diaper under Kayla's wiggling body. "What if I had squirmed around like this?"

"You might have gotten stuck."

"Ouch. I'm sure glad I won't have to use pins with her."

Thank goodness for my mother's help. She hadn't taken care of a baby in forty-three years, but I guessed it was sort of like riding a bike. We fed Kayla some yucky-looking green food and bathed her.

I could never tell if Kayla was wet or not, so I changed her numerous times that day. And on the flight, I wouldn't even accept a Diet Coke from the flight attendant. What if I had to go to the bathroom? How did mothers with babies use public restrooms?

Kayla's first plane ride was perfect — no fussing or crying. Whew! I'd sat next to some pretty loud, unhappy babies on planes. I felt lucky.

In Charlotte, I waited until everyone got off the plane before I lugged Kayla and our bags to the front. I smiled at the flight attendant by the door. "I'd like to get the stroller I gate-checked, please."

"I'm so sorry," she said, "we already sent it to your connecting flight."

Panic set in. "Oh, no. How am I gonna get her and all this stuff to the other concourse?"

"Don't worry. I'll call for assistance."

An electric cart soon arrived. Kayla's eyes widened, and she giggled as we zoomed past travelers on our way to our connecting flight.

We arrived at the gate just before they boarded the plane. This time, we were seated next to a middle-aged man in the window seat. He smiled and offered to hold my bags as I settled Kayla in the middle seat and buckled my seatbelt.

During the flight, I cuddled her in my lap to feed her. She sucked away at one of her many bottles. I sighed in contentment. This wasn't so hard after all.

The man touched my arm. "Excuse me, Miss," he whispered. "There's no milk in that bottle. It's empty."

I stifled an embarrassed laugh and thanked him.

When we landed, the flight attendant waited with the stroller for me. As I struggled to hold Kayla and push the piled-up stroller toward the waiting area, I spotted Ed and Ann. "Look, sweetie, there's Mommy."

I handed Kayla to her mother. "Ann, she was so good."

Relief. I had delivered her safely to her mom. Later that night, Ann said, "Kayla had a diaper rash before I left. Now it looks like it's completely gone."

I just smiled. Exhausted, I fell into bed after my crash course in babies.

The next day, I told a friend about my experience with Kayla.

"You don't know anything about babies," she said.

"I do now," I said with a new sense of pride.

Back in Tennessee, my father died four days later. I'd never given him a grandchild, but I was thankful that he'd spent his last week enjoying his great-granddaughter.

The experience jump-started my close bond with Kayla. I'd never been a mother. But that week, I became a grandmother.

— Linda Carol Cobb —

There's a Person in There

A grandfather is someone with silver
in his hair and gold in his heart.
~Author Unknown

I didn't mean to get involved with the kids, really. It was kind of like how I ended up being the family-dog guy. When we were dating, Kathy asked me to walk the dog, so I did. I didn't fumble it too badly, and bingo bango bongo, I became the dog guy. I walked the dogs everywhere and always had them on my lap. There's one there now, by the way.

When the first grandbaby came along, and Kathy was volunteered to take care of him one day a week, and then two, I really didn't think I would play much of an active role. I had never had kids; Kathy and I had married when hers were grown. I thought that ship had sailed. A baby would never be spitting up on my shoulder.

Then Kathy got tired and busy. I don't even know what the specific trigger was, but one day she asked if I could hold Harrison for a little while. Reluctantly, I agreed, took the little meatloaf — I mean, baby — and walked gingerly around the house.

He lived — that first time I gave Kathy a break. If we're grading, I deserved a C-.

The next time he was in our home, Kathy wanted a little longer break to get dinner ready. The transition went a little smoother. I held him more like, well, not a person, but say, a cat, and less like a glass football. My grade rose to a C+.

The third time was the real test. The first two times, Harrison was largely asleep. We just transferred him from one warm shoulder to another, and I managed to take the handoff without fumbling him. The third time, he wasn't as passive. In fact, he was downright squawky. He was fussing and crying, and Kathy handed him off more from frustration than because she had anything she needed to do. "Here. See if you can get him quiet."

I walked around the house, rocking and shushing him like every sitcom parent on television, and I was 100 percent unsuccessful. Rock rock rock, wah wah wah. Shush shush shush. Wah wah wah. Well, crap. Since other people in the house were sleeping, and the weather was nice, I decided to step outside with Harrison.

"There, there. Let's go out here and see if…" I didn't even get a chance to finish my spiel. As soon as we were outside, Harrison was quiet.

Since he'd been fussing and squawking, and an inch away from full-blown crying, even an infant-care newbie like me recognized the difference. However, I wasn't sure I was right about this, so I did a test. I stepped back through the still open door. He immediately began to twist, turn, and fuss.

Fascinating. I stepped back outside. Blessed quiet.

In what has now become a standard family joke, I turned sideways. I stepped left to go outside: silence. Step right, inside, crying. Wah-shh. Wah-shh. Magic.

And I was the baby whisperer who found this out. Ta da. Well, it was a nice enough day, and standing on the porch didn't do much for me, so we went for a little walk.

Harrison seemed to like it when I talked to him, but he also liked silence. And even though he was just a few months old, he seemed to notice things. He paid attention to the sky, passing birds, and drooping branches.

I had always liked kids. But I liked them when they were moving around, talking, etc. As I indicated earlier, I often called infants "meatloafs" because they just sat there, and also due to the size and shape of a swaddled baby. Basically, it was my way of saying, "You know, he/she's just a lump right now."

But as we walked, a realization crystallized. "Oh, crap. There's a person in there."

Before he could walk or talk, Harrison was still a person. A person with his own desires: Outside! Explore! Go! Touch!

When it became clear that I was going to be spelling Kathy regularly, we bought one of those strap-on baby carriers. It was a complete waste of money. It fit okay. It worked okay. But I couldn't let him go. If there was a chance to carry Harrison, I carried him.

I carried him out in the rain, standing under the eaves for an hour. I carried him out in the snow, letting his tiny fingers touch icicles. I carried him in the morning, when we watched the clouds. I carried him at twilight. And one day he showed me he wasn't just a person, but a smart person. It was months before he would say his first word, but when a dog howled in the distance, he tapped my T-shirt, which had a dog on it, and made snuffling sounds, like his family's Boston Terrier did when it was excited. Before words, he was connecting sound, memory and image (the stylized dog on my shirt) to tell me the howl was a dog. And he told me something else along the way: He is crazy smart.

But that wasn't the real lesson of the day. It's important, but the real lesson makes me come close to tears even now. I learned I was good with babies, and I loved Harrison more than words could say. I try to tell him that every day.

— Greg Beatty —

A Grandma at Last

Perfect love sometimes does not come
until the first grandchild.
~Welsh Proverb

My friend asked, "Are they your real grandchildren, or are they adopted?" I didn't respond. Her question didn't deserve an answer. They are my real grandchildren. It doesn't matter how children arrive in a family. It matters that we love them.

For several years, I had dreamed of being a grandmother. As the only one in my circle of friends without grandchildren, I felt left out when the conversation over lunch turned to talk of grandchildren. Out came all the latest photographs. My friends shared the name of the newest arrival. The pride and joy they felt was a feeling I hadn't experienced.

Imagine the excitement when I received that phone call. "Mom, you're going to be a grandmother. We're adopting." I was overjoyed at this amazing news from my daughter and her husband, who were about to adopt two older siblings: a seven-year-old boy and a ten-year-old girl.

I researched everything available to find out how to grandparent older, adopted children. The waiting was painful. How would I react at our first meeting? Would they accept me as their grandma? What would they be like?

A few weeks later, the new family was coming to visit us. My daughter warned me that the children might not want to be hugged. But when they arrived, both children hopped from the car and walked directly to me with the widest smiles. There was an immediate connection. The moment I hugged those two children, they were my grandchildren. My dream had come true.

We were cautioned that bonding would take some time, but we bonded that first day. The children changed our family. They altered the dynamics of our home. I can't imagine life without them.

The road forward has not always been smooth, and bumps along the way have been challenging. Unexpected situations required a great deal of patience, consistency and firmness.

When my new grandson had been part of our family for a short time, he looked up at me and asked, "Will you always be my grandma?" My heart melted.

The children have a forever home, and I'm their forever grandma. I carry their photographs in my purse and proudly join the lunch conversations with my friends when we talk about our grandchildren.

Being a grandma has been one of life's most rewarding gifts. It matters not that these children don't carry my genes. They have my heart, and they know who loves them.

At the end of the first visit, my little grandson ran back from the car to where his grandpa stood. He handed him a piece of paper on which he had scrawled his telephone number. His parting words were, "Grandpa, if you ever need me, just call."

Families are created in a variety of ways. It makes no difference who gave birth to these children. I'm their real grandma, and they are my real grandchildren.

— Lorna Cassie-Bywater —

First Things First

The beginning of wisdom is to call things
by their right names.
~Chinese Proverb

M y daughter is about to give birth to a little girl, my first grandchild. While her parents have yet to share what they will name this little princess, I am in a quandary over what she will call me.

I have been waiting many years to become a grandparent, and I want to get it right. While I ruminate over all the choices of what to be called, my husband says he has it figured out.

"So, what will your granddaughter call you?" I asked him.

"Oh, that's easy," he replied.

"Really?"

"Really."

"Okay, so what is your chosen title?"

"What my students called me for the thirty-two years that I taught school... Mr. Levin," he said with a slight smirk as he walked out of the room.

"Oh, I should have known," I sighed, and went back to the names spinning in my brain.

My list started with Grandma, Grammie, Granny, Grandmary, and Gigi, followed by Mimi and Mimaw. Bubba and Bubbe were also there along with Nana, Nanny, and Nans. They all kept whirling through my head. I had to stop this nonsense.

I had to listen to each one and how it sounded. I also had to consider what my reasons for choosing that title might be. Even though it would be at least a year or two before the baby called me anything, I knew my family would immediately start referring to me as whatever-name-I-chose.

So, I started trying on each name for size. It's not so different from trying on new dresses. With clothing, you choose the size and the styles you like and take them all into the fitting room. Trying them on is a private affair. As you slip into each one, you can tell quickly if it is going back to the rack or staying in the maybe pile. It was time to get my maybe pile going.

I started with the most popular title: Grandma. I rolled it around on my tongue a few times. It was good and honest and defined the role. As I said it, I kept seeing pictures of grandmas in the olden days with aprons, orthopedic shoes and big pocketbooks. With a start, I realized that I had just described my paternal grandmother whom I called Grandma. Even though I loved her and had good memories of her, I didn't see myself in an outfit like this. As wonderful as Grandma is, it was not going into the maybe pile.

Once I had studied Grandma, I tried on Granny. I said it aloud a few times. It had a nice ring to it, maybe a bit better than Grandma. Would I like it when my granddaughter said, "Granny, let's play?" It just sounded ordinary to me. Granny wasn't a keeper.

Then there was Grandmary. When my daughter was little, we read American Girl books. Those featuring Samantha also featured her grandmother, whom she called Grandmary. We used to wonder how it was pronounced... Mary or Marie? It certainly had a bit of elegance about it. It was going to make the first cut.

Grammie spelled with an "ie" came next. It was cute, easy, and sounded young. I liked the thought of being a Grammie. It moved to the top of the list. The more I heard it in my head or said it aloud, the more I liked it. I thought Grammie was it. But still something wasn't quite right.

Maybe I needed a different tactic. I decided to check in with some of my friends who are grandmothers. Several of them went by Gigi.

I always thought that was just a child's first attempt at pronouncing grandma. In the case of one friend, it stands for Gorgeous Grandmother. That's not a bad thing to be called. I'd consider it a maybe.

Another friend goes by Mimi. When I asked how she chose it, she told me it was what her mother had been called, so she just assumed it would be her honorific. She loved when her grandchildren called her Mimi. To my ear, it just didn't sound grandmotherly enough. It went into the discard pile.

The Memaw I spoke with had waited until her grandchildren had begun speaking and let them choose what to call her. I didn't want to wait that long. Memaw was tossed out.

Both my maternal grandmother and mother were Bubbe. I remember my Bubbe sprawled in a big chair wearing housecoats. She had a large lap for sitting and wore braids wrapped in a crown around her head. To my young eyes, she looked ancient. My own mother always said she never entertained any other title. While the memories of both these women were good, Bubbe just seemed too Old World. I wanted a name that was mine alone and not shared in the family. Bubbe didn't make the first cut.

Growing up, many of my friends had Nanas or one of its derivatives. It had a loving sound to it. Nana felt warm and comforting to me. It was going to make the list.

I wrote the names on an index card — Grammie, Nana, Grandmary and Gigi — and taped it to the bathroom mirror. As the due date of this little person got closer, I perused my list several times a day.

My husband still couldn't believe I hadn't chosen a name. He had settled on Grandpa Mike.

"We are getting closer every day, and you haven't decided on anything yet?" he said a bit exasperated.

"No, I haven't. I like these, but I am still waiting for it to hit me. I'll know it when I hear it."

And then, just before the baby was due to be born, my husband and I took a trip to Venice, Italy. Walking through a park one afternoon, we saw many grandmothers playing with their grandchildren. I was enchanted by the scene. And while I don't speak Italian, I didn't need a translator to understand that when those little darlings on the playground called out "Nonna," the women who ran joyfully to push them on the swings or catch them on the slide were their adoring grandmothers. I was smitten.

I repeated the Italian word for grandmother to myself several times. It sounded warm and loving. It sounded just right.

When this little girl is born, I am going to be Nonna.

—Ina Massler Levin—

Baby Takes All

If your baby is "beautiful and perfect, never cries or
fusses, sleeps on schedule and burps on demand, an
angel all the time," you're the grandma.
~Teresa Bloomingdale

When our first grandchild, Isabella, was born, we were so excited. But she lived clear across the country. Then her parents, Star and Joe, agreed to move from California to Massachusetts to live near us.

My husband David told them, "Move to Milton and live with us until you find a place of your own." Previously divorced and childless, David looked forward to having a baby in the house. He imagined Isabella hopping onto his lap to watch his favorite action movies — no fuss, no muss, no changes to our routine. He had no idea of future TV time filled with talking animals, pink unicorns, and squeaky songs.

David wondered why I stared at him and sighed.

Star and Joe would take an upstairs bedroom, but the question of a separate room for Isabella was David's rude awakening.

Me: "The baby will need a nursery."

David: "What? Why can't the baby sleep in the same room as Star and Joe?"

Me: "Too small for all of them."

David: "Well, where will our visitors sleep?"

I stopped stirring soup to stare at him. Classic delusional behavior. When three people move in and one of them is in diapers, it's goodbye to houseguests. Even the insane know that.

Before me was a man genuinely stumped as to why our "B&B" would be no more. My suspicions were confirmed when he said, "Their room has a big closet. Why can't they put the crib in there?"

I put down my spoon and repeated slowly, "No. The crib in a closet? Please. Besides, there will be way too much stuff for one room anyway."

"How much stuff can a little baby have?"

Let's see: a crib, layette, playpen and a field of toys. Which bathroom will sport the Diaper Genie as the washer and dryer churn 24/7? I envisioned a high chair and the floor littered with Cheerios. And the vision of a Johnny Jump Up hanging from the entrance to our formal dining room made me laugh out loud.

But I simply said, "Well, quite a bit of stuff, actually."

That alone unnerved poor David. When a man is shell-shocked, it's best to perform triage, allow for recovery time and, above all, offer hope.

"David, there's plenty of time. We can work it out." (That's code for "You'll adjust.")

That night, we talked about how the relocation would happily coincide with a New England summer. Then we'd move on to fall foliage. Wouldn't it be great to have a real family Thanksgiving for the first time in years? We imagined little Isabella's first Christmas. Happy sighs.

Suddenly, David said, "The kids should feel welcome, so let them have the entire upstairs. What the heck."

He stared off, all aglow in Norman Rockwell scenes. I surveyed the living room and mentally ticked off a to-buy list: baby gates, wall-socket protectors and padding for the coffee table. The playpen would be perfect there. We'd just get rid of that recliner that David loved so much. I'd have to ease him into that!

I smiled and nodded. The entire upstairs — well, that was a running start.

— Suzette Martinez Standring —

Grand & Great Laughs

11

Closet-Gate

On the seventh day, God rested. His grandchildren
must have been out of town.
~Gene Perret

"**H**as anyone seen the little girls lately?" my daughter Heidi
asked. The silence around the kitchen table showed that
we had to think. It had been a wonderful few moments
for my girls and me to sit after dinner, calmly sipping
coffee without the children disturbing us.

"Dad took them downstairs to watch cartoons," my second daughter
Mandi said. "It does seem a little quiet, though. They may be only
three years old, but those two are ingenious when it comes to trouble.
Should we check?"

I chuckled, "Hey, maybe they have Grandpa tied to a chair with a
skipping rope and are drawing a mustache on his face with markers."
We all had a good laugh at the thought as we refilled our cups with
the comforting, strong brew.

At that moment, my husband walked up the stairs alone. "Dad,
where are the girls?" Heidi asked.

Gord's face reflected confusion. "Aren't they with you?"

"No," Mandi spoke slowly. "They were with you."

"Well, I fell asleep, and they were gone when I woke up. I just
thought they'd come up here." He seemed unruffled, but we instantly
put down our cups as our "mother's intuition" went into Amber Alert
mode.

Heidi jumped up quickly. "I'll look downstairs."

"I'll look in the living and dining room." Mandi was already on the move.

"I'll check the garage," I said.

"I'll go upstairs," Gord offered, "but I doubt they're there or you would've seen them pass by."

Our daughter-in-law Erin grinned as she watched us scramble, lifting her coffee mug in solidarity. "I'll keep a look-out from here!"

In a few moments, we all met again at the kitchen table. We looked at each other, bewildered.

"Let's all check again. They have to be here somewhere." Mandi's voice betrayed the beginning of concern.

I decided to take a look upstairs this time, as my husband Gord has been known to require help finding milk when it's right in front of him in the fridge. He's a wonderful grandfather, but finding things isn't his strong suit.

As I walked into our bedroom, there was an unusual smell in the air. I took a moment to identify the faintly familiar scent. It smelled like... baby powder. I looked around the room and everything seemed in order, but it was somehow too quiet. Then I noticed the light was on in our walk-in closet. "That's odd," I said out loud.

I slowly opened the folding door. It took a few minutes to process what I was seeing.

It was as if it were snowing indoors. Gord's pants, socks, shirts, and shoes were completely white, as well as the air around them. Looking down through the thick cloud, I beheld two little nymphs staring up at me, completely encased in a powder coating from top to bottom. Their only identifiable features were their eyes — one set brown, and the other set green. My missing granddaughters!

They stood like frozen sentinels. One had a large but empty baby powder container in her hand; the other had an open bottle of nail polish with the dripping brush poised to paint. They spoke not a word, but as they blinked simultaneously, I realized the purpose of the dark red polish. It decorated both their eyelids and was quickly hardening to the point where that blink was probably difficult.

Gently moving the two wee girls from the closet, I stood them in the center of the room. Their terror at being found out rendered them mute.

I leaned out the door and called, "Mommies! I think you should come upstairs... right away!" My voice must have carried urgency as the immediate thundering footsteps on the stairs foretold the arrival of their mothers.

The first thing they saw was the complete coverage of white powder on their precious daughters. "Oh, no!" said one. Then they saw the nail polish. "What on earth?" exclaimed the other.

As the moms took my granddaughters downstairs to wipe their faces clean and try to remove the polish so close to their eyes, I continued my journey to the back of the closet. My section.

The snow-white film had found its way onto all my clothes and shoes as well, including scarves and jewelry. Then further mischief became evident. Four bottles of nail polish lay open and dripping on my vanity. The various colors ran down the piece of furniture, collecting in puddles on the soft cream carpet. Mascara, eyeliner, and lipstick containers were opened and used to paint the mirror, window, and vanity top. As I turned to look at the items hanging on a lower rod, I noticed long lines of nail polish down the sleeves of each blouse. Neat, creative lines had been drawn from the shoulders to the cuffs.

I moved farther into the closet to the more expensive outfits that now gave new meaning to the words "designer dress." Then I saw something else. A pair of scissors lay on the floor beside my powder-encrusted high heels.

I ignored the sounds of screeching children behind me as their mothers frantically tried to remove the polish from their eyelids and continued to gaze across the line of clothing. Almost every piece had a perfect slice cut into the sleeve, the front, or the back. Shuffling through fifteen outfits, it didn't take long to see that every one had the same damage.

I stood in utter amazement at the incredible ability of these two little souls to manage so much destruction in so little time. If I had set out to do this myself, I'm sure it would have taken me hours. These three-year-olds managed it all in just minutes, and probably without conversation or planning. Incredible! This could mean only one thing. Well, two things, I guess.

First, I would need a new wardrobe. But second, and most importantly, they must be borderline genius!

Over the following days, as the total damage was revealed, my horrified daughters kindly presented me with several gift cards to replace much of what was lost. They were generous offerings and very much appreciated.

Years have passed, and these two sweet granddaughters are now ten years old. And, yes, they are extremely creative children who will do great things in their lives. They also remember that day clearly, and on different occasions each has quietly sidled up to me and confessed that it was the other girl's idea. Ha! I love it.

That day will never be forgotten. And to give it a rightful place in our family history, we now affectionately refer to it as — "Closet-gate."

— Heather Rae Rodin —

What Goes Up

An hour with your grandchildren can make you feel
young again. Anything longer than that,
and you start to age quickly.
~Gene Perret

Our ten-year-old grandson scrambled up our backyard maple tree like King Kong scaling the Empire State Building. He stood on a limb, grabbed the one above him, and bounced. Hapless young leaves dropped under his onslaught as the branch bobbed up and down.

My breath caught in my throat, a regular occurrence for a grandparent of an active boy. "Asher, be careful. You haven't broken any bones yet. Let's keep it that way."

He stopped bouncing and plopped onto the limb. My lungs resumed their normal rhythm. "Grandma," he called in a cajoling tone, "climb up with me. Please."

I eyed the old tree. Asher and I considered it our private fortress, but the branch I normally used to boost myself up had broken off in a recent storm. Getting into that tree would take more upper-arm strength than I possessed. "Honey, I don't think I can climb up there anymore."

Asher's eyes widened as if I'd uttered a blasphemy. "But, Grandma, it's our special place. You have to try." His stricken look prompted me to grab a branch, but I was struggling. "Pull harder, Grandma. Boy, you should really start working out. You're getting pretty weak."

After multiple tries, I hefted myself onto the lowest limb and lay panting against the rough bark. Slow maneuvering brought me to a sitting position.

"See, Grandma, I knew you could get up here." Asher grinned and scooted next to me. We sat together on the branch, our feet dangling. A cool May breeze held the insects at bay as Asher told me about his school day.

I silently thanked God for the opportunity to spend time with this beloved grandson. My husband Jake and I relished our time with him. We'd forged a special bond over the years with this child.

As sunset streaked the sky, the breeze died down, and mosquitoes began attacking us. "Okay, sweetie, let's go in. Your grandpa will be home soon."

Asher shimmied down the trunk like a competitor in a lumberjack competition. I swung my leg lower, feeling for the limb I always used to descend. "Be careful, Grandma," he warned. "Your climb-down branch is gone, remember?"

I surveyed the hard surface below. Our new river-rock-and-brick landscape edging mocked me. I couldn't figure out how to get myself down safely.

"Hurry up, Grandma." Asher bounced on the patio.

"Sweetie, I'm having trouble."

Asher stopped jumping and peered up at me. "Grandma, are you stuck in the tree?"

The knobby bark bit into my protesting backside. I cautiously shifted my weight on the branch. "I don't want you to worry, but…"

"Are you *really* stuck?"

"Yes, Asher, I'm really stuck."

His eyes gleamed with excitement. "Can I call 911?" he asked hopefully.

"No, not 911. Call your grandpa."

Asher ran inside for the phone. A tiny gnat, the size of a pinhead, landed on my arm. I jerked at its needle-jab sting, and then fought to keep my balance. A red, dime-sized welt appeared where the gnat stung me. I swatted away another Mutant Robo-Gnat that was dive-bombing my face.

Asher ran back, waving the phone like a prize. "Are you sure I can't call 911?" he asked again. I could see his mental wheels turning. A fire truck or two, perhaps a rescue squad on stand-by, would make a great story at school.

"Dial your grandpa and put him on speaker," I commanded.

Jake answered on the second ring. "Grandma's stuck in a tree," Asher announced cheerfully.

"What?"

I rolled my eyes and swatted another gnat.

"Grandma told me to call because she's stuck in a tree."

I heard a long pause before my husband asked, "Is Grandma really stuck in a tree?"

"Yeah, and she wants you to come home and help her down," Asher enthused.

Jake's hysterical laughter flowed through the phone line.

"You're on speaker. I can hear you," I shouted from my perch. "Now stop cackling, come home, and get me down."

Between bouts of laughter, Jake said, "Tell Grandma to hang on. I'll be there soon."

"Okay, bye Gramps. I'll take care of things until you get home." Asher laid the house phone on the patio table and ran back inside. I smashed a Robo-Gnat attacking my leg as Asher burst through the patio door, his new cell phone in hand. "My grandmother is stuck in a tree," he said in his best news-announcer voice.

"Who are you talking to?" I asked.

"Nobody, Grandma."

Asher resumed his spiel. "My grandmother is stuck in the tree. She can't get down. Grandma, would you like to say a few words?"

The splintery wood dug into my palms. I tamped down exasperation. "Say a few words to who? Who are you talking to?"

"I'm not talking to anyone. I'm recording you. See?"

He flipped the phone around and held it up for me to view. Sure enough, a video played on-screen. A middle-aged woman wearing silver loafers, dark-washed jeans, and an exasperated glare hunched in a maple.

"Give me that!" I made a feeble swipe at the phone. Asher pulled it back and tapped buttons furiously. I wobbled on the branch before regaining my balance. Asher peered up at me through the deepening twilight. "Be careful! You almost fell. Grandma, are you really, truly stuck?"

My heart softened at his evident concern. "Yes, sweetie, but I'll be all right. Don't worry."

"Oh, I'm not worried," he said. "I just posted this online. The video already has two 'likes.' You've gone worldwide."

— Jeanie Jacobson —

13

Mammie's Doll Babies

Years may wrinkle the skin, but to give
up enthusiasm wrinkles the soul.
~Samuel Ullman

During a break at work last spring, I took a quick glance at my Facebook account. I had several notifications, and one of them was a friend request. I looked more closely at the screen and saw my grandmother's picture next to the request. "Barbara Haywood sent you a friend request," the notification stated. Maybe it was a joke. I hated to think that someone could have opened an account under my grandmother's name.

I called my mom at the end of the workday. "I have a friend request from Mammie. Is it really from her?" I asked.

"It is," my mom confirmed. She explained that my uncle Buster had bought her a Kindle Fire and my cousin Courtney had helped her set up the account.

"That is so awesome," I said. "Now I better go accept her friend request before she gets annoyed with me!"

I opened my app and wrote a welcome message on my grandmother's page. I told her how excited I was to see her on Facebook, and added that her request was the best one I had ever received.

Mammie learned about Facebook gradually. At first, she simply "liked" pictures of the family. After a while, she figured out how to add comments. But if we responded to her or asked questions, we didn't always receive an answer right away. She was still figuring things out.

Her Facebook proficiency is not of great importance. It's the fact that she's on social media and has access to pictures of her family on a daily basis.

My grandmother has four children, ten grandchildren, and ten great-grandchildren. We all live fairly close to her, but we also lead very busy lives. Collectively, our children are involved with theater, dance, soccer, baseball, cheerleading, volleyball and gymnastics. And though we invite Mammie to many performances and games, her lack of mobility limits her attendance. Now that she has a Facebook account, she doesn't have to miss a thing.

Mammie can keep up with the latest trends, view vacation pictures, and look at photos of baseball games and dance recitals. She will be able to follow her granddaughters who are heading off to college this fall and still feel very much involved in their lives.

Sometimes, Mammie's presence on Facebook makes me chuckle. One day, I woke up to thirty-eight notifications from her. She was up at 3:00 in the morning, liking pictures from two years ago. I figured she must have had trouble sleeping, and she was looking at pictures to help pass the time.

Then there's her special way of commenting on posts. She calls us all her doll babies, even those of us who are approaching forty years old, and she always signs her comments, "Love, Mammie." After I posted a picture of my kids and me on a recent camping trip, she commented, "Here are three of Mammie's little doll babies. Looks like a fun and happy time. Love you, Mammie."

A friend asked me the other day if I was going to tell her that she didn't need to sign her name at the end of her comments.

"I sure am not," I told my friend. "She can use Facebook however she wants. I'm not criticizing a thing about what she does."

Mammie seems to be enjoying her new social-media presence, and the rest of us are benefiting as well. Just a little while ago, I checked my account, and I had a comment from Mammie.

"What are you celebrating now, Miss Thing?" she wrote at the bottom of a picture I posted.

"Life!" I responded.

And I really am. I am celebrating life, family, and the fact that my eighty-three-year-old grandmother is on Facebook. And that I am one of her doll babies.

—Melissa Face—

14

Pussy-Willow Wisdom

Wisdom and deep intelligence require
an honest appreciation of mystery.
~Thomas Moore

U ntil our daughter, Reyn, turned three, her "nanny" was my father, a retired Navy pilot. After years as a strict military parent, Daddy had morphed into a different kind of grandpa. He loved without expectation, disciplined with mercy, and never criticized our parenting decisions.

Except for one.

As soon as his granddaughter learned to walk, Dad grumbled about an umbrella stand full of pussy willows that stood by our front door.

"You need to move them," he said. "Someday, Reyn will get one of those soft willow pods stuck up her nose."

That's ridiculous, I thought. She didn't even know they were there, and she seldom went into the front foyer. Why would our bright child want to pick off one of those furry buds and put it in her nose?

I ignored my father and left the branches in their brass stand. He finally quit mentioning them to me. As we approached Reyn's third birthday, I had almost forgotten his dire predictions of pending pussy-willow disaster.

One morning before my dad arrived, Reyn came into the kitchen holding her blankie and sounding forlorn. Busy unloading our dishwasher, I didn't look at her too closely.

"Mommy," she said, "something's wrong with my nose."

I lifted glasses onto their shelves. "Do you need me to help you blow it?"

"Yes."

"Well, then, let's blow it." Reaching for a Kleenex from the dispenser on the counter, I covered her nose with it. "Come on, big blow."

She tried two little puffs out of her nostrils. "How's that?" I asked.

She shook her head.

"Blow again. Harder."

"It's still there," she said, twisting her blanket and looking a bit like Eeyore holding his tail. "It's stuck."

Tissue in mid-air, I paused. "What's stuck?"

"I'll show you." She took my hand and headed toward the front door. Oh no. Surely, she hadn't. But, of course, she had. She pointed to the pussy willows.

"Did you put one of those up your nose?" I asked.

She nodded.

I bent to look her in the eyes. "Why would you do such a thing?"

Like a wounded bird, she tucked her face into her left shoulder. "I dunno," she said.

I didn't know either. But somehow my father had.

We went back to the kitchen and tried again to blow her nose. The pussy-willow kernel wouldn't budge. I got a flashlight and some long tweezers and tipped back Reyn's head. The fuzzy usurper could not be seen.

"How did it get so far up there?" I asked.

"I tried to get it out. Now, I can't breathe so good, Mommy."

I started to panic. She must have pushed the pod way up into her nasal cavity. Swallowing my pride, I called my father. When he picked up, I got straight to the point. "Don't come to the house. We're on the way to the hospital. You can meet us at the ER."

My dad remained calm. "What's happened?"

I paused. "Um… Reyn has something stuck in her nose."

There was one terrible beat of silence. At least he didn't laugh.

"What kind of something?"

"It's a stupid pussy willow!" I shouted. "I can't believe this is happening. Just get to the hospital!"

Reyn whimpered next to me.

Her grandfather took charge. "I'll meet you at the entrance to the subdivision, and we'll go together. Don't worry."

I threw my purse on the passenger seat of the car as Reyn crawled into the back. Trying to hide my fear, I buckled her into her booster. Fat tears rolled down her flushed cheeks.

"Stop that," I said. "You'll make it even harder to breathe." She bawled louder.

I lowered my voice. "I'm sorry, Reyn. Mommy's not mad at you. Please don't cry. It will be okay."

But as I whipped out of the driveway, Reyn's sobs escalated. She snorted and snuffled and coughed while I watched her in my rearview mirror. What if she choked back there? What if she stopped breathing?

We were almost to the meeting point when she let out a huge, explosive sneeze. I pulled over to the curb and threw the gearshift into park. Snatching a tissue, I leaped out and yanked open the back door. Reyn smiled at me.

"It's gone," she said.

"What? Are you sure?" I wiped off her face and glanced around for the culpable pod. I found it on the floor.

Relieved and grateful, I stood up just as my dad's vehicle appeared at the other end of the street. When he pulled alongside of us, he realized the crisis had resolved itself without injury (except to my parental ego). Oozing benevolence, he helped me into the driver's seat and followed us home.

I plucked Reyn from the car and pitched the pussy willows in the garbage before my father crossed the threshold. He never gloated or said he'd told me so. He congratulated Reyn for ejecting the seed on her own and carried her off to the playroom while I slunk down the hall to my office.

How on earth did my dad predict the pussy-willow plug-up? I

asked him that once. He smiled his inscrutable smile.

"Grandparents just know these things," he said.
And maybe they do.

—Andi Lehman—

15

Deception at the Dryer

You can learn many things from children.
How much patience you have, for instance.
~Franklin P. Jones

It's my fault. My children's incessant hankering for Dots, Swedish Fish, and virtually anything sugary and gooey; their almost unyielding preference for foods that are sweet over those that provide sustenance; and the way they become downright giddy — I mean, huge smiles and full-on cheering — when I, say, offer them a tiny pack of fruit snacks on the drive home from school.

They likely inherited all of the above from yours truly.

Granted, I wasn't a complete louse on the dietary front when I was pregnant with them. I drank copious amounts of water, consumed multiple avocados daily, and pretty much inhaled anything that contained a sizeable amount of omega-3 fatty acids during both pregnancies.

But I confess that I also ate Twizzlers and miniature Reese's Peanut Butter Cups like it was my job.

Now, nearly seven years later, I realize the error of my ways. And, trust me, I'm working to rectify it.

But my mother isn't doing me any favors.

The fact that my mother joyfully offers to watch the kids overnight so that my husband and I can have a much-needed date night is a favor more valuable than gold, indeed.

It's her kitchen pantry, which sits smack-dab across from her washer and dryer, that's the problem.

The third shelf in particular is rife with delectable snacks, and it's as if my mother enacted some sort of unspoken law, which stipulates that anything inhabiting said space must possess a minimum of sixteen grams of sugar per serving.

Naturally, Scotty and Kennedy know their way around that space like the proverbial back of their hands.

"We had, um, how shall I say it? A little issue last night," my mother confessed recently when I picked up Scotty and Kennedy from an overnighter. She glared at Scotty as she spoke; her face conveyed a mixture of grandmotherly compassion and sternness.

I turned to my son, whose face was awash with guilt.

"I'm sorry! I promise never to do it again," Scotty piped up in earnest.

I turned back to my mother for an explanation.

Apparently, while my mother was watching TV, Scotty casually pranced by, proclaiming, "I'm just going to check out the knobs on the dryer, Grandma."

That alone should have been a red flag.

Then, just as quickly, Scotty headed back to the playroom from whence he came.

A few seconds later, he returned.

"Just doing my duty, Grandma, making sure everything's good at the dryer."

Forget just red flags. If Scotty had pulled this stunt at home with me, his behavior would have elicited more flags (of all colors) than a Daytona race.

But, again, this is Grandma's house we're talking about.

It wasn't until Scotty ran past my mother for a third time — now with his little sister Kennedy in tow — that my mother finally realized something was up.

She followed Scotty and Kennedy back to the playroom and asked, "Exactly what is going on here?"

Both Scotty and Kennedy stopped dead in their tracks and faced Grandma sheepishly.

No words or further investigative work were necessary: the bulges in their tummies revealed everything. When my mother lifted their shirts, licorice sticks and a bevy of tiny chocolate bars tumbled to the floor.

Scotty and Kennedy had raided the pantry and pretty much poached all the candy their T-shirts could hide.

I confess: This is totally something I would have attempted back in the day had my mother made such sweets readily available. I could only wish to have had access to such a stash when I was a kid.

But my mother is a grandmother, and things are much different now. If Scotty and Kennedy want sweets, there is no need for trickery. All they have to do is ask.

Ironically, this past Christmas, I bought my mother a coffee mug that bears the phrase: "Everything Is Sweeter at Grandma's."

I thought the saying was cute.

I have since learned that it is also true.

—Courtney Conover—

16

Our Cemented Bond

Happiness is handmade.
~Author Unknown

"Look what I bought to keep us busy tonight!" I held up the box for my grandchildren to see. "It's a gingerbread-house kit. All we have to do is put the walls together with icing, add the roof and decorate!" Taylor, age four, was very excited. Levi, who was eight, raised a skeptical eyebrow as I opened the box and emptied the contents. His expression changed, however, when a clear bag filled with gumdrops, peppermints and other candy slid out and landed on the table.

I often babysat the children. We usually played board games or read stories until bedtime. But the charming gingerbread-house kits had caught my eye in a local store. I'd picked up the box and thought to myself: *How hard could it be?* The busy cashier rang it up and bounced it into a bag. That was the first of many hard knocks that poor house was going to take.

As usual, both kids wanted to be the first to get their hands on the project. They each grabbed a wall, and Taylor ran to a drawer for glue. "Oh, no, honey, we don't use glue! The icing will hold the walls together," I announced with confidence.

Each child held a wall as I squeezed the sweet, sticky icing along an edge. "Now put your walls together to form a corner," I instructed. They happily banged their walls into each other's. Taylor's broke into two large pieces. Levi's lost a portion along the bottom. They both turned to me, looking horrified.

"Don't worry!" I sang out. "We can fix it with icing!" I slathered icing heavily along the cracks, praying the repair would hold. We placed the broken walls down "to dry." They picked up the remaining walls, and I iced them both while they gingerly placed them together.

"We have a corner!" I told them joyfully. As we turned back to admire our achievement, both walls collapsed.

We needed stronger icing, I decided. We huddled like chemists over a bowl, adding any ingredient that we thought might work. Levi dumped in flour, which I thickened with water. Taylor added a raw egg, sugar and the gumballs from the candy bag. She got mad when I fished those out. "Gum is sticky, Grandma! We need sticky!" I explained to the kids that we wouldn't be able to eat the finished house now, but it would still be fun to build.

After spreading our "cement" generously over the cracked and crooked walls, we once again attempted the "house-raising." Again, we watched it collapse as if someone had pulled a rug out from under it. I frowned, and then had an idea. I went to the garage and came back with a cardboard box. Levi instantly understood my plan and began cutting out cardboard walls. Taylor was in charge of taping them together as I applied our mortar. We pressed the walls on and held our breath. The house leaned to the left, and we braced ourselves for the crash. Surprisingly, it didn't happen.

"It's time for the roof!" Levi shouted. We iced the roof pieces onto cardboard and placed them on top, angling toward each other. They stayed in place for about thirty victorious seconds before sliding off in opposite directions. I expected the children to give up and go watch television. They surprised me with their perseverance. Taylor went to get the real glue while Levi decided that we needed something inside the house to hold up the roof. He was willing to sacrifice Taylor's stuffed rabbit, but she wasn't. Finally, we settled on a toy toaster that nobody played with anymore.

The toaster worked well to bolster the roof. We finally had our structure, and it was standing! High-fives all around. No happy dance, as we couldn't risk the slightest tremor. We worked together diligently, patting our paste carefully into any weak areas. There were plenty.

"It's candy time!" Taylor shrieked. We were all shocked that the project had actually progressed to this point. As anticipated, I had to settle several spats over the candy. We finally drew the invisible line that every child tends to respect. Taylor got to decorate the right side of the house and Levi the left. They happily placed the treats, sampling many of them. I watched with a smile as Taylor popped a spicy cinnamon candy into her mouth. Her eyes widened in surprise and anguish. "It's hot!" she complained, giving me a look of betrayal.

"Some people like them," I laughed.

The heavier candies slid off the house moments after application. Only the tiny silver balls seemed to adhere. Levi finally got out the colored sugars and sprinkles that we use to decorate sugar cookies. The result could only be described as psychedelic.

It wasn't pretty, but it was ours. We had triumphed against overwhelming odds. The children put on their pajamas, and I told them the story of the gingerbread man. "Run, run, as fast as you can! You can't catch me, I'm the gingerbread man!" I recited.

Levi walked over to our pitiful creation. He ducked behind it and pretended it was talking. "Work, work, as hard as a mouse! You can't build me, I'm a gingerbread house!"

— Marianne Fosnow —

17

Look Who's Here

If you would have guests merry with your cheer
Be so yourself, or so at least appear.
~Author Unknown

There was a knock at the door of Great-Grandma Smith's home in Lake Placid, New York one Thanksgiving. Since she was the hostess for this family holiday, she got up, opened the door, and exclaimed with delight, "Look who's here!"

She pulled a young man into the hallway, hugged him, and said, "It's wonderful to see you again! Everyone will be so delighted!" Great-Grandma then hurried to take off his coat and led him to the table. "Oh, just look who's here!" she announced with joy. The family murmured. She moved things around and placed him in a seat between my uncle and herself. He was surrounded by family on both sides and faced Great-Grandpa Smith across the table.

"Coralie, go get us another place setting!" she commanded. "We're so sorry that we started without you. No one knew you were coming," she explained. "But you're just going to love everything. We have turkey, potatoes, squash, and cranberry sauce. Oh, you know how Fayette always teased Coralie and told her to eat more cranberry sauce so she'd have room in her stomach for more food." She stopped to laugh at the family joke about my mother's gullible nature when she had been young. We still laugh about cranberry sauce opening up extra room in the stomach each Thanksgiving. Great-Grandma gently patted his arm. "Oh, and Gladys made an apple and a pumpkin pie for dessert even! So, just dig right in. My, it's good to see you." She patted his arm again and sighed.

No one had interrupted her joyful speech from the moment she had left the table to answer the door. After looking around the table at our family, the young man turned and looked straight at Great-Grandma Smith's face, which beamed with love and joy. He said in a bewildered voice, "I don't know any of you. I just stopped at your house to get directions!"

—Melanie A. Savidis—

18

Papa's Arms

*In the eyes of their grandchildren, grandfathers are
professional pranksters and veteran comedians.*
~Author Unknown

My granddaughter, Lilith, had reached that scary but important age when her baby teeth were beginning to loosen and come out. As one would expect, it scared her. She would try to hide the fact that she had a loose tooth, not wanting us to touch it to see how loose it was or, even worse, attempt to pull it out.

No amount of sweet talk about how it wouldn't hurt would make her open her mouth to let us see it. No stories concerning the beautiful Tooth Fairy coming by at night when she was asleep would comfort her. Each loose tooth was a traumatic experience.

Eventually, she became used to the process, accepting it as a natural part of growing up from a toddler to a little girl. In fact, she began to look forward to the Tooth Fairy's visits and the coins that showed up under her pillow. She would proudly display the hole from each missing tooth like a badge of honor.

One day, after she had pretty much passed through that childhood phase, we were standing next to each other, and I noticed her looking at my arm.

"You see how my arms are longer than yours?" I asked her.

"Yes," she said.

"That's because these are my grown-up arms."

She looked down at her arms.

"Stick your arm out straight," I said, and she did.

I stooped down and stuck my arm out next to hers.

"See," I said. "Mine are longer."

I didn't realize that my wife had walked up behind us and was listening to this entire conversation. I stuck my other arm out straight, parallel to my other arm.

"Do you know why mine are longer?"

"Because you're bigger," she said.

"You're right. I'm an adult, and these are my adult arms."

Her big eyes looked from my hands to my shoulders, taking it all in.

"When you get a little bigger," I said, "and your baby arms fall off, you'll grow adult arms like me."

She took one look at her own arm sticking out and ran off screaming. I laughed and turned around to see the scowling face of my wife.

"You're paying for the therapy," she admonished, and went off shaking her head to comfort our granddaughter.

— Del Howison —

19

Love and Las Vegas

A grandparent is old on the outside
but young on the inside.
~Author Unknown

Rushing down to our white rental car, we pile in. Grampy and I sit in the back seat, my parents in the front. The towering palm trees and glimmering facades of Las Vegas flicker before my eyes on our short trip to the Roman Catholic Shrine of the Most Holy Redeemer. While we had agreed to my mother's crazy idea of spending Christmas in Vegas, good Italian-Catholics didn't skip Christmas Mass, regardless of the location.

In addition to its painfully wordy name, the church's exterior challenges my expectations for a place of worship. Rather than a dull brick facade, we are greeted by a whitewashed exterior and peach geometric archways where shadows stretch across the hot pavement. Palms trees flank the sides of the arches, their arms waving a friendly "hello" to approaching church guests.

Without discussion, we choose a wooden pew near the rear of the church, and I settle myself beside Grampy, with my parents sitting to his left.

As the Mass proceeds, I find myself fading in and out. The priest, whose accent is incomprehensible, does nothing to inspire the few scattered worshipers, let alone my family. Finally, he instructs us to share the sign of peace — a welcome break from the monotone, lifeless words that echo off the church's high ceiling.

Grampy, a seventy-six-year-old gentleman complete with handlebar moustache and dapper blue golf shirt (with khaki shorts, of course), makes his rounds. He shakes hands with me first, his handshake firm but kind, and then continues onwards to neighbouring strangers. I barely notice his initial interaction with the woman behind us, but her outfit catches my eye — a white straw hat reminiscent of the 1930s and a delicate purple blouse. In his raspy voice, Grampy shakes her hand and wishes her a "Merry Christmas," the more suitable sign of peace for Christmas Day.

Thinking nothing of it, I continue to sit in the pew, my eyes wandering between stained-glass pictures of various saints and periodic glances to my watch. Not until the final "Amen" do my ears perk up.

I link arms with Grampy, preparing to help him stand. Having undergone surgery over thirty years ago, the metal plates in his knees have begun to show their age.

With a hand resting under his left arm, I wait impatiently for my parents to exit. My mother is slowly collecting her purse, and I'm fairly certain my father has fallen asleep. Their slothful motions make us targets for post-Mass chatter, and a female voice from behind asks in a Southern drawl, "Where are you folks from?"

Turning in our pews to face the solo senior, the very same in the white straw hat, Grampy answers for all of us: "St. Catharines, Ontario." Then, after a pause, "Canada. My son, daughter-in-law, and granddaughter are from Calgary. How about you?"

"I live here." At this point, I don't really listen to the conversation. What has my attention is the woman's body language. As she continues to chat with my grandfather in a playful lilting manner, her body shifts forward in her pew until she is a mere foot away from him. How she manages not to fall off the edge is beyond me. Still, I watch, entranced.

"Anthony — everyone calls me Tony." Her name escapes me because, at this moment, she makes her move.

Leaning forward even more precariously, her lithe fingers begin to trace Grampy's ear while she coos, "It's so nice to meet you, Tony."

My dad isn't following the conversation. His eyes look everywhere except toward the two seniors. My mom and I, however, don't miss a moment. We're both a bit shocked. My grandfather is a charming man, without doubt, but in church?

I continue to watch and wish the fingers would stop at his ears, but she tickles them across his neck, her eyes aglow with a playful sparkle.

My mom breaks in, her abrupt words cutting through any hopes of future dalliances. "Well, folks, let's go. Time for lunch."

Grampy shakes his admirer's hand for the last time and, with arms linked, I escort him out of church. The scorching sun is a welcome reprieve from the odd experience; I feel as though I have witnessed a private moment in a not-so-private setting. For a second, I feel ageist; since when did I not think it possible for seniors to flirt?

My reaction becomes further complicated as I remember Grampy's actions two summers ago. Grampy had taken an interest in my parents' neighbour, a then-widowed senior named Marie. Those hot summer nights involved Grampy standing on the back deck below Marie's bedroom window — in true Romeo-and-Juliet fashion — singing the Italian version of Dean Martin's "Oh Marie." She would approach the window, her tan lined face attempting to look disgusted with my grandfather's overtures, but a smile always escaped as she closed the window and shut the blinds. A mustachioed Italian man may not have been her English cup of tea, but the romance behind it inspired a brief glow. If Grampy could romance the neighbour, why could he not also be the subject of someone's affection?

My reverie is broken by the closing car doors, but the ensuing silence is brief. I regain my focus and allow my shock to speak. "Grampy! Look at you! Picking up women... and in church of all places!"

A boisterous chuckle follows my outburst, along with confusion. "What are you talking about?"

"That woman! She was flirting with you!" I try to impress upon him the grandeur of the scenario — my hands outspread, palms up, my eyes wide with passion.

"What? No, she wasn't flirting. She's just a nice woman." Ever the kind-hearted soul, Grampy can't see that he has just recently become the Most Holy Redeemer's most eligible bachelor.

I try again. "Nice? Does nice play with your ears in church? Come on, Grampy, she was into you!"

Grampy pauses for a moment, holding onto his seatbelt with his right hand, steadying himself against the twists and turns of my father's driving. "Hey, kid, old people get lonely too, ya know? She was probably just looking for a friend."

Not feeling keen to let the adventure die, I narrow my eyes, muttering to myself, "Friend, yeah, right, Grampy...."

For a few moments, no one speaks; only the rumble of the car offers its voice. Finally, in an exhale of defeat, Grampy breaks the silence. "Damn. Maybe I should've gotten her number...."

Laughing, I rest my hand on Grampy's shoulder. From behind his wide-rimmed glasses, he eyes me seriously, shaking his head. We drive away. While a potential romance is left behind, the knowledge that Grampy still has "it" makes us smile.

— Ashlee Petrucci —

Chapter 3

Treasured Moments & Memories

My Grandma's Game Show

Dreams are today's answers to tomorrow's questions.
~Edgar Cayce

Every night after dinner, my grandparents would retire to the den, hunker down in their well-worn seats, and turn on the 6:00 o'clock news. No matter how hard I tried to act grown up and watch with them, I would inevitably get distracted — until 6:30 when *Wheel of Fortune* came on.

My grandma would play along, trying to guess the answers before the players. Her whoops of excitement when she succeeded could be heard across the house.

As I grew older, my love of reading and writing blossomed, and I would join my grandma in yelling out letters. Soon, I was experiencing the thrill of solving the puzzles faster than the contestants and even my grandma. I was hooked.

Due to constant moving around with my mom and stepfather, I started to spend less time with my grandparents, but our bond remained strong. My grandparents provided me with the stability, love and support that I so desperately needed growing up. When times were bad, I would remember those cozy nights spent safely nestled in the warmth of their den watching *Wheel of Fortune*.

Athough my grandpa passed away when I was eleven, I was fortunate to have my grandma in my life until I was twenty-seven. Through the years, she was always there for me, listening to my problems and supporting my dreams. No matter how outlandish my goals, she was always there with an encouraging word and a ready smile.

Later in her life, she was diagnosed with cancer and not given long to live. Even though I knew the end was near, her death was no less devastating. It was hard to fathom that I was never going to have another conversation with her, never see her smile again or solve another puzzle with her.

A few years later, I was living in Chicago. While watching an episode of *Wheel of Fortune,* I had a wave of nostalgia. I decided to complete an online contestant application. I didn't think much of it until I received an e-mail months later announcing that the *Wheel of Fortune* casting team would be coming to Chicago. In order to be considered for an in-person audition, applicants would need to submit a sixty-second video explaining why they wanted to be a contestant.

All my childhood memories of watching the show came flooding back, and I knew I was meant to spin the wheel for real. Immediately, I recorded a video and submitted it. A couple of weeks later, I received an e-mail inviting me to audition in person.

I was a bundle of nerves on the audition day. I couldn't believe I was trying out for "America's Game"! After two rounds of intense auditioning, with half of the hopefuls let go after the first round, it was over. We were told we would receive a letter in the mail within two weeks if we were selected.

I ran to the mailbox every day but there was no letter. After two weeks, I thought it had been delivered to the wrong apartment. After a month, the realization sunk in. I had not been selected.

A few months later, I awoke from a vivid dream.

In the dream, I was watching Wheel of Fortune *when my grandma stepped into the room. She was face-to-face with me.*

Looking at me, she asked, "Why haven't you tried out for Wheel of Fortune *again?"*

Feeling defeated, I replied, "I wasn't good enough. They didn't want me."

With a confident tone, she replied, "Laura, try again. Trust me."

I woke up with a jolt and started crying. All I wanted was to fall back asleep and bask in the warmth and comfort of her presence. It had felt so real — my grandma standing next to me and encouraging me as she had for so many years.

That same week, I received notification that the casting team was headed back to Chicago. I couldn't believe it. My grandma knew exactly when I needed her and instilled in me the confidence to submit another video.

A few days later, I received an e-mail inviting me to audition. This time, I went in more excited than nervous. I already knew what to expect and, more importantly, I had a cheerleader by my side.

I made it to the final stages of the audition process and was told to wait for a letter in the mail. Once again, I went directly to the mailbox every day and walked away disappointed. Then one morning while getting ready for work, I checked my e-mail and let out the loudest scream ever.

There it was: an e-mail from *Wheel of Fortune* stating that they had a tape date for me. I had to read it several times before I truly believed it. I was going to be a contestant on *Wheel of Fortune*!

I ended up filming my episode a few months later, and the entire experience was amazing. From meeting Pat and Vanna, to spinning the wheel and, most importantly, saying those magical words, "I'd like to solve the puzzle." It was a day I will never forget.

I knew that I wouldn't be standing on that stage if it weren't for my grandma's belief in me. She knew when I needed her, and as she had so many times throughout my life, she was there to support and encourage me.

As for that letter that was supposed to come in the mail, it was delivered months later in a plastic package from the U.S. Postal Service stating that it been lost and damaged on the journey. I just chuckled and looked up. I swear I heard my grandma chuckle, too.

— Laura Niebauer Palmer —

21

Granddad and the Lollipop Tree

Anything I've ever done that ultimately was
worthwhile... initially scared me to death.
~Betty Bender

I think about him every time I pass by a pink magnolia tree in bloom. My Irish granddaddy, tall and lean, bursting with energy and laughter, held a special place in my heart. He lived across the street with Grandma, and their home was open to us whenever we ran over to visit. We wouldn't go into their house to find him, however; we would hurry out back where he would be working in his garden.

Flowers, vines, vegetables—whatever he planted flourished. From early spring through late autumn, the immense back yard exploded with colors. Delicate purple cosmos flowers waved beside the garage. Pink and peach roses stood next to the back door. And way in the back was the vegetable plot overflowing with red tomatoes, yellow squashes and green beans.

On the side of the yard grew two apple trees and a small, gnarled pear tree. A majestic magnolia tree stood in the middle. Its shiny, dark green leaves and large pink flowers captured the attention of all who saw it. Besides being beautiful, it was perfect for climbing with its sturdy gray limbs reaching out from the wide trunk. It was perfect for climbing—if I only knew how!

My granddaddy wanted to teach me. He tried. He really tried. But I was afraid I wouldn't be able to get back down, or that I would be stuck high up in the tree, so I didn't want to try.

Except that I *did* want to try. I'd watch my friends climb up their backyard trees, or my sister settle into one of the top boughs and munch on her apple while she surveyed the neighborhood. I wanted to sit on top of the world as well!

And Granddaddy knew it. He tried cajoling, convincing, scolding, even offering to go up the tree with me — which always made me laugh! How could my granddaddy with gray hair know how to climb?

One early spring morning, the magnolia tree was beginning to open its magnificent scented blossoms. Granddaddy was standing on his front porch waiting for me when I walked outside. "Come over here! Come over!" he beckoned excitedly. "The tree is blooming lollipops instead of flowers!"

"What?" I ran across to the back yard to see a dazzling sight. Nestled into every magnolia bud was a lollipop.

"No pink magnolia flowers this year," he muttered sadly as he shook his head. "They'll all turn brown and drop down. What a waste that will be. But this is the first year ever for our tree to bloom lollipops!"

He glanced over to me. "Do you think you could scramble up — just to the lowest branch — and gather one or two? Then throw them down to me. I would love a lollipop!"

I was staring in amazement. Never in all my seven years of living had I seen a tree this beautiful — full of my favorite candy!

Ever so carefully, I shimmied up the smooth trunk, securely placed my feet on the lowest branch and grabbed two lollipops. Just as I was about to slide down, I saw some lollipops on the higher branch. Maybe I could reach them, too! Just one more branch, and then I'd slide back down. So I tossed what was in my hand down to Grandaddy and climbed up to the next branch — and grabbed more. And slowly, branch by branch, I conquered the tree!

When I was at the top, clinging to my lollipops and reaching out to touch the tip-top of the tree, I looked down to see Granddaddy beaming up at me.

"You did it, girl!" he called up to me. "Now get down here so we can enjoy the candy!"

Scrambling down, I gathered up my goodies and giggled. "That was fun!" I said, before running home to share my story.

I burst into the kitchen, hands tightly holding my treasures. "Look!" I exclaimed to Grandma, who was sitting in the kitchen with Mom. "Look what I just picked from the tree!"

"That's amazing, sweetie!" Grandma replied as she gave me a hug. I spilled the yellow, red and orange lollipops onto the table.

"But… but how did that tree bloom lollipops instead of flowers?" I asked Grandma.

"Oh," Grandma shook her head wisely, "Granddaddy can grow about anything, can't he? And did you know that he's an expert at climbing? Why, just this morning I saw him…" She stopped mid-sentence and smiled when she saw Mom shake her head. "You know, sweetie, he can make anything grow — even lollipops on trees!"

— Thalia Dunn —

22

Chirps and Chatter

There are only two kinds of people in the world:
the Irish and those that wish they were.
~Irish Saying

"I'm going to get Omama a parakeet," my mother announced. Omama was my grandmother, and at that time she was in her eighties. "It will give her something to care for," my mother continued. "Her house is so quiet. A little bird may liven things up. If nothing else, it's something to watch besides television."

I nodded my head in agreement. "Something to love," I added. My grandmother had pets in the past, and she had spoiled them properly. I knew that a little bird would get plenty of attention. Omama was a chatterbox, and she could out-talk a politician. She had arrived in America from Ireland, and her memory was fully stocked with tales from the Old Country. She loved nothing better than to reminisce, and once she got going you might as well make yourself comfortable.

Her tales were interesting and exciting, and some were downright amazing. She was a fearless woman who had bulldozed her way through life. She was always ready for anything, so she hardly batted an eye when my mother and I delivered her new roommate.

"His name is Patrick!" she decided. The coffee table was quickly cleared off, and Patrick's cage was set down gently. Omama wet a finger and held it up, checking for a draft. She shifted the cage a bit to the right, out of the sun. My mother gave her the feeding instructions.

Omama listened intently for a minute, and then waved us away. "Think I'll starve him, do you?" she asked accusingly. "He'll eat better than me!"

As we walked toward the door, Omama was plugging in her record player and promising Patrick that he was about to hear some real Irish music. "Listen well and tell me what you think," we heard her say as we stepped outside.

If ever a parakeet was loved, it was Patrick. Omama called us often to report on his charming antics. When she sat on the front porch to get some air, Patrick went along. Soon the neighbors knew Patrick and recognized his chirps blending in with the calls of wild birds. Omama was quick to show off her beautiful blue bird to anyone who passed by.

If we called to say that we planned to visit that day, Omama would say, "Hold on, please," while she announced to Patrick that we were coming.

I knew Omama was crazy about her pet and talked to him constantly. Patrick was special; Omama had assured me of that, more than once. Still, nothing prepared me for the day Patrick would take my breath away.

I hadn't visited in a while. It was chilly outside, and I came in a bit hunched over from the cold. Omama quickly offered a hot cup of coffee. "That sounds wonderful," I told her. She went off to the kitchen, and I sat on the sofa. Patrick acknowledged me by stretching a foot and giving his feathers a slight ruffle. He sidestepped along his perch and peered at me.

"Hello, Patrick," I said casually.

He straightened up and imitated my words as clear as could be. "Hello, Patrick!" he called. I stared in surprise.

"My goodness, I didn't know you could talk."

He must have interpreted that comment as an invitation because he talked my ear off for the next three minutes. "Good morning, Patrick. Hello. Hello, Patrick. Pretty bird. Pretty pretty Patrick. Sweet bird. Kiss, kiss. Hi, Patrick!"

My mouth dropped open. It was not because Patrick was talking. Living with my grandmother, I expected that he would. Patrick had an extensive vocabulary. What shocked me, and to this day makes me smile, was that every word Patrick said was spoken in a perfect Irish brogue!

—Marianne Fosnow—

23

Violet

Nobody can do for little children what grandparents
do. Grandparents sort of sprinkle stardust over the
lives of little children.
~Alex Haley

When I was a kid, I had a purple stuffed cat named Violet who I took everywhere. I slept with her, made her talk, and acted out scenes and adventures with her.

One fall weekend when I was six, my little sister and I slept over at our grandparents' house, as we did every once in a while. Of course, Violet came, too. Our grandparents' back yard bordered a field that we would sometimes walk through to see the farm animals.

When it was time to go home, Violet was nowhere to be found. We looked everywhere in the house. I was devastated. I couldn't sleep without her.

Months passed, but she did not turn up. That entire winter, it felt like I fell asleep crying every night, missing her, thinking about her being alone and scared.

Spring came, and my grandpa was out in the back yard talking to the farmer as he took a break from mowing the field. As the farmer started the mower back up, my grandfather saw shreds of purple flying out from it. He recognized them immediately.

My grandpa carefully gathered up every piece: the torn-off head, the broken tail, and the body, which was filled with bees that had made their nest inside.

He carefully removed the bees and washed the pieces. And then, this man who had spent his whole life working on cars and trucks repaired my beloved Violet. He replaced her destroyed stuffing with cotton balls and stitched her up. It turned out he could fix anything!

My grandparents came over to our house that weekend, and when I woke up and went downstairs, Violet was waiting on the counter for me. The sight of her made me sad. She had red and black stitches all over her body. She didn't have eyes anymore. But it was okay. I still loved Violet.

It took years for me to realize what a huge gift my grandpa had given me. Now that he's gone, I fully realize how much he loved me and how hard he worked on that cat. Violet might have lost her eyes, but she taught me to see.

— Elizabeth Alonzo —

Gunner's Gift

I have learned that there is more power in a good
strong hug than in a thousand meaningful words.
~Ann Hood

To get a hug from my grandson I had to chase him down, grab him and pull him into my arms before he knew what hit him. Then I had to smother him with affection quickly before he struggled out of my arms.

Gunner wasn't always like that with me, his Grandma Renee. There was a time when I would walk in the door and he would come running at me full speed. He'd yell, "Gramma Nee!" and jump right into my open arms. His enthusiastic greeting always made me feel like I was his favorite, as prized as the beloved fuzzy, filthy blanket he carried around everywhere and slept with at night.

But he became independent so quickly, not just with me but with his parents as well, preferring to do everything himself. His stubbornness was evident when he didn't want to do something, which proved to be a challenge for his mom and dad at times. But his heart would always melt just a bit for me, and I treasured it. Hugs were few and far between, but we still had a connection.

When my mother passed away, Gunner was five and a half years old, and I worried he might be too young to attend the funeral. But his parents brought him along with his three-year-old sister, Brinlee. In fact, all my mother's great-grandchildren were at the funeral.

I was full of grief at Mom's memorial, but inside I was more

Treasured Moments & Memories | 75

concerned about how others were doing. I didn't cry as we stood over her casket viewing her frail body. I didn't think I had any tears left after watching her gasp for breath for three days as she lay dying in the hospital.

I watched as Gunner and my other grandchildren viewed her lifeless form and touched her out of curiosity. I wondered how much of this event they understood. They never got to spend much time with their great-grandmother, but she always made them feel welcome and special when they came to visit. I wished I could read their little minds. They did exhibit some signs of sorrow, but mostly the gathering was about seeing their cousins and other children and running around outside.

Once the simple funeral service started, I sat at the front of the room by myself. I wanted to be close to my mom while I listened to the pastor talk about her, and her casket was just a short distance to the right of me.

Pastor Kathy talked about how Mom had touched so many lives through sewing quilts and gifting them to people. She asked the congregation how many people had received quilts from her, and three-fourths of the people raised their hands, including all the grandkids and great-grandkids. As I turned and saw all those hands in the air, I thought about the impact she had made on all our lives. She wasn't much for public displays of affection, but we knew how much love she put in her quilts.

Toward the end of the service, the grandkids and great-grandkids were all given red hearts with magnets on them to place on Mom's metal casket. They all lined up single file and walked up to leave their hearts with Grandma Sell. It was heartwarming and heart wrenching at the same time.

I watched as Gunner stood in line to put his red heart on the casket. He looked somber and a little unsure of the task. I hated that he had to experience these moments of grief at such a young age, but his parents wanted him to learn about the whole cycle of life at an early age.

One of Mom's favorite hymns, "The Old Rugged Cross," started playing. That was the same song we played at my dad's funeral a few years earlier. The combination of that song and all those magnetic hearts on the casket made me very emotional. Right at that moment, as soon as Gunner had completed the ritual of placing his heart, he came running toward me and leaped into my arms. He sat there on my lap, with his little arms around my neck, as I hummed along with the music.

I relished Gunner's presence in my lap. How did he know that his Gramma Nee needed that hug at the very moment like I needed nothing else in my whole life? Finally, I was able to cry, with Gunner embracing me through the whole song. When it was over, he jumped down and went on his way, not knowing the impact he had had on me. He might have thought I was comforting him, but really he was comforting me.

Our bond grew stronger than ever that day.

— Rita Renee Lange Weatherbee —

25

Two Gray Heads

If becoming a grandmother was only a matter of
choice, I should advise every one of you straight away
to become one. There is no fun for old people like it!
~Hannah Whitall Smith

Grammy sounded both excited and doubtful. "You're going to put me on a horse?"

I laughed. "If you're up for it, yes. I'm going to take the family on a trail ride."

As the assistant horsemanship director at a camp, I enjoyed having the opportunity to expose my family to horses. And Grammy was still active and adventurous at age seventy-one. When she came ready to ride in jeans and a worn blue jacket, I knew exactly which horse I would have her ride. Lucky was a seasoned gray gelding that would take good care of my senior citizen, but the real reason was because of his color. Grammy had a thing for white horses.

I whistled, cracked the whip, and sent the herd thundering toward the catch pen. The drizzly November day had turned the dust to mud. It sucked at my boots as I haltered Lucky and brought him over to the tie post.

"This is your horse today. His name is Lucky."

Grammy picked her way around a puddle and ran a brush across Lucky's crusty coat.

"Oh, he's white, just like Cotton!"

I smiled. "Exactly."

I was about eight years old the first time she told me the story about Cotton. I had just finished cutting all the horse photos out of her *National Geographic* magazines for my horse scrapbook.

"I loved horses when I was your age, too," she reminisced. "For a few summers when I was a teenager, my mother and I spent a week at Lake Tahoe. All year, I saved my money — babysitting for twenty-five cents an hour or picking prunes in my grandfather's orchard — so that I could ride Cotton while we were there."

Grammy's eyes brightened. "Cotton was this beautiful white horse, and I loved him. Each summer, I rented him for a trail ride. The trail took about an hour, but once we were away from the barn, we'd go fast, and then walk back so the horses weren't too sweaty."

I tried to picture my grandma as a girl like me, flying through the forest on her white horse. I couldn't, really. She was Grammy — permanently gray-haired and grown-up.

That summer, and every summer for the next four years, Grammy's birthday present to me was a week at horse camp. I lived for that one week every summer. All year, I played with my model horses and galloped around the playground on my imaginary horse, dreaming of the day I would actually get to ride.

At camp, I went on my first trail ride. My horse? A gray gelding, of course. Comanche plodded through the Blackberry Pass and Wild Oak trails, nose glued to the tail of the horse in front of him. I didn't care; I was on a horse. The best part was when he fell behind and trotted to catch up. The trail would always lead us back to the barn far too soon. Even though it was hot and dusty, I didn't want the rides to end.

My one week of horse camp in the summers turned into weekly riding lessons, a college degree in equine science, and a full-time job at the camp where it all started. The horses that taught me to ride — Miramar, Leaf, Comanche, and Manzanita — were all white like Cotton. They turned a horse-crazy girl into a lifelong horsewoman.

Grammy supported and encouraged me every step of the way. On Christmas mornings, I could count on a horse-themed gift from her. When I was a teenager, we took a special trip together to Arizona just to watch the Tucson rodeo.

When I was in college, not only did she help pay my tuition, but she trekked three hours to visit me at the barn where I competed with the equestrian team.

Now it was my turn to share with Grammy the experience she had made possible for me. She hadn't ridden a horse since Cotton, and I was excited to re-create the wonderful experience she had as a child.

Lucky turned his head to look at Grammy with the same golden eyes that had looked at me across the fence twenty years earlier. His dark dapples had faded to white long ago, and he had matured into the calm and gentle patriarch of the herd. Grammy eased herself into the saddle and picked up the reins with arthritic hands. I was grateful that the rain had stopped in time for our ride. I put Grammy right behind me, and the rest of the family fell into line as we headed out. Lucky picked his way carefully up the same trail where I had taken my first trail ride.

From my place in the lead, I turned to look behind me. Two gray heads bobbed in unison, merging past and present memories into one sweet moment.

"How are you doing, Grammy?"

"Wonderful! This is so special." Grammy raised her fist triumphantly.

Together, we were kids again, riding our favorite horses.

— Sarah Barnum —

26

Grandma's Kitchen

Grandmas are moms with lots of frosting.
~Author Unknown

Grandma and I could not talk to each other. It wasn't that we didn't want to; it was because she spoke Hungarian, and I spoke French.

My mother never taught us her mother tongue because she only planned to take us to Hungary every few years. My father thought that was okay, because Mom always translated for us.

But here I was at Grandma's house — alone with her for a couple of hours. My parents were going into town by themselves. I was only nine, and this was scary. Of course, Grandma was always nice to me, but I was afraid I would do something I was not supposed to because I did not understand her.

"Bettyke." Grandma was calling me from the kitchen, my favorite part of her house. I went in there and, to my surprise, Grandma had thought of a cooking project for the two of us. Flour, sugar, eggs, baking powder, milk, and a rolling pin had been placed on the kitchen table.

Grandma kept talking to me, and even though I did not know exactly what she was saying, I knew what I had to do. I was going to imitate what Grandma did and learn how to bake with her.

We were speaking different tongues to each other, but it did not matter as it seemed we understood each other anyway. We laughed and had so much fun; we even managed to make a delicious cake.

It turned out to be the best time I ever had at Grandma's. My parents were so surprised when they came home. After that day, I took it upon myself to learn Hungarian words related to cooking so I could have even more fun with Grandma.

She passed away a few months ago. When I learned of her passing, all I could think about was that wonderful memory of her teaching me how to bake.

Now that I have kids of my own, I am passing on Grandma's recipes to them. After all, food is the international language of love.

— Betty Farkas-Hart —

100% Cotton
Green Goblin Boxers

Hem your blessings with thankfulness
so they don't unravel.
~Author Unknown

I point my grandson toward the rows of fabrics. "Choose a material you like," I say. "Make sure the bolt says 100% cotton."

I can hardly believe that Travis is starting kindergarten. He looks so small. It seems like yesterday he sat in the basket while I pushed him around the fabric store. Now he insists on pushing the cart and picking out fabric himself. I have to wait for him by the cutting counter.

Travis returns with his selection. "Got it, Gramma."

"Hey, bud, I think you'd better pick out another," I say when I see a bolt of cotton corduroy. I am making him a pair of boxer shorts. "I know what this says, but it will make you too hot." Travis darts off to the Halloween material display and, after careful consideration, chooses a neon green goblin print.

The following Monday, I arrive at his home to get him off to school. After I present him with new boxers, he rushes into his bedroom. Soon, he comes out with the goblin boxers over white knit underwear. "I'm ready," he announces, planning to wear the goblin boxers as shorts.

"Travis, look," I say, and point out the slit fly in the front.

"Ohhh," he says and dashes back into his bedroom. When he

returns, the boxers are turned around with the fly in the back.

"Plus," I add, "I'd like you to wear long pants today since it's chilly out, and you're getting over a cold. Put your jeans on over your new boxers."

Travis frowns and stomps back to his bedroom, mumbling to himself.

I peek in his room. There he stands in front of the mirror. "Gramma is so mean. She says I have to wear long pants, and I want shorts. Look at me. I look like a dork."

As we take off for school, Travis notices bright green peeking over the waistband of his jeans. "Uh-oh," he giggles and pokes his new boxers down. "I don't want people to see my won-doe wear!"

* * *

My front door swings open. Travis slips an arm around me and rests his chin on top of my head. He grabs a pencil and writes on my calendar: "Travis's High School Graduation, 7:00 p.m." Then he opens my refrigerator door. "Hey, old gal, got anything good to eat?"

As he bends over to look in my refrigerator, I get a nice view of his "won-doe wear." Like most boys, he wears low-slung pants. My mind drifts back. How come these blue plaid undies I'm staring at aren't as cute as that 100 percent cotton green goblin pair was?

— Sharon Landeen —

Nana's Secret

Everyone is the age of their heart.
~Guatemalan Proverb

Please, don't show this to Nana! If she knew her secret was out, I would have one heck of a time redeeming myself.

You see, Nana has always been ageless. Not only would she never tell her age, but no one dared to ask. We all knew that, for a reason known only to her, this subject was taboo. It was not until Nana broke her hip that anyone ever needed to know her secret. So a scavenger hunt was launched, one that would unearth some very interesting items from Nana's schoolgirl years.

First discovered was a wonderful class picture with very solemn-faced young girls in bustles and stoic-looking young boys in knickers. We knew this represented Nana's eighth-grade class because that information was clearly legible on the chalkboard along with the name of the school, the teacher and the city. Notably missing on the board, however, was the day and date traditionally found on boards in classrooms everywhere. Upon closer inspection, the portion of the photograph where the date would have been found, had clearly been scratched out with a sharp object.

The next object found was Nana's diploma… with a hole in it. Hmm… Since moths do not usually have much of an appetite for paper, we assumed that this, at one time, was the date.

Nana did not drive so there was never a driver's license. A birth certificate was never found, and a request to obtain one from the State of New York was unsuccessful… some technicality that only requests from the named would be honored.

The only solid lead was a dated baptismal certificate. Well, not so solid when we discovered that the ink on the date didn't quite match the rest of the writing on the document. A letter to the church in New York City finally cleared up the confusion. The parish priest replied with a note stating Nana's exact date of baptism and the age that she was on that day.

Pieces of stories heard long ago were finally beginning to fit together.

Around the year 1915, a young woman working in a factory sat at her sewing machine piecing together parachutes that would be shipped overseas for the war effort. Concentration was difficult as the workday was almost over, and her mind was on the next day's island picnic.

It was an early rising for Nana that summer day of the picnic so there would be plenty of time to meet friends and catch the first boat. They wanted to be certain to stake out their claim for the best spot on the beach.

In contrast to the bikinied volleyball games of today, the crowd on the beach would appear rather sedate as they tried to keep the sun off their bodies. Only the most risqué of the ladies present would inch up their swim skirts and roll down their dark hose to expose their knees. I never did figure out whether Nana was in the latter group.

What I do know is that, sometime that day, Nana was attracted by the good looks, charisma and radiant smile of a ukulele player named Robert. They spent that day and several days later together, enjoying what Nana always referred to as "keeping company." In fact, they kept company so well that day on the beach that they missed the return ferry with their group and had to wait for a later shuttle.

All went well until Nana discovered that Robert was five years younger than she, which at the time was an embarrassing, even humiliating position for either party. So, a choice was made. Nana axed six years off her age that day and set out to destroy or alter any evidence that would prove otherwise. It was quite a task, but this determined lady was convinced that no one like Robert would ever come her way again. She would forever spare him the humiliation of the time:

marrying an older woman.

Nana is napping in her wheelchair now as I sit by her. Her eyes flutter open just long enough to catch mine, and there is a hint of a smile before she dozes off once again. I kiss her forehead as I turn to leave her room.

Sleep well, Nana.

Your secret is safe with me.

— Kathleen Steele —

29

A Sticky Situation

*Grandfathers are magicians who create wonderful
memories for their grandchildren.*
~Author Unknown

Both of my parents worked full-time — my mother as a nurse and my father as a state cop. Sometimes, they worked the same shifts, which caused issues in the summer when we were out of school. My grandfather often stepped up and took us for those full days.

We never really knew what adventure lay before us at Grandpa's. It could be fishing in ponds we didn't have permission to be at. Or he could hand us each a $10 bill and take us shopping at the mall. Or we might hang around his place, the basement or garage that held so many interesting trinkets. The options were endless.

One day, Grandpa loaded the three of us into his Ford Escort hatchback, the ugliest yellowish-beige color you ever did see. I had never seen a car that color before, nor have I since. I have no recollection of where we were headed, nor do I know if we had a set destination in mind. All I remember was that the three of us were loaded up with Grandpa, and we were headed toward Broadway.

I remember coming up to 34th Street. Grandpa talked about gum and asked if any of us wanted some. My grandfather was the Gum King and always had multiple flavors stashed in his pockets. My sister, Charity, seated up front, took a package. Angie, my other sister, and I were in the back seat. We both voiced our desire to have a piece, too. Grandpa turned around to hand us a package, and we were suddenly airborne!

Grandpa's Escort had climbed the curb. The passenger side was on the curb, and the driver's side was still planted firmly on the street.

My grandfather whirled back around and grabbed the wheel. I remember all of us, Grandpa included, screaming as we saw a SPEED LIMIT sign suddenly appear in the windshield. He only had moments to react. Just as quickly as we had gone up, we came crashing back down. We were headed back toward Broadway, miraculously avoiding a collision with a metal sign.

I remember Grandpa looking up in the rearview mirror at me and Angie as he said, "We'll hold off on the gum for a bit."

That right there would have been enough to call it a day, but we weren't through yet. We continued to travel up to Broadway and then turned to head east down the main road. We passed Casey Middle School and crossed the tracks approaching the stoplight that sat there. Grandpa turned around again, only for a moment, to pass back that ill-fated package of gum. I remember trying to reassure Grandpa that we could hold out until the stoplight, but Grandpa was not having it. His grandkids needed gum, and we were going to get it.

That's when we hit something. Something SOLID.

I looked up to see the Stan the Tire Man ad to my right. The woman in the ad was glaring down at us. And what was the solid thing in front of us? My grandpa had just hit a BUS! He calmly told us to "Stay put" and climbed out of the car. By this time, two men wearing cowboy hats had exited the bus and come to the back of the large vehicle. They approached my grandpa, and all three of them began talking. I watched from the back seat of the car, trying to get any of the conversation I could, but I couldn't hear anything. That's when my twin sister noticed something.

"Look!"

She pointed to the bus. The back window curtains parted a bit, and we saw someone looking out at everyone below. I could make out what appeared to be a female with long hair. A slight wave came from the window, and I watched my grandfather wave back. That's when I

noticed something: a name ran across the back of the bus. It read…
Loretta Lynn.

My grandfather had just rear-ended Loretta Lynn's tour bus!

I remember my grandpa shaking the men's hands and waving one final time at the window in the back of the bus. It appeared as if there was no damage to the bus and surprisingly no damage to grandpa's Escort. Grandpa opened the door to the car and slid in. He shut the door and then let out a long sigh. After a few moments of silence, he turned to all of us and smiled.

"So, who needed gum?" he asked, pulling out a package from the pocket of his shirt.

—Jeremy Mays—

30

My Lunchtime Grandfather

Many people will walk in and out of your life, but only
true friends will leave footprints in your heart.
~Eleanor Roosevelt

I had been waitressing for a couple of months, earning some extra money for college. "Since it's not too busy, go see if Ray wants any more coffee," my boss said to me as he pointed to an older man sitting in the corner.

Ray was taking small sips from the cup in his hand as he stared out the window. He was a regular lunch customer on Mondays and Fridays. He always sat by the window, and he seemed to be thinking about something far away.

"Can I warm that up for you, Ray?" I asked. He looked up with a peaceful smile and held his cup out toward me.

"You know, I've been coming in here for several years, and I have to say you have the nicest smile," he whispered.

"Thanks," I laughed as I held up some cream. He shook his head and looked over at my boss behind the counter.

"I'm going to borrow her for a couple of minutes… Okay, boss?" Ray shouted across the empty room to my boss, who nodded.

"Only for you Ray," he answered, and then he walked into the back room.

Ray tapped the table across from him. "Can you sit for a couple of minutes… please?"

I sat down hesitantly, and he smiled and touched my hand. "Don't worry, I'm not some crazy degenerate. It's just that your smile reminds me of my granddaughter."

I relaxed in my chair. I liked Ray's smile, too. There was something about him that made me feel at ease. "Well, thanks. What's her name?"

"Sharon," he said as he pulled out his wallet from his pants pocket. He took out a picture of her and handed it to me. "She graduated from college last year."

"What a nice-looking girl," I said. "Does she live near you?"

Ray shook his head as he glanced at the picture and then put it back in his wallet. "They moved across the country last year. I miss her a lot. She and I used to have lunch together on Mondays and Fridays."

A flash of lightning and a burst of thunder rumbled outside the window. I jumped a little, but Ray didn't move an inch as he looked at his coffee.

"Any chance she went to that college across the street, Ray?"

Ray grinned at me shyly. "You're too smart for me. We'd meet up here so she didn't have to drive off campus."

"That's where I go now," I said. "It sounds like you two were close."

"Sharon was my daughter's first, so I got to spoil her rotten. I used to pick her up every day after grade school, and we would hang out in the park, get ice cream…" He laughed a little. "We did pretty much anything we felt like, including getting into trouble with her mother."

He put down his cup and touched my hand again. "You probably did the same thing with your granddad, too."

I looked out the window for a split second and then back at Ray. "I wish. I never got to know my grandfather except from some pictures my mom had of him. He died when I was two."

Ray touched my hand softly. "Oh… I'm sorry. He missed out, too."

I could feel warm tears welling in the corners of my eyes, but I fought them back quickly.

"She wants me to move out there to be closer to her," Ray said.

"So, why don't you?"

"I don't know if I really want to move. I've been here all my life," he answered.

I heard my boss clearing his throat from behind the counter. We both looked over at him.

"I guess that's meant for me," I said as I stood up.

We smiled at each other. "Ray… if my grandfather had been like you, I would have bugged him day and night to move closer to me, too." I patted his shoulder. "Don't wait too long. Nice talking with you… See you on Friday?"

Ray patted my hand and nodded.

For the rest of the day, I thought about our conversation and wondered what it would have been like if my grandfather were still alive. In a way, I felt cheated that I didn't get that opportunity to know him.

For the next couple of weeks, Ray continued to come in on Mondays and Fridays. He always stopped by the counter and asked how my week was going.

When he was in the dining room and it was slow, I would ask to take my break so I could sit with him for a while.

He showed me pictures of his family out west and told me their latest tactic to get him to move. I told him about college and asked him questions about his life.

Ray became the grandfather I never knew. When Thanksgiving was around the corner, I felt moved to get him a card.

On that Monday of Thanksgiving week, I waited for Ray to come in, but he never showed. First, I thought maybe he wasn't feeling well. If he had gone to visit his granddaughter, I thought he would have said something to me. With no number to call him, I said a small prayer that he was okay and put his card in my glove box.

One Wednesday afternoon, I was getting off my shift. Walking out to my car, I heard a voice yell my name from across the parking lot.

It was Ray, hustling to catch up to me.

"I thought I missed you," he said, catching his breath as he stood in front of me.

"Everything okay, Ray? Didn't see you on Monday."

Ray pulled out a folded piece of paper and handed it to me with a grin on his face. It was addressed to Ray with a California return address.

"Go on, open it." Ray was excited.

"…So I'll be flying in on Wednesday at 7:10 p.m. Hoping you can pick me up if your car isn't too packed. I can't wait for our adventure… Love ya, Sharon."

Ray looked as happy as a kid in a candy store. "Adventure?" I asked.

"The moving truck left on Monday and is arriving there today. Sharon's coming here to help drive my car… I'm finally going."

"Wow!" I said as I gave him a big hug. "What made you change your mind?"

"Well…" looking down at the letter as he folded it back up, "you did." Our eyes teared up as he took my hand and smiled.

"These last couple of weeks, you reminded me of how important being a grandfather is… I kind of forgot that when Sharon moved."

I gave him another hug and whispered, "And you gave me a chance to have a grandfather. Thank you."

— Kam Giegel —

Through the Eyes of a Child

31

Grace to Live in the Moment

There is a saying: Yesterday is history,
tomorrow is a mystery, but today is a gift.
That is why it is called the "present."
~Oogway, Kung Fu Panda

My granddaughter Madison was three years old when my flower garden drew her in. She stood in front of a rosebush and leaned close. Cupping a Barbie-pink blossom with both hands, she nestled her face into its petals and breathed deep.

"Meema, your woses smell so so good."

"Madison! Don't smash it!"

I knelt in the dirt, yanking at weeds. The day before, I came home from a relaxing weekend trip to a cluttered home: toys tossed about the living room; wet towels on the bathroom floor; dirty dishes with last night's dinner stuck to them.

So, the overdue weeding got to me. *I have to do everything around here. I live with the laziest people on earth. And why am I raising my granddaughter?* I, the victim. I, the under-valued. I, so sweet and blessed just yesterday at a women's retreat. I. I. I.

In the middle of my pity party, I suddenly realized it was a bit too quiet. Looking up, I saw a rosebush stripped almost bare. My face flushed hot. I was about to get angry.

But then I saw Madison twirl.

Her face was toward the sun and her pigtails stuck straight out. With little arms raised and her palms to the sky, silky rose petals fluttered from her hands and floated to the ground. Shades from pink to white blanketed the brown mulch and wound around the other nearly naked bushes. Dizzy from her dance, Madison wobbled and then steadied herself. Her eyes were wide-open as she admired her work.

"Oh, Meema. Isn't it bee-u-tee-ful?"

Watching my granddaughter changed my toxic thoughts. My self-focus and snarky attitude lifted. I saw my brown-haired, blue-eyed little burst of energy as a gift. Though it was sometimes difficult and exhausting, I was blessed to tuck her in at night with stories, hugs and kisses while her daddy was deployed with the Air Force. It was a privilege to say the words she wouldn't hear from her biological mother, who had left because she wasn't ready to be a parent.

"Yes, Madison Grace. You are absolutely beautiful."

Like the weeds in my flower garden, life's messes can distract me from what's most important. If I'm not careful, in a nano-second, my blessings become burdens. When it's all about me, I whine and blame and complain about my plans, my comfort, my happiness. But a me-centered world is quite small, and it yanks the joy right out of life.

I've heard, "Life isn't made of years; it's made of moments."

My moments with Madison remind me to grab life with both hands, breathe deep, and be thankful. To not let difficult challenges choke out the everyday blessings. I'm reminded that roses grow back, and children grow up. Boom. Just like that. And it's so easy to miss it.

Sometimes, I still mumble and grumble. But each morning and throughout the day, I try to choose the right thoughts and attitudes. I pause and breathe a prayer because I do not want to miss one more precious moment.

— Robin K. Melvin —

32

Hoohoo Fraks

I want to take all our best moments, put them in a jar,
and take them out like cookies and
savor each one of them forever.
~Crystal Wood

My grandson Josh is a train freak. Thomas the Train is his favorite toy. He has several of the other toy engines featured on the TV show as well. In the weeks leading up to his fourth birthday, when I came home from work, he would meet me at the door and say, "PawPaw Mike? Thomas birthday." He was so excited that his speech impediment would become worse, and I would have trouble understanding him.

For his birthday, I decided to take him on a train ride. The train I picked runs from Jersey City to Newark, New Jersey. It takes about forty minutes to make the trip in one direction. I chose this train because, for the first part of the trip, it runs underground. The remainder of the trip is spent above ground. Even better, we could get in the front car and look out the window at the tracks as we rolled over them.

Down in the subway, Josh saw the tracks. "Fraks! PawPaw Mike! Fraks!" He would only take his eyes off the tracks when a train passed. We got on the first car of our train and walked to the front to stare out the window. I explained to the gentleman sitting there, "It is my grandson Josh's birthday. He loves trains, and this ride is my birthday gift to him."

The gentleman got up and let us have his seat by the front window. The train began to roll along. It made several stops underground, and then the part I was waiting for came. We blasted up out of the tunnel, and there in front of us were rows and rows of tracks and even a few trains parked on sidings.

Josh began to screech with delight. "PawPaw Mike! Fraks! Look at the fraks! PawPaw! Look at the fraks!" Then he saw the parked trains. "PawPaw Mike! Hoohoos! Look! Hoohoos," he squealed.

My little grandson stood in the window and would not take his eyes off all the tracks and trains. It was one of those moments when I could not stop smiling.

At Newark, we transferred to the returning train. Halfway home, the train had to stop for a few minutes until a train ahead had been switched to another rail. As we waited, the conductor of the train opened his door and saw Josh staring out the window.

"Hey, little man! How are you?" he asked.

I explained it was his birthday, his first time on a train, and that he was a big fan of trains. "Come here then, Josh! I'll show you something." He sat Josh in the conductor's seat and let him blow the horn.

Josh got back in my lap, a grin splitting his face, as the train continued its journey. At that moment, I looked to the back of the car and saw a sea of smiling faces. Everyone was watching Josh and grinning.

Children give such a beautiful gift — innocence. Josh was yelling and squealing about the "hoohoos" and "fraks" without a clue as to how he was affecting the other passengers. It was impossible not to smile. They all watched this little train fanatic enjoy his first ride on a train. His pure, innocent joy was a beautiful thing to witness.

I have ridden that train many times and hardly ever saw a smiling face. People usually sit quietly, waiting to get to their destination. They read or stare straight ahead, ignoring their fellow travelers.

Josh was only four, but I doubt he will ever forget his first train ride with his PawPaw, and I doubt many of our companions that day will forget it either. Josh taught us all a lesson. If we could only see things through the eyes of a child, see them new and fresh every time, life would be more interesting. If I ever feel bored over the things I see every day, I am going to think of "hoohoos" and "fraks," and remember to see them through Josh's eyes.

—Michael T. Smith—

Penny Power

Children make you want to start life over.
~Muhammad Ali

Taylor was standing sideways like a baseball pitcher, her right arm poised in the air. "Are you ready, Grandma?" Taylor called to me.

I stood beside her and imitated the pose. "I'm ready now," I said.

"Okay, make your wish and throw your penny," she instructed. I peeked at Taylor before I tossed my penny into the fountain. Her eyes were closed, and she seemed to be deep in concentration. With a satisfied nod of her head, she flung the penny. Quickly, I did the same. Our coins landed in the water with a gentle *plink* and then slowly sank. They joined the silver and copper mosaic that blanketed the bottom of the fountain.

I took Taylor's hand, and we walked over to a nearby park bench. We perched together like pigeons, taking in the scenery. The warm sun brought a sense of contentment, and we snuggled together.

"What did you wish for, Grandma?" Taylor asked me.

"Oh, I wished for a new dishwasher," I answered. "My old one has been making a funny noise."

Taylor looked at me quizzically, and then looked down at the ground. She seemed disappointed.

"What did you wish for, honey?" I asked. Immediately, she stood up and held my face in her hands. She does that when she wants to ensure my full attention. Taking a deep breath, she whispered, "I wished for a butterfly to land on my finger." Her eyes sparkled as she added, "That would be amazing!"

I stared at her. Once again, I had learned something important from this tiny teacher. How foolish grown-ups can be, wasting our wishes...

I reached in my purse for another penny. Taylor followed as I walked back to the fountain. She watched me close my eyes, concentrate, and toss. This time, my penny seemed to dance on its way down.

I won't tell you what I wished for, but you can be sure it wasn't a dishwasher!

—Marianne Fosnow—

Naptime with Grandma

Babies are bits of stardust,
blown from the hand of God.
~Debasish Mridha

Today, I sat and held you while you took a nap
I just sat and stared at you, this bundle in my lap
I could have laid you down and gotten a few things done
But let me tell you something, my precious little one
The years flew by with my kids, one of them your dad
And I wouldn't change a thing and all the fun we had
But sometimes I let life rush me, and I didn't take the time
To store up precious memories, treasures in my mind
I won't make that mistake again; this is my second chance
I'm going to take the moment, to take that second glance
It's not wasted time I spend admiring your sweet face
I know in just a short time, changes will take place
Babies don't stay babies; this phase passes much too fast
I'm making me a memory; these days will soon be in the past
I'm looking forward to it all! Life for me is good!
I've entered a special time called grandmotherhood
Your parents have the advantage; I'm at their beck and call
But here's the best part about it… I don't mind at all
I'll gladly be there for them; I've been waiting years for this
There's not a thing in your childhood that I want to miss
Oh, I'll try not to crowd them; they need their family time, too

But I'll be sitting by the phone if there's something I can do
I'm older and I'm wiser; there are things that I have learned
Grandkids are like a "do over," I get a second turn!
So you just keep on sleeping, maybe I'll nap, too
I'm going to need the energy to keep pace with you
I'm storing memories in my mind; you're already in my heart
I close my eyes and smile; for me and you, it's just the start.

— Kala F. Cota —

Grandma Saves the Day

A child needs a grandparent, anybody's grandparent,
to grow a little more securely into an unfamiliar world.
~Charles and Ann Morse

One lovely spring morning, my new granddaughter, Tricia, age five, was helping me sort through some pictures to place in the family album. When we came upon a photo of me posing by an old, rustic water pump, I was surprised when she asked if she could have the picture.

"Of course, you can, honey. But what are you going to do with it?" I was curious since none of the other grandkids had ever asked for my picture.

"I want to put it in my new wallet so you can be with me all the time, Grandma," she replied.

My heart melted.

Our son, Jeff, and Tricia's mother, Tammie, had dated in high school, but went their separate ways upon graduation. Fate brought them back together a few years later, and they were now happily married.

Since Tricia's birth father was not involved in her life, she was overjoyed to have a new daddy and a large, loving family.

The couple had been living in an apartment in town nearly ten miles from us, but they longed to move closer to our home in the country.

Coincidentally, my recently widowed mother (who lived just up the private gravel road from us) had a workshop adjacent to her home. She offered it to the couple if they were willing to do some major renovating to convert it into a small house.

Jeff and Tammie jumped at the opportunity and began working on their new home immediately. Their plan was to move in by the time school started in September.

Mom was looking forward to having them close since her house was at the end of the road and somewhat secluded from her neighbors. It was the perfect fit for all.

They worked diligently all summer, with many motivated family members spurring them on to meet their September move-in date. While working on some finishing touches on a late August afternoon, I overheard Jeff call out to Tricia.

"Will you please run down to the house and get my tape measure off the kitchen table, Tricia?"

Thrilled at having been asked to do a favor for her father, Tricia smiled broadly, hopped on her little purple bike and took off down the gravel road.

When Tricia didn't return as quickly as she should have, we became concerned. Tammie and I walked down the road toward my house to look for her. We didn't see her along the way, and she wasn't at the house when we got there.

We checked around the property, calling out her name, with no luck. The neighbors were few and far between, but we decided it would be smart to walk down the road in the other direction and ask if anyone had seen her. When we didn't find her by the time we got to the main road (about a half-mile from the house), panic ensued. We hurried back to call the local police.

As we approached the front porch, we could hear my phone ringing in the house. Tammie ran through the door and picked it up, praying for good news.

It was an officer from the county police department asking if we had a little girl named Tricia. Tammie gasped and answered, "Yes, she's my daughter. Is she alright?"

It was great news! A man and his wife had found Tricia crying beside her bike in front of their house on the main road leading into town. The officer gave us the address and said he'd wait for us to arrive. Without inquiring further as to how she got there, we hopped in my car and hurried down to pick her up.

I recognized our neighbors Ron and Toni standing with Tricia and the officer. Ironically, their son and Jeff had been soccer teammates several years prior.

A little ashamed at having allowed a five-year-old to get this far from home on her bike unattended, we quickly explained that she was only supposed to ride a very short distance down the gravel road. When we asked Tricia why she rode so far, she sobbed, "Dad told me to go down to the house and get his tape measure."

It hadn't occurred to us that Tricia wouldn't know when her father said "the house" that he was referring to the house in which he grew up. It was only natural that she would assume he meant the apartment where they were living — and that's where she was headed.

When she reached a steep incline and couldn't pedal her bike any farther, she got scared and started to cry. Luckily, the couple spotted her quickly.

Since Tricia knew me only as Grandma, I asked the officer how they made the connection, which led to his phone call.

Ron laughed and said, "Tricia showed us a picture of you, Connie. And, of course, we recognized you. We thought it would be better to contact the police before putting her in our car and trying to find your house."

"She had the picture with her?" I asked, slightly embarrassed.

"Yes," Toni laughed. "She had her little purse in her bicycle basket, and yours was the only photo or identification of any kind in her wallet. She was so proud to show us the picture of her grandma!"

Wow, I never would have guessed that the picture Tricia requested months earlier would have played such an important part in finding her safe and sound. Her words were truly prophetic when she said, "I want to put it in my new wallet so you can be with me all the time."

Thirty years later, our bond has only grown stronger. And though I'm certain my photo has been replaced in my granddaughter's wallet

with those of her three beautiful young daughters, I continue to be
with her in spirit all the time.

— Connie Kaseweter Pullen —

36

Panic Button

A smile is a curve that sets everything straight.
~Phyllis Diller

The horn's sudden blare shot me so high out of my seat that I smashed my head on the visor, causing a stream of giggling from the back seat. Instead of being frightened, my grandkids, two-year-old Carson and four-year-old Maddy, shrieked with glee along with each horrendous beep.

Unfamiliar with modern automobiles, I had no idea that a car fob had a "panic button" or that my daughter (who had safely locked us in the car) had unknowingly hit it when she'd entered the building.

Of all the places to get trapped in a honking car, this was the worst! My daughter had parked in front of the courthouse on Main Street during the busiest part of the day.

Shoppers and business people scurried by on their lunch breaks, but still found time to gawk at us. Most couldn't help tossing a disapproving look my way. After all, I'm sure they thought that, as the "adult," I should have done something to stop the noise.

Blushing from embarrassment, I ducked on the floor so that no one could see me. Once down, I popped back up, afraid that a well-meaning citizen might decide that my daughter had abandoned her children and would call the police. My actions caused an extra-loud explosion from my grandchildren, who thought I was playing hide-and-seek with them and the people who glared at us.

Even though the children swore that they hadn't touched anything,

I fiddled with buttons and knobs on the dashboard, trying to silence the noise. The more I fumbled, the harder the children howled. They thought I was a riot.

Turning around in my seat, I watched my grandkids, their bodies shaking uncontrollably, cackling so hard that they could barely breathe. Suddenly, it hit me — I was the grandma, and these were my grandkids — not my children. Who cared if my daughter's car irritated everyone on the street or if I looked irresponsible and crazy? The kids were having the time of their lives, and I wanted in on it. After all, it isn't every day that we're locked together in a car making a spectacle of ourselves.

Once I realized the humor of our situation, I laughed so hard the tears ran down my cheeks. I even snorted, causing a fresh uproar from the back seat. We started waving at everyone who passed by, causing the children to squeal with delight. And even though we still got plenty of disapproving looks, people also smiled at us and waved back.

Thankfully, my grandchildren have always had a magical way of bringing out the wonderful, goofy, youthful parts of me that I thought I'd lost forever. At that moment, I didn't have to act my age, be responsible, or solve our dilemma. They had a mother who would soon end the madness. But for now, we were the stars of the show, having a ball, and it felt fantastic!

— Jill Burns —

Through the Eyes of a Child

37

Chicken Soup for the Soul

Doll Baby

What's in a name? That which we call a rose by any
other name would smell as sweet.
~William Shakespeare

G randparents often have interesting names. My sister-in-law was known as Mimi. Her husband goes by Peeka. Why? Their firstborn grandchild decided on those names.

My firstborn grandchild named me as well. He called me "Doll" or "Doll Baby." I will never forget the day he cuddled close to me and, in front of a roomful of people, called me "Doll."

"What's her last name?" my daughter prompted.

Joshua put his little hand to my cheek, patted it and said, "My Doll Baby."

From that point on, I was known as Doll or Doll Baby. Even my sons-in-law call me Doll. Friends of my children and grandchildren call me Doll. It's a given.

For the most part, it's fine, even endearing, to hear my grandchildren call me Doll. But there was one time…

My daughter and her husband were going out of town, so the plan was for me to pick up five-year-old Spencer from kindergarten, take him to their house to wait for Joshua's school bus, and bring both boys home to spend the night with us. Spencer and I arrived long before the school bus. While we waited for Joshua, Spencer wanted to show me a new trick he learned on his skateboard. We opened the garage, and he brought out the board.

Spencer was pretty good. He had learned how to step on the back of the skateboard so that the front tipped up, and then slam his front foot down on the board and take off. Way cool.

Then it was my turn. I had played around with skateboards in my day. Of course, they weren't the high-tech kind of toys my grandchildren enjoyed. Ours were made by mounting the wheels of our old sidewalk roller skates to the bottom of a plank of wood. Still, I had this. I put my right foot on the back of the board and tipped up the front. So far, so good. I brought my left foot down with every intention of rolling forward.

Good intentions. Bad form. I fell hard on my elbow as the skateboard flew across the concrete driveway. My injury was minor, but Spencer raced into the house and retrieved Boo-Boo Bunny from the freezer to bring me comfort. It helped my arm, but not my pride.

"Do you realize how bad that could have been?" my husband asked when I made my way home safely with the boys. "I mean, what if you hit your head and were unconscious?"

He was right. That evening, Spencer crawled up between us in our bed. Tom commended him for getting the Boo-Boo Bunny and taking care of me.

"What if Doll had been badly hurt, Spencer? Do you know what to do in an emergency?" Tom asked.

"Yes! Call 9-1-1!" Spencer was proud he remembered what to do.

"Right! Let's practice. Pretend Doll hit her head, and you had to call 9-1-1. I'll be the operator. Ring, ring." Tom put up his hand as if it were the phone, his thumb the earpiece and his pinkie the mouthpiece. "9-1-1. What's your emergency?"

Spencer brought up his pretend hand phone and spoke clearly into his fingers. "Help! My Doll fell on the skateboard and hurt her head!"

Tom and I smiled at each other. It was hard to keep from laughing. "Uh, Spencer," Tom said. "There are probably times you need to call her Grandma."

— Rebecca Waters —

38

Black Doggy

*There are no seven wonders of the world in the
eyes of a child. There are seven million.*
~Walt Streightiff

I had undergone deep brain surgery two weeks prior for my Parkinson's disease and was scheduled to have my unit turned on and programmed. It was a two-day drive down to Arizona to my Movement Disorder Specialist and two days back home to Southern Oregon.

"Why can't I go?" my granddaughter asked.

"The doctor is trying to fix my brain, and it won't be any fun," I replied.

The day before I left, Boo (my name for my granddaughter) informed me that she still wanted to go with me to the doctor. Boo also informed her mother when she came to pick her up. When her mommy said "no," her little lips began to quiver, and she started to cry.

"Boo, the ride is really long, and you wouldn't like it. The next time Grammy goes to her regular doctor here, you can come with me, okay?"

That appeased her for the time being, and she and her mom left for home.

Later that evening, my husband and I drove over to Boo's to say goodbye to the family because we were leaving in the morning. As we were getting ready to go back home, my son said, "Boo, isn't there something you wanted to give Grammy to take with her to the doctor?"

Her face lit up, and she ran to her room.

"She was still upset when we got home today about not being able to go with you to the doctor," her mom told me as we waited for Boo to return. Then she came around the corner with Black Doggy, her prized little friend. Boo cannot sleep without Black Doggy. Boo cannot live without Black Doggy.

Boo gave me Black Doggy.

"You can take Black Doggy with you to take care of you," she told me as she handed him to me.

I fought back tears. "Oh… but what will you do when you go to bed?" I asked.

"I'll use Brown Doggy," she said. My son winked at me and nodded his head.

"Okay," I said and then asked, "Do you want to have Black Doggy's picture taken with the doctor?"

Boo was beside herself. "Yeah, Grammy! Yeah!"

I gave Boo another big hug and we left. *Okay,* I thought, *so how am I going to pull this off without feeling utterly ridiculous?* Who cares? I decided. Anything for Boo.

Two mornings later, I saw my doctor. Re-entering the exam room after doing some tests, my husband sat waiting and holding Black Doggy and the camera.

"Okay," he said as he stood up, "this is for Boo."

"Oh, the grandchild! We can do that," my doctor laughed and then smiled for the camera, holding Black Doggy.

Boo was so pleased with her picture.

And I must admit, having Black Doggy along made everything just a little bit better.

— Sherri Woodbridge —

39

The Joy of Now

*When you look at your life, the greatest happinesses
are family happinesses.*
~Dr. Joyce Brothers

I had been answering e-mails and adding the final touches to an important document. Then my daughter Alicia called with a request for which I had no ready answer. "Mom, do you think Jordan can stay with you this summer?"

I squeaked out a quick response. "Let me get back to you."

It was February. In four months, school would be out for the summer break, and my ten-year-old granddaughter's plans needed to be set. Previously, she had spent the summers with my parents, Jordan's great-grandparents. But since they were getting older, an alternative was needed. I had wanted to spend more time with my only granddaughter. But I had a busy career that required long hours and significant travel.

I sat at my desk mulling this over when I thought *Yvonne, you may never have this opportunity again. Take it now!* I decided to take an early retirement from my job of thirty-two years.

Although Alicia and I both live in the Washington, D.C., suburbs, there are twenty-five miles separating us. So when Jordan joined me that summer, there were plenty of new things for us to do together.

One of our first big activities was an early-morning train ride to New York City. Jordan had never been on a train, and she had never been to New York. For someone who had never been to the Big Apple, she sure knew a lot about it, suggesting we go up the Empire

State Building, get hot dogs from a cart in Central Park, and eat New York-style pizza.

The one thing I had not considered — and Jordan was quick to remind me of — was that we were doing a lot of walking. Fortunately, we both wore comfortable footwear. However, it wasn't long before fatigue got the best of us, and we began searching out a place to sit and chill from the ninety-degree heat.

We had browsed every floor of the American Girl store, and were now headed to FAO Schwarz and Central Park. But my eyes were still searching above the crowd, looking for a place to rest when Jordan tugged my arm. We briefly stared at each other and, without saying a word, the two of us ducked into a church, sat in the back row and enjoyed the blasting cool air.

But soon the horror of our dastardly deed took over. Jordan and I had inadvertently joined an in-progress mass at the famous St. Patrick's Cathedral. We quietly exited back to the street.

However, much sooner than we anticipated, the day drew to a close, and we were returning to Penn Station, joining other travelers heading south. While waiting for our train, Jordan and I couldn't help but happily review our day. "That was such fun in FAO Schwarz," Jordan said, hugging the teddy bear she had purchased. "And Central Park was just like on television. And those hot dogs, they were fantastic, especially with all the toppings."

I smiled in agreement. Indeed, it had been a great day for us. However, it was while we were on the train rolling toward Maryland that I received my greatest surprise. A bit groggy from all the activity, Jordan tapped my arm.

"What is it, dear?"

Jordan's smile was wide and deep, and her eyes glistened with joy. "Nana, thank you."

"Honey, you've already thanked me," I reminded her. "You thanked me over and over again today."

Jordan sat straight up in her seat, her dark eyes now fixed on mine. "No, Nana. The trip was great, but I'm thanking you for loving me so much that you want to spend the whole summer with me."

Overwhelmed with joy, I held Jordan tightly as tears welled in my eyes. Little did Jordan know that the honor she had bestowed on me was much greater than any of the university degrees that once graced the wall behind my office desk.

— Yvonne Curry Smallwood —

That Mutual Unconditional Love

Transformative Support

Encourage, lift and strengthen one another. For the
positive energy spread to one will be felt by us all.
For we are connected, one and all.
~Deborah Day

My husband and I squeezed hands as we stepped off the elevator on my parents' floor. It was odd to be visiting them without our kids, their grandkids. But we'd told them we needed to talk to them alone about something going on in our family. They knew nothing more than that. My stomach did a flip as we walked toward their door. I wondered if the talk would change everything. How would they respond?

We hugged my parents and gathered in the living room. I jumped right in and said we needed to talk with them about our nine-year-old, their grandson. My mom nodded, as if she had a feeling it was about him. This sweet child had been struggling for some time, and I explained that we'd come to a clear understanding of the reason in the past few weeks. I showed my parents his journal from the past year. On each page, scrawled in childish handwriting, was some version of: "I don't feel right. I know I am a girl. I hate having to be a boy."

The tears spilled from my eyes as I explained to my parents that he had been talking with me for over a year about what he called "my gender problem" and "my ache." They already knew he had been getting headaches and stomachaches regularly, crying a lot, missing school, and not sleeping well. They did not know that he talked to

That Mutual Unconditional Love | 119

me about this problem every single night.

My parents and husband had tears in their eyes, too, as I explained. We had taken our nine-year-old to a trusted psychologist/child-development professor, to whom he expressed unequivocally that he knew he was a girl. The only thing keeping him from asking to live fully as a girl, he told the doctor, was what other people would think. Especially his family and friends. Especially his beloved grandparents.

After asking many questions, this experienced therapist was confident: We have a child who is transgender. Our child, the doctor said, is not a "he" but a "she" in her mind and heart. In fact, research has shown that the actual brains of transgender people match their gender identity, not their bodies. So, our child's brain looks like mine, not my husband's. This dissonance causes transgender people deep sadness, anxiety, shame, and other negative emotions. Honoring their gender identity is a first step toward helping them, the therapist said. I had been reading about it for many months and knew in my heart this was my child's truth.

As my parents processed this information about their grandchild, they were silent, still, and listening. I'd wondered if they would question, doubt, resist. They were usually big conversationalists. They are academics, well-read, questioners. But at this moment, they were just quiet, with tears forming in their eyes. I didn't know how much they knew about what it means to be transgender, or how much they were ready to accept.

Being transgender is not a new human condition. In fact, there's evidence of transgender people in ancient times, and indigenous tribes have long honored them. But it's new in our culture to accept transgender people as part of the innate LGBTQ spectrum. Would these grandparents, who grew up in older times, be open to this newer understanding?

I took a deep breath before telling my parents my final point. The scariest part for us, I said, is the attempted suicide rate for transgender people: between 41 and 56 percent. This compares to around 2 percent for the general population. However, I told them, our greatest hope is that when transgender people have support — most especially family support, but also community support — those numbers plummet, and they can live contented, productive lives.

"We've made the choice to fully support and honor her as the girl she is inside," I told them. "We're helping her to transition socially as a first step. We can already see her relief and happiness." I paused. "And we hope you will join us."

This was the moment when we'd know if our child's cherished grandparents were truly with her on this path. I held my breath as I held my husband's hand. I heard the clock ticking on the shelf.

Then, at the same instant, my parents both nodded emphatically, wiping their tears. "Of course," they both said, without hesitation. "Of course."

We all exhaled, cried, and chuckled together at the thick emotion in the room. We held hands in a circle and nodded at one another, knowing that we were a team in supporting this child we all love. We talked for a long time that night, validating what we'd all seen with her, agreeing that we wanted her to live authentically and happily. My parents said they would support their transgender grandchild to extended family, friends, and neighbors, and would support us. My heart swelled with gratitude, relief, and pride.

The next day was my dad's seventieth birthday, and we all gathered together. My parents hugged my kids, squeezing our transgender daughter extra tight. My mom offered to take her shopping for new clothes — in the girls' section where she had always longed to shop. My dad handed her a card that told her of his unconditional love for her. They called her "she" for the first time.

A day later, my parents were on a plane to Europe, and my dad sent me an e-mail from the sky. It said: "I just keep thinking: She is the bravest person I've ever met." My tears overflowed, and I thought, *The apple doesn't fall far from the tree.*

— Diane Page —

My Biggest Fan

*Grandfathers give us not only wisdom and
encouragement, but they are an inspiration to us.*
~Kate Summers

My grandpa was my best friend. Maybe that sounds strange
for a kid, but because my parents and I had a complicated
relationship, I spent a lot of time with him. His wife, my
grandma, had died when I was ten, and my parents led busy
lives.

Whatever chance we got, my sister and I would spend time away
from home. My sister was a social butterfly, so she spent her time out
with her friends at movies, parties, or other gatherings. But I chose to
spend my free time with my grandpa. He supported everything I did
and encouraged me with enthusiasm. He attended every play, concert
and assembly I was involved in and took pictures. I would often peek
out through the curtains from the wings, and as soon as I saw Grandpa
sitting there, I could smile and get on with the show.

One of the things I enjoyed most was music. I loved listening to
it, but I loved singing most of all. In fifth grade, I sang Neil Diamond's
"America" to audition for the choir. In junior high, I sang Stevie Wonder's
"I Just Called to Say I Love You" to get into the choir. My parents came
to a few of my concerts back then, but my grandfather came to all of
them.

I loved singing so much that I would practice the songs in the
shower, between classes, and in my room. Unfortunately, my parents

didn't share my enthusiasm and would often shut the door if they thought I was being "too loud." So I went over to my grandpa's house, where he would listen to me sing song after song with rapt attention.

I got into the high school choir, but I set my sights on the chamber choir. I got in, but then came the biggest audition of my choir life — The Spartanaires. Every high school in town had a group like them. It was made up of equal parts men and women because they not only sang, but they danced as well. The men wore tuxes, and the women wore fancy semi-formal dresses. Only the elite singers made it in. I was sure I didn't have a chance.

I spent weeks preparing. One of the current Spartanaires, who was a friend of my sister's and played piano, helped me pick out a song — "Babe" by Styx — and accompanied me as I practiced. I sang it countless times to my grandpa, who told me I was a "shoo-in." I loved him for saying so. And I loved him for being my biggest fan.

I thought the audition went very well. I sang and danced my heart out. I remembered all the words and all the choreography. But I also knew that I was up against people far more talented than I was. All I had to do was wait for the letter that would arrive in the mail sometime before school started that fall, which would give me the good news or the very bad news.

That summer, I spent my evenings and weekends watching movies and reading books with my grandpa — and singing a few songs, of course. One day, he asked me if I would mind bringing my cassette-tape player over to record myself singing for him so he could play it when I wasn't there. I was pleasantly surprised at his request and was happy to comply. The weekend after I had dropped off the player and recorded all the songs, I arrived to find him sitting at the kitchen table listening to the tape.

"This is my favorite song on this tape," he said when he saw me. It was "Oh Shenandoah." He leaned back in his chair and closed his eyes. I laughed.

"You know, I could sing it for you now if you want so you can hear it in person," I said. He smiled and nodded, so I sang it for him.

A week before school started, I arrived home to find a letter addressed to me on the dining-room table. This was it! I tore open the envelope, my heart racing. But I couldn't bring myself to look. I needed some courage. And I knew just where to find it.

I burst through the kitchen door to find my grandpa reading at the table.

"It came!" I cried, waving it in the air. He put down his book.

"Well, open it," he said calmly.

"I did, but I just couldn't read it by myself," I said. I slid the letter back out of the envelope and unfolded it. I took a deep breath and read it.

"I'm in! Oh, my gosh! I made it!" I danced around the kitchen, laughing, crying and waving the letter. My heart felt like it was going to burst through my chest. I looked over at my grandpa.

"That's great!" he said, smiling widely. "When will your concerts be starting?"

"Um, I'm not sure. Why?" I asked curiously.

"Because I wore out the cassette player."

My mouth dropped open. "How?"

"I played the tape of you singing too much."

I was momentarily speechless. I thought about all the times my parents had told me to "be quiet" and shut my door, or made excuses not to go to my concerts. Then I thought of my grandfather who went to every concert, saved every program, and loved for me to sing for him — so much so that he wore out the tape player. He was looking at me apologetically. I walked right over to him and gave him a big hug.

"What was that for?" he asked in surprise.

"Because you're the best, and I love you," I said and kissed him on the cheek.

He came to every choir and Spartanaire concert. He even bought a new cassette player, and I made him a new tape. It was the least I could do for my biggest fan.

— Kristi Cocchiarella FitzGerald —

Joe

Grandfathers are for loving and fixing things.
~Author Unknown

J oe lived behind the laundromat. All the neighborhood children were afraid of him. We steered clear of Joe when he came out of his cabin, which was small enough to be a playhouse. He kept his car parked outside the fence that separated the alley from his tiny yard. His car was nicer than most cars in the small town, and Joe kept it spotless. He even wiped off the door handle with his handkerchief when he closed the door and locked it. I played in the alley and the vacant field with the other children, but we tried to stay away from Joe's car.

One day, while riding my newly obtained, used bicycle, I hit a mud puddle near Joe's car. I was so concerned about splashing mud on his clean car that I wrecked. I panicked as my handlebars slid down the side of Joe's Buick. The other children ran away.

Joe trotted out of his cabin, where he had been sitting at the window, playing solitaire and watching. "Well, child," Joe said. "Was it worth it?" He paused, looking at the big scratch on his perfectly kept car. "Are you hurt?"

I was hurt. My knee was bruised, and my leg had a deep scratch from the rusty pedal that had no pedal pads. "I'm okay," I said. "Please, I'm sorry. I tried to miss your car. I did. I really did."

"First things first, little girl," Joe said. "You come with me."

I didn't dare disobey him. He led me into his cabin while holding to the back of my T-shirt.

"Sit here," Joe said. Then he went into another room.

The only thing in the room was a small table with one chair near the window, where he had seated me. There was a refrigerator and a sink in the corner, and a really small cabinet was mounted to the wall above a tiny stove. The wooden floor looked like barn wood, but it was spotless. The ceiling was so low that I could have reached it with a short jump.

My heart raced so fast that I paid no attention to my pain. I was so frightened that I could barely breathe. Then Joe came back into the room carrying a dish pan, a towel, some bandages, and a bottle of peroxide. He told me to hold my leg out over the pan so he could put the liquid on my leg. I obeyed.

After Joe cleaned my injury and bandaged it, he kneeled on one knee in front of me. "I don't think this will keep you out of school. You need to be more careful and take better care of your body. You also need to be more aware of your surroundings. Cars cost a lot of money."

I started to cry. "I'm sorry, sir, I really am. I can work for you. I can mow the grass, run to the store for you, and do your laundry, your ironing…"

"No need to cry, little one," Joe said. "We all have accidents. I will consider what you can do to pay for the damage to my car, and I'll let you know tomorrow." Joe opened the door and said goodbye to me.

I realized that Joe was not even as scary as my dad would have been. In fact, I didn't want my dad to know about it at all. He would punish me severely.

The next day, I went to Joe's to ask if he wanted me to clean his car. He answered, "No, you stay away from my car. I want you to take this list and go to the company store for me. First, I want you to let me look at that bicycle." Then he checked it to make sure it wasn't damaged by the wreck. He went to the trunk of his car, pulled out a brand-new basket and attached it to my bicycle. "You will be doing my grocery shopping for a month."

I didn't tell the other children anything about Joe. They asked plenty of questions, but I remained silent. Sometimes, after delivering his groceries, I visited Joe and played cards with him. I didn't ask him many questions, but during my month of running errands I learned that he was divorced. His son had sided with his mother and refused to allow Joe to see his only granddaughter. He didn't miss his wife or his son, but he did miss his granddaughter. "She's a lot like you," Joe said. "She's your age, tomboyish and rambunctious."

The month passed quickly, and I wondered if Joe would still be my friend after I stopped shopping for him. So, I continued to ask what he wanted from the store when I ran errands for the neighbors. We played cards almost every day after school, and sometimes Joe fixed a plate for me when it was time for him to eat. In the wintertime, when the snow was too deep to ride my bicycle, Joe took me in his car to run errands for the neighbors. "I can't let you tread the snow," he said.

At Christmastime, I bought Joe a box of candy with the money I had earned from the neighbors. He loved chocolate. "That wasn't necessary," Joe said, "but it sure was nice of you."

"Isn't that what granddaughters are supposed to do?" I asked. After I said that, I wondered if I had overstepped because Joe didn't say anything else.

When my school had its spring play, I had no one to attend for me. My parents both had to work, and they weren't interested in attending anyway. I was surprised to see Joe in the back row. After the play was over, Joe stood outside waiting for me. "What a performer you are!" Joe said. "You are a natural-born actress." He kissed me on the forehead.

"Thank you, Joe," I said proudly. I wondered if he realized that he had made my day. I really wanted someone besides the teachers to see me do my part on stage.

"Well, what do you expect? Isn't that what grandpas are supposed to do?" Joe asked, as he took my hand and walked me to his car. "Let's go get some ice cream and celebrate."

—Joyce Carol Gibson—

Photos in My Mind

Gratitude is not only the greatest of virtues
but the parent of all others.
~Cicero

"In order to thrive, a child must have at least one adult in her life who shows her unconditional love, respect, and confidence. For me, it was Abuelita," writes Justice Sonia Sotomayor about her grandmother in her memoir, *My Beloved World*. I know how she feels because, for me, it was my Grandma Etta.

I was two years old when my mother left my father. She took my older brother and me with her to our grandmother's one-bedroom apartment in Queens, New York. Grandma Etta had always hated my father for his "horrible" behavior, and she welcomed us, although space was tight. My crib was put in the bedroom beside two beds for my mother and brother, and Grandma began sleeping on a studio couch in the living room. Soon, my mother got a job to support us, and we stayed at Grandma's for the next ten years.

Life had a calm predictability in Grandma's home, where comforting routines counterbalanced terrible battles between my parents, whose angry voices resounded in the hallway whenever my father tried to see us. We were not like other families in the building, especially in the 1950s when "divorce" meant something humiliating and shameful. But Grandma was there at the beginning and end of each day, and she would be the best parent I had.

She managed all the housework and sewed beautiful dresses for me. She helped me with my homework and insisted that I do well in school. "That's your 'job,'" she'd tell me. "Work hard at school, and don't worry about anything else." Unlike my mother, who disliked clutter and disarray, Grandma didn't mind the mess of children's things. Coloring books fanned out on tabletops, dolls lounged on chairs beside miniature soldiers, and shoeboxes crammed with crayons, puzzle pieces and baseball cards piled up everywhere.

I have no photographs of my grandmother cooking or cleaning, kneading pie dough with her arthritic fingers or bending over the bathtub to rub my back with a warm, soapy washcloth. But I remember her doing all those things. She kissed me goodbye when I headed off to school or my father's waiting car, and her eyes fell on me like a sweet benediction, which helped untie the knots in my stomach. Coming home was always easier than leaving.

There is no picture of my mother rising early to shower and dress for work before dashing off to the subway. Nor is there a picture of the dressing table where she transformed herself, before my eyes, from a pretty woman to a most beautiful one. But I can see these women, and the rooms they occupied, as clearly as if they were pictures in an album.

I was obstreperous and edgy, and I never missed a chance to answer back when scolded. I'd learned early that words were the only weapons I had against a sometimes intimidating brother, high-strung mother, and menacing father. Sometimes, I talked back to Grandma Etta, too, but I knew that nothing I ever said would lessen her love for me.

When I was eleven, my mother remarried and moved into her new husband's apartment a few blocks away. My brother and I stayed with Grandma Etta. My mother and stepfather saw us on weekends and sometimes in the evenings on their ways home from work. A couple of years later, my brother and I moved with them to a new house on Long Island.

Being part of a new family was exciting but also difficult for me. My mother continued to work, and our house was sadly empty when I came home from school. Even worse, she had made it clear that my brother and I had "better behave" lest our stepfather walk out on her.

I returned to Grandma's frequently for entire weekends or just for dinner. My stepfather turned out to be a good man, but it took a long time for me to know him well, and even longer before I fell in love with him.

I was nineteen when Grandma died, and I knew that I had lost my best friend.

I was lucky to be raised, primarily, by a grandmother who always loved me no matter how I behaved. Without her, what would have happened to us?

— Susan J. Gordon —

Roommates

*Grandmothers always have time to talk
and make you feel special.*
~Catherine Pulsifer

My parents announced I was getting my own room. I was so excited, because my sister was not great at sharing. Unfortunately, my new bedroom was down in the partially unfinished basement. And basements are scary places when you're only five years old. My room was warm and comfy, but I had to go through the shadowy unfinished part to get to it. Because of that, I was a little apprehensive — until I found out my great-grandmother was going to live with us and would have a bedroom next to mine.

My great-grandmother was one of the sweetest, kindest, warmest people I've ever known. And she loved her family. She raised three kids and took turns staying with them to help raise her grandkids. But she had a soft spot in her heart for my mother and then, as it turned out, for me. So she decided to spend the remainder of her life with us instead of continuing to switch families.

She was like a live-in nanny for my sister and me, and we couldn't have been happier. She made delicious cookies, and when she wanted a favor — especially needing her pills or a sweater from her bedroom all the way downstairs — the reward was always a kiss or a big bear hug.

But even with her staying in the bedroom next to mine, I was still afraid of sleeping in that big bed, in that big bedroom, in that big, old, scary basement. She understood completely and started letting me crawl in bed with her.

It worked out well for both of us for a while. I could even put up with her snoring because I loved snuggling up next to her. But when my parents found out, they were not happy. They wanted me to learn to sleep by myself. They thought if I continued to sleep with my grandmother, I would never be able to do it alone.

Of course, I screamed, cried and threw temper tantrums. It didn't work, but at least I had put up a good fight. So I went back to my bedroom and lay in bed, wide awake, for hours. I didn't want to get my grandma in trouble, but I was too afraid to go to sleep. So when I was sure enough time had passed for her to fall asleep, I got up and crept as quietly as I could into Grandma's bedroom. She wasn't snoring, but her breathing was steady, so I lifted the covers and slid into bed. Her back was to me, thankfully, so I curled up and fell asleep.

It seemed like only minutes had passed when I was suddenly being shaken awake. I was disoriented at first — until I saw my grandma's anxious face. I sat up quickly. She squeezed my hand reassuringly.

"You need to get back to your room," she said softly.

"What?"

"You need to get back to your room before your parents get up. If they find you here, we'll both be in trouble. Now, scoot."

She pushed me gently off the bed. I ran back to my room just in time as I heard movement upstairs. I crawled into my own bed, pulled the covers up to my chin and pretended to be asleep. I heard footsteps come down the stairs and my door opening. I didn't move. When the door shut again, I looked up and breathed a sigh of relief. It worked!

That night, I crept into Grandma's room when I thought everyone was asleep. Just as I was shutting the door, I heard Grandma say, "Not yet."

I jumped, but turned and made my way back to my room. Just as I shut the door, I heard someone come downstairs. My door opened, and my mom sat down on the bed.

"How's it going down here?" she asked. I looked up at her innocently.

"Great!" I said and smiled. She patted my shoulder and left. After the sound of her footsteps receded up the stairs and there were several minutes of silence, I went back to Grandma's room and crawled into bed. Her back was to me again, but this time I snuggled right up to her. She had known I was there all along, so there was no point in hiding it. And once again, in the early morning, before either of my parents got up, she shook me awake and made me go back to my own bedroom.

My wonderful grandmother saved me while we lived there. She continued to patiently wake me up every morning to go back to my own bed. Because of her, I never had to sleep by myself, and I still had the benefit of my own room.

A little over a year later, we moved to a different house. My mom told me that I would no longer have a room to myself, and I was really disappointed — until she told me I wouldn't be sharing with my sister, but with my great-grandmother. I was ecstatic! Since I'd already essentially been sharing a room with her, this just meant we could do it officially. I breathed a sigh of relief.

"Thanks, Mom," I said happily.

"No problem," she said with a twinkle in her eye. "And just think, you don't have to sneak in to sleep with her anymore."

— Kristi Cocchiarella FitzGerald —

45

Maria

Act as if what you do makes a difference. It does.
~William James

I was starting kindergarten when we were told my father would be stationed in Korea. At the time, we were stationed in Lubbock County, Texas on Reese Air Force Base, far away from extended family. My mother worked nights at the Pancake House, waitressing to make ends meet. Suddenly, she was faced with the challenge of having to balance everything on her own for an entire year.

I'm sure this had to be stressful for her. But I was a kid, and as such unaware of the very daunting trials she'd face alone.

Kindergarten was a huge step, and my teacher was extremely cold and distant. She was very pregnant and didn't seem to like kids all that much. A day didn't pass that one child or another, including myself, was left in tears because of her abrasiveness.

I remember the babysitter who paddled me for saying a naughty word. I was only repeating a story about pranking my dad and his reaction, and I didn't really understand why I was in trouble. Her children were given full cups of milk, a plate full of potato chips and entire sandwiches. We were given Dixie Cups half full of watered-down Kool-Aid, a quarter of a sandwich, and six potato chips. She loved her own children well enough, but the rest of us were only a paycheck to her.

After that mean babysitter struck me, my mother had to find a new babysitter. I'm sure it created a huge predicament. She confided in me as an adult, much later, how lean those times were for us as a family.

Like a heaven-sent angel, Maria arrived. She was beautiful, wrinkled and smelled of cigarettes. I don't recall how my mother met her or how she came to be our babysitter. With my father gone, my teacher distant, and my poor experience with the other sitter, I was feeling more than a little bit alone.

Maria was a neighbor and just about the coolest adult I'd ever met. Her superpowers were kindness, crafts and empathy. When Mom worked extra late, we'd get to have sleepovers with Maria. She often made us gifts such as doll quilts or ceramics. She took us to her church when Mom was tired and needed extra rest on Sunday mornings. Her door was never closed to us. She was everything my mother needed, and everything my sister and I needed. She became our grandmother in all the ways that mattered, and I will never forget her hugs, kisses, tuck-ins and snacks.

Shortly after my father returned, Maria's husband was reassigned, and they had to move. I recall the very last hug she gave me. Her skinny arms were strong around me as I cried. "You'll be fine," Maria assured me in her deep, raspy voice.

I don't know what became of her, but forty years later the ceramic Poodle she made as a gift for my mother sits atop my curio cabinet as a reminder to always be a safe harbor for the children who come through my life. While they cannot understand all our adult issues, it is up to us to understand that they are experiencing issues of their own, and it is our job to support and nurture them, even if they aren't our flesh and blood.

— Nicole Ann Rook McAlister —

46

Happy Dances

The greater the obstacle,
the more glory in overcoming it.
~Molière

C layton was a perfectly healthy little guy with a cheery disposition and a love for learning—until he started having seizures at age four. Although our family was devastated when we learned he had epilepsy, we were grateful when the correct combination of medicines finally stopped his seizures several months later. But the side effects included aggressive behavior, attention deficit disorder, and hand tremors.

Before Clayton started kindergarten, my daughter Jill spoke with his teacher about the problems my grandson faced. Ms. Bonnie promised to let her know how he behaved. And whenever Clayton was good, she would reward him with a certificate.

To everyone's surprise, after the first day of school, he handed his mom a certificate that said, "Clayton had a great day." He brought home three awards that first week, and then they stopped cold. His teacher explained that Clayton refused to stay at his desk and wandered around the room, stopping to scribble on classmates' papers. She also said that Clayton had a meltdown every time he tried to write his name, a feat he'd mastered at age three.

At his next session, Clayton's occupational therapist gave him a fitted glove and weighted pencils to help him with his grip. At first, Clayton was excited about his new tools, but later he refused to use the aids at school because he wanted to be just like the other kids.

My heart broke. That was exactly what we all wanted for him.

Since Jill lived next door, she dropped him off at my house every day. While I prepared him an after-school snack, I nonchalantly asked if there was a certificate in his backpack from his teacher.

He shook his head and grumbled, "Grandma, I don't have a clue what her problem is."

Weeks went by without an award. One afternoon, Clayton stomped into my kitchen with a big scowl on his face.

When I asked him what was wrong, he replied, "It's Ms. Bonnie. She wouldn't give me a certificate. So I walked around some. I did my work. What more does she want?"

I tried convincing him it would be okay as long as he tried his best.

His teacher devised tactics to help Clayton stay on task. She made index cards depicting eyes, ears, and a chair to remind him to focus, listen and stay seated. Whenever he misbehaved, she held up one of the cards. As an added incentive, I placed an empty picture frame on my kitchen counter and promised him I'd frame his next certificate.

After school the next day, a horn blared in my driveway. I rushed outside as Clayton bounded from his mother's car. He was grinning and hiding his hands behind his back.

He shoved his prized certificate at me and said, "Here, Grandma. I did it for you."

It read: "Clayton had a pretty good day."

I grabbed his little hands and twirled him around and around as we did our "Happy Feet Dance" moves. A wide smile stretched across his face as he watched me ceremoniously place the certificate in the silver frame.

The next day when I heard the horn honk I broke into a big smile. The twinkle in his eyes said it all. A certificate two days in a row! It read: "Clayton had a fairly good day." After putting it in a different frame, we did our jig once again.

When he got his third one, we hooted, hollered and danced before displaying the certificate and lining it up next to the others.

On day four, Clayton didn't stop by. Assuming that meant he

didn't get an award, I called his house to assure him I wasn't the least bit disappointed.

After a long silence, he squealed, "Tricked ya! Got another one."

His mom got on the phone and read what the teacher had written: "Clayton had an okay day."

I shuffled my feet in rhythm, imitating our dance, and heard giggles on the other end of the phone, followed by little feet pounding the floor in the background. Before hanging up, I mentioned how awesome it would be if he got five awards in a row.

But the next day, the horn didn't toot. His mom called later that afternoon and said Clayton was in tears, worried I'd be mad.

When he got on the phone, I said, "Honey, I don't expect an award every day."

"Besides," I added, "I'm running out of frames."

Eleven years later, Clayton is seizure-free. He has achieved numerous academic and sporting awards. Every time I dust the frames displaying Clayton's treasured kindergarten certificates, my heart, and sometimes my feet, dance for joy, knowing my sweet grandson is doing better than okay.

— Alice Muschany —

The Grandson

Thank you… for gracing my life with your lovely
presence, for adding sweet measure
of your soul to my existence.
~Richard Matheson

The Alzheimer's wing of the skilled nursing facility where I worked was buzzing with the daily routine typical of such places. Staff moved through the hallways, sometimes stopping to talk with one of the residents in an awkward, too-saccharine way.

I shied away from that, wanting to relate honestly to the residents with whom I worked. It was my first real job, working in the activities department, and I was getting to know the residents. Harriet was one of the residents on the wing who could still interact meaningfully with others, and I liked her immediately.

"You remind me of my grandson," she said as she smiled up at me from her wheelchair. "He started losing his hair early, too."

Feeling the color flush into my face, I asked Harriet if she would like to attend the social scheduled for the afternoon. "There will be ice cream," I said with my highest-wattage smile. But Harriet was studying my face intently. She didn't seem to have heard my question.

Her silver-white hair was pulled up into a tidy bun, and the colorful scarf around her neck struck a stylish note. Matched with earrings of some emerald-colored stone, it set off the rust-colored knit top she was wearing quite admirably. Harriet knew how to put an outfit together, no doubt about it.

Finally, she spoke: "What's a big galoot like you doing here? My grandson played football. You look a lot like him. You should be playing football, not asking little old ladies if they want ice cream." I couldn't help but be charmed by her. She was definitely not the typical resident.

We formed an instant bond, something that other staff members had warned me against. "It makes it tougher when they die," they said. It didn't matter. I loved Harriet; she was outrageous. "Button the top button on your shirt," she said to me one day. "I can see your chest hair poking out, and this old lady doesn't need her heart racing so fast." She shut her eyes dramatically and placed her hand against her forehead.

"Besides," she added, eyes still shut and hand still dramatically posturing, "you look too much like my grandson, and thinking frisky thoughts about you makes me very uncomfortable."

And so our days went, with a lot of laughter and her constant teasing. She asked me if I was married, and upon hearing that I wasn't, affected horror. "What's the matter with you? You aren't one of those types out tomcatting around, are you?" I assured her that I was virtuous and would not risk sullying anyone's reputation. "That," she said with a sniff of mock disdain, "will get you sent to hell, lying like that."

I worked hard to give my time equally to all the residents, but I found myself spending extra time with Harriet, usually off the clock. For one thing, she received no visitors. Ever. I didn't ask her about it, but I did notice that her records had no relatives listed — no children, let alone grandchildren. It nagged at the back of my mind, but I pushed away the concern.

Harriet eventually began to show in her personality the diagnosis of Alzheimer's that was listed in her chart. Sometimes, she would forget where she was. One morning, I found her in tears. "Harriet, what's wrong?" I asked.

Pulling me close, she asked in a whisper, tears brimming in her wide blue eyes, "Why am I here in prison? What did I ever do?" I faltered in trying to comfort her. It wasn't so difficult to tell her that she wasn't in prison as much as it was to explain to her exactly where she was and why.

But we carried on, and Harriet never stopped comparing me to her grandson.

One day was particularly bad for Harriet. She had seen herself in the mirror and was startled. "It isn't me," she said. "I think I've been stolen." It was after my work hours, and I was sitting with Harriet in the day room as the setting sun cast shadows around the empty furniture. We were the only two in the room at the time.

Harriet looked down at her hands and wrung them over and over. Her hair wasn't as tidy as usual, and her blouse had some dried food on it. In truth, she didn't look like herself. "Tomorrow will be better, Harriet," I told her. "I know this has been a rough day, but tomorrow will be a good one."

She looked up at me then, her face shadowed but her eyes bright. "Jack, you're gay, aren't you? I mean, you are a gay man, isn't that right?" I was startled to the point of speechlessness. She was right. "It doesn't bother me," she said quickly. "I've known gay men my whole life. I thought you were, right from the start."

As quickly as the lucid moment had come, it passed, and her eyes clouded over, no longer sharp. She began humming absentmindedly, forgetting me and what she had just said.

The progression of the disease accelerated, and the Harriet I knew was less and less in evidence. She stopped speaking almost entirely, and it was difficult to focus her attention. Eventually, she was confined to her bed most of the day.

The staff had been right; this was hard. One day, a nurse pulled me aside and said, "Jack, you have to face the fact that Harriet won't be here much longer. I know it's hard, but there will always be another resident." But I knew there would never be another one like Harriet.

And then, the end came suddenly, but not before Harriet had one final flicker of her old self.

It was four days before she died. I had not been in to see her all week because she was never awake, but this day I heard her call my name. "Jack," she said in a voice like an echo. "Come here, please."

Astonished, I hurried to her bedside. Her eyes were, one last time, clear and focused. "I am so sorry," she said quietly.

"Harriet, what do you mean? Sorry for what?"

She looked away from me. "I have no grandson, Jack. I have no children and never did. I just wanted someone to give some attention to." And then she was sound asleep, a peaceful look on her face. She never spoke or awakened after that. In a few days, she was gone.

Decades have passed since Harriet's death, or even since I have worked with Alzheimer's patients. But Harriet showed me that the capacity to love is never lost. Speech and memory may fade, the body and mind decline, but the spirit still lives, seeking only to love.

And I remember a stylish woman with bright blue eyes who just wanted someone to give some attention to. "You remind me of my grandson...."

— Jack Byron —

Boomerang

A grandma is warm hugs and sweet memories.
She remembers all of your accomplishments
and forgets all your mistakes.
~Barbara Cage

Every day, I walk past the gallery. Numerous times, in fact. Pictures of our kids are scattered on the wall. Our grandchildren smile as I move from the main part of the house to the bedrooms and smile again as I return.

I stop and stare at the frame that holds a piece of artwork. I place my hand over the imprint of my granddaughter's hand. How tiny. Her hand barely fills the palm of my hand. I trace her tiny fingers stamped onto the paper with red paint. The red handprint is framed by a yellow handprint on the left and a blue one on the right. The yellow and blue hands are slightly larger than the red one.

I let myself go back in time.

The smell of baby comes to me first. Then I feel my lips brushing her soft scalp. In my memory, I hold that tiny hand in mine as my thumb brushes across her infant skin. I close my eyes and remember the rhythm of rocking her tiny body.

***

We call our oldest daughter our boomerang kid. She is the only one of our seven children to have returned home to live for a period of time.

When she returned, we still had our two youngest children living at home. They were in high school, so we had just begun to imagine a life without children in our home. Of course, we'd miss them. But after seven children, we felt more than ready to become empty nesters.

The boomerang kid didn't return for the classic reasons — divorce, money, emotional problems. There were no issues, no lack of independence. Our daughter only wanted to live closer to home, so she returned, with her husband and three children.

The day they arrived, we went outside to greet them. Our granddaughter, just three months old, smiled at me from her car seat. Alex — wonderful, exuberant, two-year-old Alex — threw himself into his grandfather's arms. Four-year-old William grinned shyly as he scooted past us and into the house.

The timing was perfect to make this move. Our daughter was on maternity leave. She'd be available to care for the children and search for a new teaching position. Our son-in-law had just received his CPA and began an immediate job search.

Ironically, that same year, my brother arrived on our doorstep as well. Struggling through a difficult time in his life, he needed a soft place to land.

Cooking for a crowd became the norm. The house was noisy and disorganized. But every time I turned around, our daughter was cleaning and cooking while caring for her children. And our son-in-law, off to work at his new job, often returned with little gifts of appreciation in the evening.

On the weekends, our son-in-law worked side-by-side with my husband building a tree house for the children to play in.

It was a wonderful privilege to have them with us, and while it all blurs together now, there were some standout moments. I got to watch the oldest head off to his first day of school with a backpack bigger than he was. I remember coming into the kitchen one morning in an old nightgown — a turquoise, satiny thing with white polka dots — only to hear Alex say, "Grammie, I love your dress!" And I had the rare opportunity to see our daughter in action as a young mother.

And I remember rocking that baby.

***

I realize I'm still standing in the hallway staring at the framed artwork. The red handprint belongs to our granddaughter, Sadie. Below is her name and age. One year old. The yellow one belongs to Alex. His name is written in a three-year-old's scrawl. The blue handprint belongs to Will, five and proud of it. The children gave it to me after the year ended, and they were once again in a home of their own.

A well-known verse fills the top of the page:

Our dirty little handprints
we've left on every wall,
and on the drawers and tabletops
we've really marked them all…

Any marks on the walls are long gone. There are no little shoes lined up beside the front door. The house is quiet. The only marks that remain are the ones on my heart.

— Catherine (Cat) Moise —

Chicken Soup for the Soul

No Genetic Connection Required

To a small child, the perfect granddad is unafraid
of big dogs and fierce storms but absolutely
terrified of the word "boo."
~Robert Brault

I t happened again today. We were at the park with our fifteen-month-old grandson, and someone commented on how much my husband and grandson looked alike, going on to exclaim how their eyes are the same bright blue and how they have matching dimples. I've often marveled at their remarkable similarities. Why is it so unusual? Although they do look the same, my husband and grandson share no biological connection, only love.

Steve missed the early stages of parenting. We married when my daughters were eleven and twelve. He had never had children, but adapted to the role of parent smoothly. In a short time, they became "our girls."

We never used the "step" term, but we also didn't force the girls to address him as "dad." They found their own affectionate nicknames for him, the main one playing off his name and the perception of step-parents — "Evil." Imagine their friends' surprised faces when their cell phones would light up with Evil calling! We were one of the fortunate stepfamilies that didn't face many problems with the blending of Steve into our family. It was a natural fit. Witnessing Steve's love and devotion to my daughters convinced me that love doesn't have to contain a genetic connection.

With a grandchild, my husband is now getting a chance to be a part of a child's early years. He's learned to change diapers, burp a baby, and support a newborn's head. He's even learned how to get a cranky, overtired child to go to sleep.

Our grandson won't inherit Steve's mathematical aptitude or athleticism, but what he will get from his grandfather is his most valuable asset: a heart full of unconditional love. Does Callister care that the man who reads him books, takes him on walks and plays catch with him isn't his genetic grandfather? Of course not. He does know that he is loved and cherished, and nothing else matters. Recently, after a visit to see our grandson, Steve said, "I expected to love our grandchild, but I never knew I would be so totally smitten." That sentence captures our experience as grandparents and makes me fall in love with Steve a little bit more.

Because of divorces and remarriages, my grandson has more grandparents than most kids. Each one serves a unique and special role in his life. Having lots of loving, invested people in his life can only be beneficial for him and his parents. They have a strong support system and will probably never lack a babysitter. I predict my grandson will have a full audience for whatever he chooses to do, whether it's sporting events, plays or spelling bees. He'll have a cheering section made up of biological grandparents and step-grandparents. Sorting through the tangles of relationships may seem a little confusing, but having lots of people who love and support you is a wonderful gift. Genetic connection not required!

— Diane Morrow-Kondos —

Proud of Each Other

Grandchildren are the dots that connect the lines from
generation to generation.
~Lois Wyse

Jaden was welcomed into a large, loving family. He was the grandchild we had wanted for years, and he would carry the family name into the next generation.

I was so proud of him as he grew. He was handsome and he excelled in school. I never had a grandfather, so I prayed simply, "Lord, help me." I wanted to be a great role model for him, by word and deed.

In ninth grade, he had a class in Social Studies. The class had been given an assignment to choose a story from a *Chicken Soup for the Soul* book, and then present an oral report about the story they chose. The teacher wanted them to understand how much true stories can change a person's outlook.

Jaden chose *Chicken Soup for the Soul: A Book of Miracles*. He selected a story called "Escape from Hell." In this story, a firefighter is trapped in a building that is fully engulfed in flames. When the building explodes, the firefighter is sure his time has come. He can't find his way out and he is disoriented. The firefighter asks for help from Jesus, and then he suddenly knows exactly how to escape the flames, through the only possible way out. He makes his way through the blinding smoke and his fellow firefighters can't believe it when he emerges, burned but alive.

The intensity of the story made Jaden's presentation quite emotional, and the class felt it. When he finished, as he tried to regain his composure, his fellow students whispered to each other about the story. The teacher said, "Jaden, obviously the story had a big impact on you. Please explain why it moved you so."

Jaden cleared his throat and replied, "The firefighter involved in this story is my grandfather. I'm proud of him and thankful he escaped the fire." First, there was a hush, and then applause broke out.

He got an "A" on his report and a big hug from his teacher.

He got a big hug from his grandfather as well.

—Herchel E. Newman—

Gifts & Gratitude

How to Save a Life

Grandchildren are lovely reminders
of what we're really here for.
~Janet Lanese

My grandson and I were sitting across from each other in a booth at Perkins Restaurant. I had invited Aidan to dinner, but after our food arrived, he announced he would pick up the tab. "I want to treat you," he said, "to thank you for all you've done for me."

"You know, you saved my life," I responded.

Aidan's eyes widened. "What? How did I do that?"

We were there to celebrate the recent exciting events in Aidan's life. He had become an Eagle Scout, graduated high school and was about to leave for college. I was elated he had won a full scholarship to a Texas university, but that elation was tempered with concern. He would be moving more than 1,000 miles away from family and friends. I wondered how he would fare on his own, and worried about how difficult his departure would be for his parents and me. I worried I would see him less and less as his life in Texas blossomed and evolved. He was an intelligent, sensible young man, but I was anxious, as only a grandmother can be.

The truth is, I had never aspired to be a grandmother — at least not when I was younger. I mean, how many twenty-somethings say, "I want to get married, have kids and then have grandkids!" I really didn't even think about grandkids until my son Justin was in his late twenties. Dedicated to his career as a scientist, and spending weekends as a guitarist in a band, Justin seemed to spend more time in the lab and on stage than he did on dates. As the years wore on, I would joke, "I want a grandchild by the year 2000!" And Justin would quip, "I just want a date by the year 2000."

As it turned out, Justin met Valerie in 1998 at one of his gigs. It was love at first sight. She was a nurse, a willowy blonde with large green eyes and a beautiful smile. When I met her and she turned to say hello, I was struck with the prescient thought that she was family. And, indeed, she became my daughter-in-law a year later. A year after that, my first grandchild, Aidan, was born.

But Aidan did not arrive gently. Valerie endured a long, arduous labor. Family from both sides waited at the hospital, praying, laughing, crying, sipping coffee, gnawing on red licorice and watching *My Fair Lady* as it ran several times throughout the night on a local TV station.

A few hours before Aidan made his debut, and before Rex Harrison could utter another precise syllable for the fourth time, I wandered out of the hospital to the parking lot to smoke a cigarette. Inhaling deeply, I felt the tension of the difficult night ease just a bit. The fact is, I needed that cigarette.

Remembering that night long ago when he was born, I looked across the table at the handsome young man Aidan had become. "Before you were born, I was a smoker," I said. "I had smoked for many years, and I had absolutely no intention of quitting."

Aidan was incredulous. "You smoked? I didn't know you smoked!"

"Yes, I did, and I never thought I would quit," I said.

"What made you quit?" he asked.

"You made me quit," I replied. "You saved my life. And I thank you for that. You see, after smoking a cigarette on the night you were born, I tried to return to the hospital, but the guard was not going to let me in."

I could still see the guard's frown as he firmly stated, "The hospital is closed. I can't let you enter."

At his words, I felt tears welling in my eyes. "I'm going to miss the birth of my first grandchild," I cried.

And here is where I'm not sure exactly what happened. Was it my own voice? Or was it an angel? Or the voice of God? I clearly heard the voice whisper in my ear, "You will miss everything in your grandson's life if you continue to smoke."

At that moment, the guard relented and let me enter the hospital. I rushed upstairs just as Aidan was born. I listened outside the delivery room for that first indignant cry and then heard Justin exclaim with wonder, "Hey, he's looking around!"

"I quit smoking that night," I told Aidan, "and I'm proud to say I never smoked again."

"So," he said after hearing the story, "I personally didn't really save your life."

I reached across the table and placed my hand over his. "Just by being you, you gave me a reason to live the longest and best life possible. I hope to dance at your wedding, Aidan. What do you think? I'm not getting any younger. Maybe a wedding by 2029?"

He gave me a mischievous grin so like his dad's and said, "I just want a date by the year 2029."

— Nancy Johnson —

52

Arcade Prizes

There are grandmothers out there who would move
heaven and earth for their grandchildren.
~Janice Elliott-Howard, *Being a Grandmother*

T he arcade on the Balboa Peninsula—sandwiched between the pavilion and the Ferris wheel—always had the best prizes. After a few minutes of Skee-Ball, I could score enough tickets to get a slingshot or a cup of green goo. The teenagers who worked behind the counter weren't all that pleasant to kids younger than them, but they always gave us what we wanted. For me, that was usually the green goo.

When I was about five, my family went to Balboa for the weekend. After eating clam chowder at the pavilion, the adults took me and my cousins to the arcade. We were pretty loud—and obnoxious—so most of the adults waited outside. My mom and aunts were talking and laughing in the sunshine, their permed hair shining in that early-1990s way. My dad and uncles stuck around the entrance, watching us but mostly arguing about who was going to pay for the next meal.

That just left Nana Shirl to stay with the grandkids. There were six of us—three boys and three girls—and Nana watched us like a hawk. She was a beautiful woman, with big, gray hair. She wore an emerald-colored brooch that always looked magical to my five-year-old eyes. Her brooches seemed to shine right at me, as if they were trying to tell me something like some sort of sparkly Morse code. The other cousins weren't interested in that sort of thing, but I was. I was different from the rest of them — not drawn to the sort of boy stuff that I was supposed to like.

My boy cousins were playing racing games, and my girl cousins were taking turns on the cassette-tape claw machine. As usual, I was doing my own thing: playing some ball-rolling game, sort of like Skee-Ball but with rows of holes that represented the face cards in poker. I wasn't very good at it.

Nana stood behind me. I didn't see her at first, but I smelled her perfume, which completely overpowered the salty ocean air. She asked if she could try once, so I gave her a ball, and she rolled it right into the queen of hearts. Thanks to her, I got twenty tickets.

She asked me what prize I was going to get, and I told her that I would probably get more green goo. She reminded me that I'd already ruined three T-shirts thanks to my last few cups of goo, so I begrudgingly agreed to get something else. Something special.

When it finally came time to cash out, my cousins pushed their way in front of me. They got the typical prizes — slap bracelets, racecars and shoddy stuffed animals. When it was finally my turn, I slid my tickets across the glass counter. I looked up at Nana, and she smiled back down at me. "No goo," I promised her.

The other adults were also behind me, not-so-patiently waiting for me to get my trinket so we could leave. "Let's go," one of my uncles urged me. "Don't you want to start swimming?"

I looked through all the shelves of prizes. I wasn't interested in anything. My dad pointed out the racecars. Didn't I want to be like the other boys? Didn't I want to have a car of my own? I really didn't.

I knew I was taking too long because no one looked happy. Even my aunts were tapping their feet. My oldest cousin nudged me in the back. One of my uncles loudly declared that it was time to go to the beach. I had to make my decision fast.

I scanned the glass cabinet. Most of the prizes were above my ticket budget, but one section had all the little twenty- and thirty-ticket items. Nothing stuck out... until I saw a pink and purple ring. It was tacky and fake-looking, with a plastic gem that was as big as a penny, but I loved it. It reminded me of Nana's brooch. It was magical. I wanted it more than anything.

As soon as I pointed toward it, everything got silent. The arcade machines kept clinking away, but my family seemed frozen in place. For a long moment, I thought that the ring really was magical, that it had somehow done this to everybody except me.

But that wasn't true. Everyone froze because they were embarrassed that I'd done something wrong. I knew I'd made a mistake, even though I wasn't old enough to understand what that mistake was. It had happened to me before, when I was caught singing *Little Mermaid* songs in the park, or when my dad saw me having a tea party with the neighbor girls.

Dad didn't say anything at first. He put his hand on my shoulder and silently nudged me toward the other side of the glass case, where there were pens, erasers and other gender-neutral prizes. I looked up at him because I wasn't sure what he wanted me to do, and he said, "Look at all the other cool prizes. Those are probably better for you."

Before I could say anything, Mom whispered something to my dad. "Maybe we should…" I couldn't hear the rest of it.

Then my cousins started laughing at my "girl ring," and my aunts and uncles started talking over each other. That stupid ring had created a big family problem, and I didn't know why. The only thing I knew for sure was that it was my fault, and I had to fix the situation. So I very quickly told the arcade girl that I wanted a handful of polka-dotted erasers instead.

That was when Nana spoke up. She pushed her way through the others, grabbed my handful of tickets, and slid them across the glass. She took the plastic ring and placed it right in my hands. "Let's go swimming," she said.

And we left.

As I walked with my family down the busy boardwalk, I slid the ring onto my left pinkie finger. As expected, it sparkled in the sunlight, and I knew that it was magical.

I didn't realize at the time what a big moment this was, both for me and my family. As we walked together, everyone kept looking at me. My dad seemed a bit embarrassed. So did my older cousins. They were interpreting this situation in a way that I didn't understand, that I wouldn't understand until at least five years later.

I noticed the looks of embarrassment, but none of them bothered me. The only thing that mattered was that Nana Shirl was leading the way, and she held my hand proudly.

— Evan Purcell —

53

Miracle Boy

A grandchild is a gift from above,
one to cherish and to love.
~Author Unknown

Hockey arenas are cold. But that doesn't matter to me. What matters is that this frosty morning, I get to watch Miracle Boy play his heart out at just one of the sports he loves.

Here he comes, streaking down right wing, head up, deftly handling the puck. He dekes an awkward defenseman. One too many moves. The flummoxed opponent can't react, and they collide accidentally. The size difference is enormous. Nick goes down hard, but he is up instantly and skating again.

The puck slithers to a teammate in the corner. A pass out, a quick one-timer, and it's in the net. Arms raised signalling the goal, my grandson celebrates with teammates, and then looks at me (he knows where I always stand) and flashes the big "See that?" smile that's melted our hearts for ten years. Miracle Boy's done it again.

I call him Miracle Boy because it's a miracle that he's with us at all. When he was born, an astute nurse recognized signs of hyperinsulinism and ordered tests to confirm it. If she hadn't, things could have been very different.

His first five months were spent in hospitals in Toronto and Philadelphia with a tube up his nose. A painful operation followed. The care was wondrous. It gave us this bright, handsome, courageous ten-year-old who lives life with exemplary vigour and zest.

Back on the ice, the third period winds down. Nick's team scrambles to tie the game. Doesn't happen. Disappointed, the boys leave the ice for the change room. I head there, too. Hockey is just the beginning of his long, amazing day.

Minor hockey change rooms are noisy… and stinky. At this age, though, there are few frowns. Kids get over the outcome quickly and, at a decibel level emulating a departing jetliner, they rib teammates about errors or underwear or whatever. Nick contributes heartily.

Still sweaty, he has already changed into his basketball uniform for Act Two of today's saga. He smiles brightly when he sees me… just like that baby used to in the hospital bed.

It's the eyes. They light up. They tell you he's happy to see you. That life's good. That he just played hockey, and now he's ready to drive an hour to a basketball tournament.

"You played well," I say.

"Thanks, Papa. I'm hungry. Can I get a drink?" he says. Same thing every week.

"Have you tested your sugar?"

Out comes the diabetes kit. Finger poked… not a flinch. Levels examined. "It's good."

I admire the kid. He takes charge of what he has to do. No complaints.

Then he stands up, gives me a hug, and says, "Okay, let's go. I need a drink."

Choruses of "See ya Nick" usher him out the door.

His physical stature doesn't match his heart. Walking behind him, I'm astonished that he can even lift, let alone lug, that giant hockey-equipment bag. How does that little guy crash into bigger kids on the ice, leap up and fly back into the play? It seems he's been exploding through obstacles since he was a baby.

"Need help?" I ask.

"Nope, I need that drink," he says, laughing at his clever retort. I chuckle, too. He just tickles me.

As I drive us north, the only sounds in the back seat are from Nick munching snacks and slurping water.

I ask, "Everything okay?"

"Yeah, great food, thanks!" A pause, then, "Guys still ask how I got the big scar on my stomach."

"What do you tell them?" I reply.

"I had an operation when I was a baby. Hey, Papa, how long till we're there?"

From back there, he cannot see me grin. We, his grandparents, can't shake the memory of that baby in neonatal intensive care. Seems like that baby can. Other stuff's more important than self-pity.

Like basketball.

Nick's a tad short for this game, but so what. His mom and dad, both accomplished athletes, have nurtured and coached this great kid and constantly remind him that he can do anything he wants and is willing to try. I attempt to echo that.

We arrive at the tournament site.

The place is jammed. We're early, so there's time to chat. Unlike with hockey, he's nervous. We sit on the floor in a quieter hallway to talk about the game and sip a drink. I carefully offer calming advice.

Memories are funny things. As we converse, I look at him and still see that baby in the hospital. But I remind myself to speak directly to this precious boy in front of me and enjoy the fact that I can.

No place for pity. Help him stay as strong as he is.

The first game is rough. Every kid is bigger than Nick, yet he never takes a backward step. He's good, but driving to the hoop is difficult. Almost every attempt results in a crashing visit to the hardwood. A glance at me follows every rough landing. (He knows where I sit.) I get a smile through a grimace and a thumbs-up. Never a complaint.

His courage is admirable.

I nod. "Good job, Nick! Keep working. Stay tough."

Terrific game. Next game is 8:00 p.m. Won't be home before 11:00. Long day. He doesn't care. Neither do I. I get to spend my time with him.

Nick's the tenth of eleven grandkids. I've made a concerted effort over the years to spoil every last one of them. Love them to pieces. Buy them anything they want… almost. My money is finite, but my love for them is fathomless. They know it.

They're my real legacy... how I'll live on. People will interact with them and never mention my name or think of me, but I feel certain that all eleven will be loved and admired for what they achieve long after I've slipped away.

Game two. The other team's never in it. Nick scores on some slashing drives. Once, I told him that he's better than I ever was. He laughed like he does when he thinks he's hearing BS from Papa. He doesn't care about that. That's just Papa.

Mercifully, the game ends. Nick, a towel around his head, pulls on a sweatshirt, and we head to the car.

We call his mom. "We won. Home in an hour."

In fifteen minutes, he's asleep in the back seat. After one hockey game and two basketball contests, is it any wonder? In the rural setting where we live, driving at this time of night is peaceful. I glance in the mirror often to check on that handsome boy sleeping back there. The baby's grown up.

When bad stuff is happening, you pray it will stop. Moments like this, you hope will never end.

This is good.

We're home. My daughter's there to greet us. Nick, groggily awake, sees his mom and hugs her.

Then those sleepy eyes smile. He gives me an unprompted hug and then turns toward the door.

He looks back.

"Love you, Papa."

I've been paid.

— John Volpe —

54

No Regrets

Your greatest contribution may not be something
you do but someone you raise.
~Author Unknown

I can still picture the day seven years ago when Mary Ellen grabbed my hand and said, "Grandma, don't ever leave me." She followed me around the house, never letting me out of her sight. When I sat, she sat in my lap. Her parents were preoccupied with an illness my husband and I had yet to acknowledge for what it was, and she had asked to come home with us. She was two years old.

The situation in her home got better after a time, so she went back.

Three years later, my husband and I became her legal guardians. So, we gave up the fun of being grandparents and took on the hard job of parenting a child who was hurting in ways I've never known. A child who was angry because her family was torn apart. A child who couldn't understand why. A child who had to grow up too fast.

She, of course, didn't remember the earlier time. But she did remember loving her parents. She remembered that they loved her. So, she asked, "Why must I live with you? Why can't Mommy and Daddy take care of me?" And always, "When can I go home?"

The answers never sounded complete or adequate. "Mommy and Daddy are sick because they put something in their bodies that isn't good for them. It keeps them from making good decisions that keep you safe."

"When will they get well?"

"I don't know. They're working on it."

Then tears, always tears. Great sobs for which there was little comfort.

Twice that first year, I saw her acting out a story. Both times, she was running around, obviously taking care of a bad situation. When I asked what she was doing, she told me her parents' house was on fire. She needed to rescue them and put out the flames. My heart hurt for her. I wanted so badly to tell her that her parents were fine, that they were well on their way to recovery, and she would be going home soon. But I knew none of that was a guarantee and that false hope was worse than no hope.

The three of us were very fortunate to have great support. Her school counselor assured her that she wasn't the only child in her situation. Her teachers stayed in close touch with us and always insisted she work hard and follow the rules. Her principal wrote notes of encouragement on her classwork.

Our friends at church knew her name. They talked to her and listened to her responses. Once, we saw her religious-education teacher at the grocery store. Two days later, Mary Ellen had a note from Miss Maisie saying how nice it was to see her at the store. Mary Ellen was thrilled!

She became involved in Brownies, art lessons, and sports — finally settling on soccer. Her PE teacher told me she held her own against four boys at recess. There was probably something therapeutic in kicking a ball and running.

But, in some respects, every day seemed like what Mary Ellen called "opposite day." Papa and I helped with homework, listened to her read, hosted overnights, and attended kids' birthday parties — all the things we had done before as parents.

Along the way, she was told that I wasn't her real grandmother. It's true, sort of. Her father's my stepson. It's sometimes hard to put all the branches on a family tree. So, I asked her if she loved me. She said yes. I told her that I loved her, too. And if we chose to be grandmother and granddaughter, we could be. That works for both of us.

After a couple of years, she gave me a great gift. She said, "Grandma,

I would rather live with my parents, but I'm happy." That made me happy, too.

Someday, Mary Ellen will realize that she is one of the fortunate children who has been removed from her home. Her parents made a mistake, but through everything they loved her — loved her enough to get well.

After three and a half years, Mary Ellen went home. There will no doubt be hard times ahead. Parenting isn't easy for anyone, but her family has the love and support of an extended family and many friends.

After loading her bicycle into her dad's car, my husband walked inside and said, "Now we can be old." And grandparents — the kind who can play and give too much candy and send her home.

A friend asked me if I ever regretted agreeing to take custody of her. Not for a minute.

As I write this, I am looking at a handwritten note on a background of geometric shapes colored with pink and orange pencils and taped to the bookshelf above my computer. It was penned by a seven-year-old. It reads: "Hi, I just wanted to say 'I love you' and thank you for everything. With love, Mary Ellen."

Regrets? Not for a minute.

— Vicki Schoen —

55

Key Lesson

I love those who can smile in trouble…
~Leonardo da Vinci

As soon as he saw me, Pawpaw rose from the plush red chair in the hotel lobby. I'd escaped for a short walk and some much-needed alone time. "Hi," he said, smiling brightly. "Hey, have you seen the key to my suitcase?"

I shook my head and grimaced inwardly. *What now?*

From the start of our two-week trip, it had been one mishap after another. When I'd first said "yes" to going, I knew I'd need a truckload of patience to survive. But how could I turn down my grandfather's generous offer of joining him on a guided tour of Denmark, Norway, Sweden, and Finland? With two years of college journalism behind me, I was eager to see the world. I just wasn't so keen at doing it with a ninety-one-year-old man dressed in khaki pants, a turquoise eagle bolo tie, and a Dallas Cowboys cap. At least I didn't have to worry about his health, though. My spry grandfather could easily out-walk anyone half his age.

"Oh, dear," Pawpaw said, shaking his head sadly. "I was hoping that I'd given it to you."

Me, too, I groused silently to myself.

For nearly an hour, we searched our hotel room, turning over couch cushions and peering under the beds. I dumped out my purse on a table, examined every corner of my suitcase, and dug around in my green shoulder tote. No key. For several long minutes, I even tried my luck at picking the locks on Pawpaw's brown hard-side suitcase with a bobby pin. No luck.

"I'll go down to the front desk and talk to them," Pawpaw proposed. "Maybe someone can help."

I nodded as I threw back the bed sheets and searched under the blankets. In the bathroom, I inspected the floor and the inside of Pawpaw's toiletries bag. Still no luck.

"Look what the desk porter gave me," Pawpaw announced upon his return. He held up a large metal ring looped with what looked to be more than fifty keys of assorted sizes and shapes. With a sigh, I plopped down on the carpeted floor and bent over Pawpaw's suitcase. One by one, I tried each key in the lock. Surely, I'd get one to work, right? But none did. Not knowing what else to do, I tried them a second time. With every failed attempt, I lost a bit more of my patience. Instead of seeing Copenhagen, I was stuck in a hotel room because my careless grandfather couldn't hold onto one darn key.

Finally, I'd had enough.

"I give up, Pawpaw. Here," I said, handing him back the key ring. I was sure he could hear the childish frustration in my voice, but I didn't care. "I don't know what else to do!"

"Oh, it'll work out." He patted my arm with a liver-spotted hand. "Small stuff. Don't worry about it. I'll be right back." Pawpaw disappeared out the door with the key ring jangling in his hand.

It wasn't long before he showed up again, this time grinning hugely.

"Look what I have," he announced, holding out a familiar silver key. My spirits lifted as I eased the key into Pawpaw's suitcase lock. Voilà — both latches clicked open! Like a monstrous clam, the suitcase unfolded to reveal Pawpaw's neatly folded shirts, pants, undergarments, and travel books. Our passports turned up, too, tucked away in a zippered pouch.

"I told the porter that none of those keys on that ring fit," Pawpaw said. "Then I asked if anyone had turned in a key to the lost and found, and he handed me that one." Pawpaw laughed. "Now why couldn't he have given it to me in the first place?"

Really? We'd wasted all that time?

Then I laughed, too. Pawpaw was right—the past few hours did have a comical side. I'd fussed and fumed over that silly suitcase lock all because Pawpaw hadn't worded his request just right. What could I expect? As they say, we were foreigners in a foreign land. Miscommunications were bound to happen. Mishaps and misadventures, too. Come what may, I'd best rely on my sense of humor to enjoy traveling with my grandfather to the fullest. What's more, Pawpaw most certainly needed a strong sense of humor of his own to survive traveling with me.

On our last morning in Copenhagen, we had our suitcases packed and ready to be picked up in the hallway outside our hotel room.

"Wait, Pawpaw. You forgot to pack these," I said, holding up his extra pair of walking shoes. "I'll put them in your suitcase."

"No, no," he protested in his typical gentlemanly fashion. "Let me do that."

I was already out the door and unlocking his suitcase. Pawpaw followed. As I was shoving the shoes inside the suitcase, a door clicked shut behind us.

"Uh, Pawpaw, did you bring the room key out with you?"

"No. Didn't you?"

I shook my head. Then I laughed. Pawpaw laughed, too.

After the housekeeper unlocked the door, we gathered up the rest of our stuff and joined the tour group. In the days ahead, we saw colorful Danish garden homes, Norwegian sod-roofed cabins, massive Swedish palaces, and lush Finnish parks. Along the way, Pawpaw gashed his finger on a razor, lost his Dallas Cowboys cap, and vanished for a while on an overnight ferry. But I didn't worry. Pawpaw had taught me to laugh, no matter how tough the circumstances get—a key lesson that's stuck with me ever since.

— Sheryl Smith-Rodgers —

56

Grandparents' Day

Grandmothers are just antique little girls.
~Author Unknown

While in my thirties, I gave birth to my daughter. She grew up to have her first baby not long after she turned thirty, a darling, blond-haired boy named Henry. It doesn't take a math genius, though, to realize these facts put me in the position of being an older grandma.

The point hit home clearly the first time I attended Grandparents' Day at Henry's preschool. Surrounded by a sea of toddlers, the other grandparents in attendance looked tan, fit, and far younger than me. Yet I nodded at them pleasantly and felt I could hold my own. That was until we were invited to sit down with our grandchildren for snack time. I got in the miniature chair and the tiny table without a problem. But getting up was another matter. Both my knees creaked in an alarming way. For a minute, I thought one would completely lock up until a pony-tailed young grandma lent a hand to get me to my feet.

One of the teachers turned on a merry tune I vaguely recalled, and we were encouraged to sing and dance with our little ones, who mostly galloped in a hundred different directions. I did my best to keep up with Henry as he giggled and darted around the room with the others. Before long, the effort had me huffing and puffing louder than the Big Bad Wolf. Fortunately, a teacher directed us to plop on a thin layer of carpet covering the floor. We listened to her read a story and then worked on a coloring project. By this time, my back ached, and I gazed longingly at the miniature chair, but none of the other grandmas appeared the slightest bit fazed to sit cross-legged on the rug. Was I the only one with perspiration on my forehead? A glance around the room confirmed my suspicion, and I sighed.

How I longed to be a lively grandma like these ladies, who all appeared capable of running a 5K with a two-year-old balanced on their hips. But those days were long gone for me. I looked at Henry, his brows furrowed in concentration as he scribbled with a red crayon. The sight made me feel a little melancholy. He deserved an agile grandma, not one who felt the not-too-distant need for a mobility scooter and extra-powerful magnifying glasses.

The more I thought about it, the lower my mood dipped. I felt sorry for myself, but even sorrier for Henry. The lead teacher interrupted my state of self-pity to hand out cute thank-you cards to the guests, signifying Grandparents' Day had come to an end. The other grandmas scooped up their grandkids and headed for the exit with a bounce in their steps. But before I had a chance to start the slow process of getting myself off the floor, Henry climbed right into my lap.

His fingers, still sticky from the cookies we'd shared earlier, gripped my hand, and he tucked his head under my chin. The aroma of lavender-scented lotion that my daughter always smoothed on him melted me. I put an arm around Henry, and his soft hair tickled my cheek. He snuggled against my chest and yawned, content to be still for a few moments.

As I held that dear little boy, I forgot about aches and pains. My eyes misted despite the smile on my face. Maybe I wasn't the most athletic grandparent in town, but did age or fitness level really affect the quality of a relationship with my grandchild?

On the spot, I decided not to dwell on what I couldn't do. Instead, I'd concentrate on the things I could and be the best grandma possible for Henry. One who spends time reading with him. Or taking a walk. Creating fanciful animals made from soft, doughy clay. And, best of all, gathering Henry in my — let's admit it — ample lap to rock, just as my own grandmother had once rocked me.

Yes, I might have a few creaky joints, but older means wiser.

And like most little ones, Henry is a sponge waiting to learn. This is a challenge even I can handle while we enjoy each day as though it were Grandparents' Day, which, after all, isn't limited to an annual event. Our time together will be spent discovering delights and making memories that I know will stay with him forever.

—Pat Wahler—

57

Chicken Soup for the Soul

Unstoppable

*More and more, when I single out the person who
inspired me most, I go back to my grandfather.*
~James Earl Jones

It's 1991, and I'm in fourth grade, wearing a dress that itches and shoes that pinch my feet. It's my first Sunday serving as an acolyte at church, and my stomach is in knots because I'm so nervous. I don't like crowds or being the center of attention, but I like the thought of being grown up enough to actually participate in the service instead of being asked to sit quietly in the back.

We practiced how to light the candles in Sunday school, but the teacher forgot one important detail. My flame goes out when I'm halfway down the aisle, and I freeze. My partner, the redheaded boy whom I think of as my future husband, marches right past me and lights his candle with no problems. I have no idea what to do next, but I can feel the tears welling up in my eyes. Then Grandpa Norm steps up next to me. He lights my flame and whispers in my ear, "It's okay. You've got this."

Nine years later, I'm completing a summer internship at my tiny hometown's newspaper office. Grandpa and Grandma, who've lived in the community for nearly forty-five years, are ecstatic. They invite me over for lunch at least once a week, enjoying the opportunity for some one-on-one time before I head back to college.

Grandma's cooking is delicious, as always, and Grandpa's enthusiasm for my reporting assignments makes me think that I can make it as a writer after all. My boss has me writing human-interest features on prominent community members, which means most of the people I spend the summer interviewing knew me when I was six and still refer to me as Norm and Minnie's granddaughter. Grandpa's probably heard all their stories before, but he eagerly awaits the publication of every issue to savor my byline.

Today, I'm a wife, mother, full-time freelance writer, and Grandpa's de facto IT girl. Grandma passed away almost ten years ago, but Grandpa is impressively active for a man in his early nineties. His interest in technology never ceases to surprise me, which is why I juggle my schedule for these impromptu visits to log him back into Facebook and help him print pictures of the great-grandchildren he adores. Somehow, deadlines seem insignificant compared to my favorite senior citizen's social-media addiction.

When the solution to the latest tech issue only involves a few keystrokes, I take my time. I make the text on the screen a little larger so it's easier to read with his failing eyesight. I add three new bookmarks so there are fewer clicks for him to make while checking his favorite websites. He watches in amazement, and then asks if my son is ready for the middle-school band concert next week.

At the end of our visit, we step outside to see his next-door neighbor and fishing buddy heading over for a chat. Grandpa brags that I'm a "computer expert" who is smart enough to fix anything. I blush, and then think of all the ways that my tech skills are still in need of improvement.

Suddenly, it occurs to me that this moment perfectly encapsulates our relationship. He's always believed in me, even when I didn't believe in myself. I give him a hug, promise I'll stop by next week to make sure the computer still works, and drive away thinking how lucky I am to have someone in my life who remains convinced I'm unstoppable.

— Dana Hinders —

Grandma, I've Got You Covered

Being deeply loved by someone gives you strength,
while loving someone deeply gives you courage.
~Lao Tzu

As a result of chemotherapy, I lost most of my hair. Being hairless felt strange, but the thing I minded most was having a cold head at night while sleeping. I tried covering my head with a nightcap, but it was tight and gave me a headache by morning.

Dissatisfied, I rummaged through my coat closet in search of winter hats. I experimented with each of them to find a proper covering. Unfortunately, they were all either too warm or too stiff. The warmest ones made my head sweat and then get itchy. The stiff ones slid off at night, leaving my bare head exposed. I was miserable.

During the day, I usually put on a scarf at home. However, I wore a wig when I was away from the house. The hairpiece certainly improved my appearance, but it wasn't comfortable enough to wear for long periods of time. It tended to ride up on my scalp and be scratchy at times.

When my grandchildren visited me some months later, I wore my wig all the time. I put it on when I got up in the morning and didn't take it off until bedtime. Since the piece looked similar to my natural hair, the kids weren't aware of the difference.

All went well until my four-year-old granddaughter unexpectedly walked into my bedroom one morning. I was taking a shower and had temporarily placed my wig on top of a lampshade to keep it from flattening. My granddaughter saw the wig dangling over the lampshade and shrieked in terror. She tore out of the room, sounding the alarm that something terrible had happened to Grandma. She grabbed her brother and dragged him back into my room to investigate.

Wondering what all the commotion was about, I emerged from the bathroom, wearing a bathrobe but nothing on my head. I couldn't understand why my granddaughter was looking at me as if I were an alien from outer space.

She continued to stare at me in horror, as if wondering why this hairless creature was wearing her grandmother's robe. Where had her grandmother gone, and who was this strange person with the bald head?

My grandson, who was seven at the time, understood a few things about wigs. He had heard about chemo and realized that my hair would grow back later. He tried to calm his sister, but she was still too upset to recognize me.

I finally convinced her after much persuasion that I was truly her grandmother. I explained to her that the wig was fake hair, and my real hair would grow back soon. Then I showed her how I could put the wig on my head and remove it as I pleased. Quite a few minutes passed before she finally believed that her grandma hadn't been scalped!

Several weeks after my grandchildren returned home, a small package arrived in the mail. I hadn't ordered anything. Where had this package come from, and why had it been sent to me? I did a double-take after I checked the return address. My little grandson's name and address appeared in the upper left-hand corner!

Although delighted to receive something from him, I couldn't imagine why he would have sent me a gift. I turned it over, wondering what the package might contain. Then, without waiting to bring it indoors, I ripped it open. I reached inside and pulled out a cream-colored, crocheted hat. My fingers caressed the softest yarn I had ever known. With trembling hands, I held up the crocheted piece and stared in awe at the fine workmanship. The yarn had been expertly formed into coils and sewn together to form a beautiful head covering.

When I placed this creation on my head, I let out a satisfied sigh. The soft yarn cuddled my head as if someone were giving me a warm hug. The size was perfect. It was snug enough to stay on my head, but loose enough to wear comfortably. In fact, the hat was so light and airy that I didn't realize I had anything on my head. What a prize!

Later, I learned that my grandson had been troubled during his visit. My bald head had bothered him, although he hadn't expressed shock the way my granddaughter had. He hadn't said anything at the time, but I found out later that he had thought a lot about it.

As soon as he returned home from his visit, he resolved to do something to help his grandma. When he remembered how I had difficulty keeping my head warm at night, he decided to make a covering for me. He purchased some yarn and a kit containing a loom. Then he taught himself how to use the circular loom to fashion a hat for my head. Although he had labored on this project for several days, he never mentioned it. He had wanted the hat to be a surprise.

Tears came to my eyes when I realized that my grandson had created this hat all by himself. He had sacrificed several days of play in order to create something that his grandmother needed. My heart warmed when I held the hat and felt his love.

My hair has grown back now. I no longer get a cold head at night, so I don't need to wear that cap anymore. However, I keep it safely tucked away in my drawer along with my special treasures. Every time I open my dresser, I see the awesome hat my grandson made. I marvel that a determined seven-year-old boy would create a gift like that to help others. His thoughtful present is one I will always cherish.

— JoAnne Check —

59

Handheld Mixer

There are few things that are more beautifully
infectious than true kindness. It spreads
like a magnificent wildfire.
~Keith Wynn

E very time I need to use my handheld electric mixer to make a batch of frosting or a bowl of creamy mashed potatoes, I smile and think of Grandma Beth.

Grandma Beth isn't my grandmother. She's my husband's deceased grandmother. But she welcomed me into the family as though I were her own blood, and for that I'm forever grateful.

Bill's mother didn't want him moving so far away, so she'd responded to the news of our engagement by asking him if he'd thought about buying a dog as a companion instead of getting married.

I had looked forward to doubling my circle of relatives by marrying Bill, so I was devastated by his family's at-best lukewarm, sometimes outright hostile reaction.

Grandma Beth became a refuge from seemingly never-ending wedding drama, as nothing Bill and I decided on was ever "right" according to his immediate family. In her nineties and residing in an assisted-living apartment, Grandma Beth happily had no way of knowing what was going on behind the scenes.

Visits with her, during which she would walk slowly with Bill and me to the cafeteria and back to the kitchen table in her apartment, were a peaceful oasis from stress.

The bright spot in my weeks were the many days I would commute home to find a beautiful card waiting in the mail with her lovely, handwritten notes describing her life and the books she was reading. She frequently enclosed cards with family recipes or newspaper clippings she thought I would find interesting. I wrote back faithfully every time, feeling that I had a new grandma and a new friend.

Bill liked to joke that if we ever broke off our engagement, his grandmother would never forgive him.

I would have given anything for her to be at our wedding, but her fragile health made that impossible. She sent us the handheld electric mixer as her wedding gift. Always frugal—a trait she and I shared—she proudly told us that she had purchased it at no cost, thanks to her credit-card points.

After we were married, she and I continued our pen-pal relationship. When I was pregnant with our first son, she was the person Bill and I were most excited to share our good news with, and we drove the six hours to tell her in person.

As soon as our son was born, we sent her a coffee mug with his newborn photos on it and the words, "I love my Great-Grandma!" According to Bill's Uncle Jim, who opened the package for her when it came, that coffee mug was her pride and joy, and she took it with her to show all of her neighbors on her daily walk to the cafeteria.

Sadly, Grandma Beth never got to meet our baby, as she passed away shortly after he was born. Holding him at her funeral, I cried bitter tears of regret for waiting two weeks too long to make the drive with my newborn. But Uncle Jim told Bill and me that just the news of our son's birth had brightened the last weeks of her life and helped her to die happy.

It is a simple, off-brand, handheld electric mixer, but I'll never be tempted to replace it with a shiny, stainless-steel, countertop model. To me, my handheld mixer represents love and a grandma I'll never forget.

— Teresa Murphy —

60

Grandma's Gratitude Boxes

Gratitude is the memory of the heart.
~Jean-Baptiste Massieu

When our first grandchild was born, we were over the moon with excitement. I honestly don't think I slept soundly during the final days leading up to her birth. I had the outfit I was going to wear to the hospital all picked out months before her arrival — a soft pink blouse with matching pink hoop earrings and purple sandals.

The day Avery was born, I stood in the delivery room and, through tears of joy, witnessed my younger daughter deliver my first grandchild.

The day after she was born, I sat down to write her a love letter, welcoming her into our world and sharing my gratitude for her safe arrival. I decorated the envelope with Cinderella stickers. I had to laugh at myself afterward because the letter would, hopefully, be read by an adult granddaughter. But, at that moment, I was focusing on this new little life, and Cinderella made sense.

I began writing letters for every special occasion — her christening, first birthday, and first day of school. In each letter, I shared what was going on at that moment in time. My motivation was simple: I wanted to leave her with a piece of my heart — my memories of her milestones to cherish in the far-off future. I stored them in a fancy box and placed it in the back of my closet.

Nine years and seven grandkids later, I have a collection of fancy boxes stacked neatly in my closet.

Each grandchild has his or her own box. Along with my personal musings are favorite photos, their drawings, and any trinkets they have surprised me with. I save everything.

Avery's box contains a sprig of dried flowers in a Baggie that she picked for me on one of our walks around the neighborhood.

Little Billy's box contains a painted rock and a self-portrait complete with red hair — the brightest red in the crayon box. And there is also a paper with the first time he wrote his name. His mom, when teaching him to spell his name, would go over and over the letters by repeating, "BILLY: B, I, two Ls, Y." He listened intently and wrote just what she spelled out: BI2LSY!

My Grandma's Gratitude Boxes are a work in progress. They keep me focused on what is really important — the gift of grandchildren. I look forward to writing many more meaningful memories to be shared — hopefully, many, many years from now.

Avery, Gemma, Billy, Danny, Jack, Silas and baby girl Vada are my reasons for my putting pen to paper. My wish is that they will feel the love that overflows for them — my beautiful grandchildren who call me Nonnie.

— Kathy Whirity —

Chapter
7

Play Dates

61

That's a Grandpa

I wish I had the energy that my grandchildren
have — if only for self-defense.
~Gene Perret

Their parents were out for the night. Ginny and I were the senior babysitters. Oh, joy!

"Poppa Mike, I want a banana," three-year-old Elizabeth demanded.

"You what?"

"I want a banana."

I frowned at her. "Excuse me, young lady. That's not the way to ask."

"Poppa Mike, can I have a banana, please?"

"Better! Yes, you may." I handed her a banana.

"Not that one, Poppa."

"What's wrong with this one?"

"I want one with a sticker."

"Oh!" I looked at the bunch on the counter and saw one that had a blue sticker with the brand name on it. I handed it to her. "This one?"

"Yes, Poppa!" She smiled and accepted the banana. "Thank you."

"You're welcome, Elizabeth."

Before she peeled the banana, she took off the sticker. "Here, Poppa Mike."

"You want me to have the sticker?"

"Put it here," she said and pointed to her forehead.

I took it and reached to put it on her head.

"No!" She stepped back. "Yours!"

"On my head?"

"Yes!"

"You do it!" I told her. She took the sticker and stuck it on my forehead. "Make sure it's on good," I warned her. "We don't want to have it fall off." She slapped my head hard. I pretended to fall over.

"You're silly, Poppa."

"Of course!" I smiled and hugged her.

Later in the evening, Ginny said, "Well, let's get these kids fed!" She clapped her hands. "Boys!" she called. "Time to eat!"

Elizabeth put in her order, but her three brothers hadn't come to the table yet.

"Boys, put that game away and come eat," Ginny yelled.

We listened to the stomp of six feet and a chorus of arguing over who got to play the video game next. They burst into the dining room with all the grace of a pack of dogs on the scent of a rabbit.

Ginny and I refereed the meal until they finished eating (bickering) and we managed to get Elizabeth to eat at least some of her meal. I looked at Ginny. She looked at me. We sighed. "Ginny, is this what being a grandpa is all about? I don't know if I can get through this," I whined and turned to help with the dishes.

"Tag! You're it, Poppa!"

I turned, saw Elizabeth running away, looked at Ginny and said, "Well, I guess I better play. She's been begging to play tag all day." I ran after the fleeing, giggling little girl. I caught her in the hall. "Tag! You're it!" I yelled and ran the other way.

The three boys joined in. It was mayhem. We ran through the house. No room was sacred. The game went from tag to a new version we called hide-and-tag. I hid in the laundry room. I heard Seth, the oldest, approach. He was "It." I held my breath. The door began to open. I threw it open and screamed. He yelled, fell backward, hit the wall, and slid to the floor. "Ha!" I yelled, and ran off with him in pursuit. He cornered me in one of the bedrooms.

Now I was "It." I tagged Elizabeth. She caught one of her older brothers, who chased after me. I was the grandpa and the favorite target. I didn't make it easy. I opened the door to the garage and slipped inside. On the floor was a large box. I got on my knees, pulled the box over me and waited. The thumping of their feet passed the door and back again. I waited.

Benny, age seven, opened the door. "He's not in here!" He closed the door.

I waited.

Josh, age nine, said, "It's the only place we haven't looked. He has to be here."

They opened the door again. The box moved. They stepped back. The box stood six feet tall and growled. The boys screamed. The box burst through the door after two screaming boys. For two hours, we wore a path in the carpet chasing each other.

It was time to tuck them in for the night. The house was quiet. I hugged Ginny. In the bathroom, I washed up, brushed my teeth and looked in the mirror. In the middle of my forehead was the sticker from the banana. It had been there for three hours. Did I care? No! I looked in the mirror and thought, *That's a grandpa.*

— Michael T. Smith —

62

The Magic of Scented Markers

Imagination is more important than knowledge.
Knowledge is limited. Imagination encircles the world.
~Albert Einstein

It was a simple box of scented markers. For those who do not have a young child around, let me explain. These are magic markers, each with a distinct smell. They are also a gateway into the imagination, and I have proof.

On a recent drive with Grandchild #5, I gave her a brand-new box of those scented markers. She was very excited. Her words tumbled out in a big rush. "Grandma, this is the best present ever. I have wanted these markers for my whole, entire life. Plus, my mother always says 'no' when I beg for them."

Then she proceeded to open the box and give each marker a sniff, relishing each one's unique scent. When she got to the one labeled "Marshmallow," she exclaimed, "This is my favorite one because it smells like heaven!"

I could have let it go, but I knew there was more to this observation, so I asked the obvious.

"How do you know that heaven smells like marshmallow?"

I heard a deep sigh come from the back seat, a sigh that meant, "How can you not know this, Grandma? It is so-o-o obvious."

And so she led me through the explanation.

She pointed to the sky and asked me, "What is up there?"

Me: "Heaven?"

Child: "Correct! Now, what else do you see up there?"

Me: "Clouds?"

Child: "Correct! Are those clouds white and puffy?"

Me: "Yes."

Child: "Well, those white and puffy clouds look like...?"

"Marshmallows?" I guessed.

"Bingo!"

With a great deal of drama and some deep breaths, she finally concluded, "So, if there are white puffy clouds up there, there must be white puffy clouds in heaven. Since clouds are like giant marshmallows, heaven must smell like marshmallows!" She lay back in her seat, exhausted from the effort of educating Grandma.

It actually made perfect sense... I think.

Now my backseat friend started to more fully investigate the remaining markers. "Here's pineapple, cherry, lemon, orange, apple, candy cane, and grape." As I watched her, I could tell that seven more stories were already being imagined.

I can't wait for her to share.

— Diane St. Laurent —

63

Stars in Winter

Grandchildren are like stars... they sparkle and shine.
~Author Unknown

"Come, Grandma! Come see!" my two-year-old granddaughter Kara urged excitedly, grabbing my hand the second I opened the door. Her excitement almost made me forget the brutal winter snowstorm I'd braved to babysit her.

My son and daughter-in-law hurried past me to run some important errands that couldn't wait — blizzard or not.

"We won't be long," my son David promised. "She's had lunch and will need a nap in about an hour," he called over his shoulder.

"We'll be fine. Drive safe," I cautioned.

"We will," he promised. "Thanks, Mom," he threw over his shoulder, closing the door against the wind and snow that were swirling into the foyer.

I removed my boots, shook off my coat, and hung it up after prying my fingers from Kara's for a second. Immediately, she grasped my wrist again and began pulling me toward her room.

"Come!" she demanded urgently.

I laughed as I let her lead me, wistfully eyeing the steaming cup of coffee on the counter that my daughter-in-law had prepared for me moments before I arrived. When we got to my granddaughter's bedroom door, she proudly pointed to the little pink tent her parents had just erected next to her bed.

"Inside, Grandma!" she urged, almost propelling me into the

little shelter.

I struggled to enter, ignoring my aching knees. I crawled in to one side, making sure she had room to follow me into the cramped space.

As soon as Kara joined me, her voice changed. In an almost reverent whisper, she pointed to one of two matching pink foam mats. "Sit, Grandma."

"What a pretty tent you have here," I told her, trying to make myself comfortable. She placed a finger to her lips, indicating I should lower my tone to match hers. Evidently, this was hallowed ground to her and deserving of muted respect, so I complied.

After making sure I wouldn't try to escape, she scrambled out, ran to the door, and closed it. She strained on tiptoe and turned off the overhead light. The room, with its window blinds still drawn, became enveloped in moderate darkness. She joined me again for a moment to adjust a pillow on the mat, patting it and demonstrating that I should lie down.

When I did, she held out her palm in the universal symbol for "stay" and once more toddled out. This time, she dragged in her oversized stuffed dog, Fouff, that we bought her for Christmas. The length of him was twice her height. I sat up to help her, but she stopped me.

"Me do!" she insisted, and with the determination of a toddler who believes she can accomplish anything, she managed to wriggle into the already crowded enclosure with the dog. She pushed him into the space beside my head to use as her pillow.

I watched as she reached behind me for something dangling from a supporting pole. She manipulated a button, which turned on a string of stars that hung all the way around the top of the tent. Staring at it with awe, she peeked my way to see if my expression matched her appreciative one. I dropped my jaw in feigned surprise and let out a low coo of wonderment. The stars began to twinkle intermittently, illuminating the tent with their glow. Finally, she lay down herself, her head touching mine. She nestled so close that the scent of baby shampoo and soap filled my nostrils, taking me back to the days when I rocked her daddy to sleep.

"Étoiles," she murmured, quietly using the French word for stars, which she learned at her daycare. With a sigh of blissful contentment, she looked upward while I gazed at her sweet, relaxed profile. Turning to look at me, she repeated the word again, lifting a finger to her lips and then patting my cheek and pointing upward — my cue to look at the stars in silence. As I did, she snuggled even closer.

"Kitty cat!" she said moments later in hushed tones, and I raised my head to look quizzically around us. "Kitty cat!" she echoed.

I followed her intent stare and noticed that, as the stars blinked, a shadow that looked remarkably like a cat formed on the tent ceiling.

"Yes, kitty cat," I agreed softly, settling back against my pillow once again.

We lay there together silently side by side for a long time — so long that I thought she had fallen asleep. But when I turned to look, she met my gaze with a smile.

"Do you want me to sing you a song?" I asked quietly. She nodded.

Keeping my voice to a murmur, I began, "Twinkle, twinkle, little star..."

She curled up even closer. When I was finished, she asked for another and another. She didn't seem to mind that I sang off-key or may have gotten a word or two wrong. She was simply content to be the center of my world. Before long, her eyelids drooped a little, and she went back to looking at her stars. In moments, she was asleep. I pressed the little backlight button on my wristwatch and realized it was her naptime. Reaching for a small blanket crumpled in a ball in the corner, I covered her gently. Instead of leaving her, I lay back down beside her and continued to look at the stars.

I thought back to all the times, I'd had the opportunity to do something like this with her father, but passed. Work, responsibilities, household chores — they all took precedence back then when my husband and I were young parents. And though we didn't ignore our son and tried very hard to give him special, undivided time, I always felt it was never enough.

At that moment, the child of my thoughts, now a man, opened the door a crack to peek in, perhaps questioning the silence. They were back. Sitting up carefully, I leaned my head into the crack of daylight emanating from the kitchen and pressed my finger to my lips, motioning that she was sleeping. He nodded and closed the door gently.

I could have gotten up and joined them in the living room. Instead, I stayed in that little tent and watched my granddaughter, taking in her perfect features, her relaxed body, and the tiny, smiling curve of her mouth as she lay dreaming of whatever toddlers dream about.

When I was convinced there was little chance of her waking up, I leaned over to kiss her warm cheek. Then, glancing at the stars one more time, I reached over to turn them off. Slowly, and as silently as possible, I crawled out of the tent to join the adults waiting in the other room, but not before I said a silent prayer of thanks for the precious child who gave me a second chance to stop and enjoy the simple beauty of a quiet room, a lullaby, and gazing at stars in winter.

— Marya Morin —

64

Blowing Bubbles

If nothing is going well, call your grandmother.
~Italian Proverb

He calls me Bama. He has always called me Bama. When my daughter-in-law, Crescent, was pregnant with him, people used to ask me what my soon-to-be-born grandson was going to call me. I always told them it was up to him. When Eli was born, people asked, "Is he going to call you Grandma or Nana or Grammie or Gram?" And my answer to them was always the same. I would say that I had no idea; he would call me whatever he wanted to call me. It was up to him to name me.

We think Bama could be a combination of my name, Barbara, and the word Grandma. Before he could talk, he heard people calling me Barbara, and he also heard people referring to me as Grandma. Maybe, just maybe, he put the two words together, and they came out "Bama." That seems logical. Or maybe it wasn't like that at all, and he just named me whatever he wanted. Whatever the reason, when Eli calls me Bama I answer!

He is now seven years old, and we have such fun together. He is so smart, has a terrific sense of humor and teases his papa and me right back when we tease him. I try to teach him things I think he should know, and he tries to teach me to play some of the games that I have for him on my iPad. He is very patient, but so far no success with that. It's all just foreign to me.

The other day, Eli and his dad, Mike, arrived at our house for a visit with Papa and me. I could tell that something was bothering him. We sat together outside on our deck, and I asked him what was wrong. At first, he just shrugged and said nothing was wrong. But his body language told me a different story.

I asked again — pushing a little. Eli said that he was having a problem. He was trying to learn how to blow bubble-gum bubbles. It seemed like all of his friends could blow bubble-gum bubbles, but he just couldn't do it. I tried to explain how to do it, but aside from making funny faces and sticking out my tongue, nothing got accomplished. He tried to do what I said. His checks puffed out. His face got red. He made funny noises. He accidentally spit his gum out a few times, but he quickly picked it up and stuck it back in his mouth. The five-second rule, you know! But no bubbles.

Finally, we were both so frustrated we were ready to give up. But then I had an idea. I asked Eli if he had another piece of gum — and not the ABC (Already Been Chewed!) kind. He did. He gave it to me. Now, I hadn't chewed a piece of bubble gum for years. Wow, it's sweet. Blech! And one piece is huge. It filled my entire mouth, and I felt like I was gagging. I don't remember a piece of bubble gum being that big. I chewed and chewed and chewed. Finally, that piece of gum became more manageable. It was time to blow bubbles, or at least try.

Eli and I sat in chairs facing each other — with our gum in our mouths. I worked that piece of gum around in my mouth and over my tongue, and then I slowly blew a bubble. Nice! I guess it's like riding a bicycle. Even though I hadn't tried blowing bubbles with bubble gum for years, I completely remembered how to do it… on the first attempt. Eli was amazed. And might I say… impressed! Here was his grandmother, his very own Bama, chewing bubble gum and blowing bubbles.

We sat there for a while. I tried every which way to show him how to blow bubbles.

"Try this." No luck.

"Okay, try to do it this way." No luck.

"Move your tongue like this." No luck.

"Let the air out of your mouth slowly." Nothing.

He tried and tried and tried to blow a bubble, but nothing worked.

And then, just when we were both about to give up, he got this look on his face — that knowing kind of look. He moved the gum around in his mouth and wrapped it around his tongue. He sat up straighter, and then he slowly, very slowly, blew. His face got red, and his cheeks puffed out. Slowly, very slowly, a bubble emerged.

It was a very tiny bubble, to be sure, but it was still a bubble. His first bubble… ever. His beautiful blue eyes just lit up, and I could tell he wanted to smile, but the bubble was in the way. And then, "Pop!" As quickly as he blew it, it disappeared. But it didn't matter; Eli was so excited.

"Bama, did you see that? I blew a bubble."

"Oh, yes, Eli, I saw. It was a perfect bubble, too. Please do it again."

And he did — over and over and over again. Eli and I were blowing bubbles together and laughing. Each time he blew, the bubble would get a little bigger. Sometimes, the bubble would pop. Sometimes, mine did, too. We both wound up with bubble gum on our noses and chins! That made us laugh. Sometimes, the bubbles got really big and didn't pop. Picture-perfect bubbles. Eli had finally learned to blow bubbles with his bubble gum. And his very own Bama had the pleasure of teaching him!

— Barbara LoMonaco —

65

A Game of Jacks

*For myself, one of the sweetest words
I have ever heard is "Nana."*
~Zelda Rosenbaum

Every time either of my granddaughters has challenged me to a game of jacks I've stopped everything and plopped down on the floor to play. In the early days, I would intentionally fumble the ball or illegally move a jack to make the games more exciting. But those days are long gone. Now, even when I try my hardest, my thirteen- and ten-year-old granddaughters, Ella and Hallie, both beat me at the game I taught them.

Nor can I win against them anymore at spit, casino or gin rummy — three of the many card games I've introduced them to over the years. Thank goodness I can still call myself the family champion at jotto, a word game I learned from my dad and played with him for hours at a time — one of my fondest memories.

Sometimes, in a quiet moment, I wonder what Ella and Hallie will remember most about me when I am no longer here.

When they reminisce about our annual Christmas vacations in Mexico, will they think about our days together on the beach, building sandcastles, getting their hair braided, and stuffing themselves with chips and guacamole? Will they appreciate how I taught them five new words in Spanish every morning during our weeks there? Or will they laugh at how I embarrassed them when I sang along in Spanish with the guitarist who serenaded us at dinner?

I wonder what they will remember most about our recent trip to Israel, when we went as a family to celebrate Ella's Bat Mitzvah. I hope they will treasure the memories of standing side by side at the Western Wall to honor her rite of passage. Maybe they will also chuckle at the memory of my terrified face as I rode on top of a camel in the Negev Desert.

I wonder.

Will Ella remember seeing *The Lion King* with me — our first Broadway show together? Will she remember that during our sleepovers, I always let her have my side of the bed, and lay next to her scratching her back until she fell asleep?

Will Hallie remember the times we lined up every pair of my shoes around my bedroom and played Shoe Store? And how I carried her on my back through the streets of Manhattan, even while insisting that she was getting too heavy for piggyback rides?

Will they each remember the nicknames of Ella-Boo and Hallie-Bean that I loved to call them?

Both the important milestones and the smallest moments create the sweetest memories.

I also want my granddaughters to remember the silly things that still keep us giggling together. Although their Poppy — my husband — takes credit for teaching them how to throw grapes up in the air and catch them in their mouths, it was this nana who showed them how to tilt their heads back and squirt their mouths full of Reddi-wip.

Then there are those experiences we shared when they were quite young, which they remember only through the stories I've told them.

Ella never gets tired of hearing about the time she rolled off our bed while I was in the next room watching TV. I thought I had lost her… until I found her sleeping peacefully under the bed. She also loves to hear about the afternoon when her mom and I were pushing her in her stroller through Bloomingdale's while trying to teach her to put two words together. Over and over, I kept coaching her to repeat after me: "Hi, Mommy," and "Hi, Daddy." Finally, just when my daughter and I were about to give up on that lesson, Ella turned to me with a big grin of satisfaction and blurted out, "Hi, Nana!"

Hallie's favorite bedtime story is about her birth, when I got the call from my son-in-law that our daughter was having a hard time in labor. He asked me to come to the hospital to comfort her. There I was, trying to calm my daughter when Hallie suddenly decided it was time to enter the world, and I accidentally ended up in the delivery room helping the doctor deliver her!

Some stories never get old. Nor does squirting whipped cream into our mouths. Or playing card games together… or word games… or jacks.

And one day, when my granddaughters get down on the floor to teach their own daughters — or granddaughters — how to play jacks, I hope that they will think of their nana.

— Linda Saslow —

66

The Magic

In every walk with nature, one receives
far more than he seeks.
~John Muir

It was that special time of the evening when my grandmother and I took our nightly walk to the harbor. I grabbed my flip-flops and sweater, waiting patiently at the front door for Gram to come. My favorite time of day was about to start.

Off we went, starting down the winding path through the woods, hand in hand. As we walked, Gram pointed out the treasures that the woods held — a cluster of lady's slippers reaching out of the earth; an old, gnarled apple tree filled with fruit; a tiny chipmunk scampering across the path; and birds, so many beautiful birds, each with its own special call.

Gram took these things we saw and created a story for me, one that was different each night. The lady's slippers might be parasols or balloons for the fairies who dwelled in the forest. The old, gnarled apple tree might be a secret hiding place where gnomes lived. The scampering chipmunk might be a royal ride for a princess, and the beautiful birds were guardians of the forest, magical creatures who cared for all the animals who made the woods their home.

The setting sun shimmered through the tree branches, dappling the ground in front of us, as our nightly adventure continued. Gram shared her secrets about all that we saw as we walked along. The path opened up in front of us to reveal a clearing that overlooked a shining harbor. Gram said mermaids lived there, taking care of the seas and the boats that were anchored there.

As we walked along, enjoying our time together, Gram told me how lucky we were to be surrounded by the magnificence of the world around us. "There is magic everywhere. Always look for the magic."

As the years went on, Gram and I continued our walks, sharing in the beauty that we experienced together. It became woven into the fabric of our lives, into the very way we perceived life and its many gifts. It was central to our relationship and created a special bond between us.

The time came when Gram could no longer go on our walks. I would bring our walks to her, reading stories and poems that captured the essence of the world around us, the beauty of nature, and the memories we shared together. When I finished reading, Gram would always say, "Always look for the magic." That phrase had become a powerful constant between us, one that epitomized all the love and adventures we shared.

Gram passed away surrounded by family and loved ones. As I was leaving her side, ready to steel myself for the grief and longing that would settle in, my cousin came to me with a small, foil-wrapped package tied lovingly with gold ribbon. My name was written on the top. Gram had given her strict instructions about the handful of treasures she was to put inside — acorns, small stones, colorful leaves, and a small conch shell, like the ones we had seen so many times at the harbor. A small piece of folded paper was also inside. I opened it tearfully and read the words, "Always look for the magic." At that moment, I knew I had not really lost Gram. She would be with me always, in the magic she had taught me about, in the simple beauty that surrounded us. I would look for the magic… always.

— MJ Keenan —

My Grandchildren Make Me Brave

While we try to teach our grandchildren about life,
our grandchildren teach us what life is all about.
~Author Unknown

I don't like heights. I can't dance. I have a horrible singing voice. I snort when I laugh. I don't like playgrounds that have netted bridges. I am convinced that my feet will slip through, I'll be stuck in the netting, and my chubby legs will dangle for everyone to see.

I never had to worry about conquering these things until my grandchildren arrived. But when they did, I resolved to enjoy every moment with them... unless they took up skydiving. I was not going to be a downer grandma. I'd be the fun, adventurous grandma if required, although I have to admit that I hoped my grandchildren would be quiet, reserved little people who liked sedate activities.

Enter my grandchildren, and I am swinging on ropes, dancing in the street, belting out songs, snorting more than ever, and crossing netted bridges with glee. What has happened to the old me? My grandchildren's daring spirits have morphed me into a wild grandma, or Gigi, as I am known.

When my first granddaughter was three, she loved the highest slides at the playground. This required me to climb to the top with her.

Me, who is afraid of heights! I was embarrassed that a three-year-old was cheering me on. "Come on, Gigi, you can do it!" And I did do it. My hands were sweating, but I dared not taint her adventuresome spirit. I got my big, old legs in gear and finally sat my rear on the slide. I shot down the slide like I had silicone on my rear. My granddaughter gave me a high-five, cheered and clapped as if I'd won a gold medal.

My second granddaughter arrived dancing out of her mom's belly. She dances everywhere. If there is music, her hips are wiggling. I am self-conscious about my dancing skills. I should say I *was* self-conscious. Now if we are at a store, and music comes over the speaker, I am a dance queen. She grabs my hand, and we are wiggling, shaking and singing along. I have no shame. I copy her moves with wild abandon. "Watch this, Gigi," she'll say as she shimmies down the aisle. "Now it's your turn," she laughs. I have learned to do one mean shimmy, if I do say so myself. I glide down the aisle. Well, at least I think I do.

My first grandson arrived, and in his second year, I crawled in the mud looking for worms. They fascinated him. I don't like worms. I don't like mud. I don't like getting dirty. Yet there I was inspecting the earth, searching for chubby worms. Bugs were a bonus on our mission. Big, long-legged bugs crossed right in front of us. We were nose to nose, counting their legs. Bugs with hard shells and tentacles followed. I didn't scream. I wanted to, but I couldn't ruin his fascination with these underground creatures. He was enthralled with nature. Who was I to ruin it for him? I admit to being covered in goose bumps. A grasshopper arrived, and that calmed my nerves a tad — until it jumped at me.

My second grandson introduced me to bopping. He bops to hard rock. Usually, I'd turn that music right off. Now I bop along with him. We jam and stomp to the music. I even pretend to play a guitar. He has turned me into a hard-rock grannie. I know the words to Metallica songs. I even hum them when I'm with my other grannie friends. Naturally, my head is bopping, and I'm strumming my air guitar. They think I have a strange disorder, but I keep bopping.

All of my grands like the twenty-foot-tall inflatable slides. I still don't like them, but I pretend I am not afraid as I stand at the top looking over the landscape of miniature people watching below. Gingerly, I squat into position and close my eyes. One of the grands will grab my hand, and off we go flying, hair blowing in the breeze. I usually scream. They laugh all the way to the bottom. "Let's do it again!"

Over the years, I've overcome my fears. I am supposed to be the one teaching them, yet I am the student now. It's amazing how such little people can know so many things.

"Gigi, they made the ropes so even kids' little feet won't slip through. You are not going to get stuck," my granddaughter counsels as she pulls me across the ropes bravely.

"Gigi, you don't wiggle hard enough. Watch me," she says as she shakes her entire body. "I know you can do it. Just try. Now put your hands over your head and shake. You'll like it." I glance at myself in a mirror, and it's really not a pretty sight. There is way too much shaking going on, even when I'm standing still.

"Gigi, these worms are really cool. Look at their color. Some look like they have hair. Is this a ladybug or a beetle? How do bugs have babies?"

"Gigi, rock on!" The little one would say if he could talk.

I really thought I was going to teach them about life. I had so much wisdom to impart. I was going to sit in the garden and watch for butterflies. I'd tell them the story about how the winds of the world began with the flutter of a butterfly's wings. Then I'd continue to explain that little things we do make way for larger things. I'd have them imagine us walking down the path of life, hand in hand, finding adventures along the way. It was supposed to be a glorious moment, but they had other information to share:

"The girl who has the biggest belly in a ballet tutu has the most brains."

"If you have a tea party, you add so much sugar that it's called a sugar party with tea."

"You can never have enough toys, ice cream or hugs."

"The best place in the world is Gigi's house."

How could I not follow these kids if they want to jump out of an airplane? Maybe skydiving is going back on the list.

— Anne Bardsley —

Babysitting 101

Grandparents are there to help the child get into
mischief they haven't thought of yet.
~Gene Perret

It's not often that Christy asks me to babysit the grandkids. "It'll only be a few hours. You don't have to do much. Really."

"No problemo," I said. She looked a bit pensive, but left.

"You want chili fries with your pizza?" I asked Leila and Charlie.

"I thought we were going to have an after-school snack," Leila said.

"That is a snack."

"Mommy said we are supposed to have healthy snacks like fruit," Charlie said.

"Got you covered." I handed them a package of cherry-flavored Red Vines.

"But isn't this candy?"

"Perish the thought. For over 3,000 years, licorice root has been used as a remedy for peptic ulcers, sore throats, and coughs in eastern and western medicine."

"Wow."

We all gnawed on a piece of history as I closed the American Licorice Company website. Hint to grandparents: The Internet makes you look really smart.

"After snacks, you wanna play baseball?" Charlie asked.

Charlie likes to hit the ball as far as he can and score every time. If I try and tag him out, he often makes up his own baselines, which can be up to a couple hundred yards wide. Leila is like greased lightning. Last time we played, I ran the equivalent of a marathon and never got either of them out. Not only did it take me hours to recuperate, but I never got up to bat.

"How about we just watch TV? We could watch *The Three Stooges* marathon I have on DVD." I did my famous "Whubwhubwhubwhubwhub" and "Nah-ah-ah-ah-ah-ah."

"Mommy said we shouldn't watch *The Three Stooges* anymore. She thinks they are too dumb and violent," Charlie said.

"What?" I stopped noogying Leila's head. Hard to imagine anyone thinking ear pulling, nose grabbing and forehead slapping are dumb and violent.

"We're supposed to do our homework anyway," Leila said.

"Okay. I could help you with that," I said enthusiastically.

They looked at each nervously. "You're not going to draw, are you?"

Apparently, Leila's teacher didn't appreciate the rendition of an old hippie guy that I taught her how to draw. Art is in the eye of the beholder, I guess.

"We'll worry about art later. I did buy some stickers, permanent paint — not that watercolor stuff — and glitter, lots of glitter. So, what's the assignment?"

"We're learning fractions," Leila said.

"Great! I love fractions. How about you, Charlie?"

"I have to read a paragraph and figure out the main idea."

"Perfect." I started with Leila's homework.

"If you had one brownie and cut it into four pieces, what would one piece equal? Huh. Not much." I read the next problem. "If you had one brownie and divided it into eight pieces, what would one piece equal? Diddily, that's what."

Leila wrote down "diddily." I went to the kitchen and whipped up some so-easy-even-a-stooge-could-make-it brownie mix. Then I read Charlie's paragraph, something about a kid sharing his lunch money with a friend.

"You know, loan sharks lend money out to people who need it, and then they charge a really high vig."

"Why?"

"So they can make more money. The more they lend, the more they make."

"Cool," Charlie said, and wrote this down. I took the brownies out of the oven, cut them into sixteen pieces and divvied them up.

"This is the best way to do fractions ever," said Leila.

A short time later, Christy came to retrieve the kids. She surveyed the remains of brownies, pizza, popcorn, and soda. Then she asked Leila, who was covered with stickers, glitter, and several coats of Day-Glo paint, what she was drawing.

"It's a hippie chick to go with the hippie guy. See, Ernie said they all had hair under their arms."

"Want to borrow some money, Mommy? I need to make some vig to buy more Red Vines."

Christy gathered them and headed for the door.

"Call me if you need help again," I said.

"Right," she said, mumbling something about never understanding men if she lived to be a hundred.

— Ernie Witham —

Technology 101

Technology is anything that wasn't
around when you were born.
~Alan Kay

Grandparenting these days is all about technology. I'm not talking about e-mail, Facebook, iPads and tweeting. We're pretty good at that. It's those strollers and car seats. When our kids were little, life was simple. We had carriages that got pushed around the block, but never entered an automobile. They were as big as a car themselves. And we used lightweight fold-up umbrella strollers when we travelled by car or bus, and then switched to a child carrier when we got where we were going. Sure, babies slumped over like a sack of potatoes from little support in those strollers, and fingers got pinched when they folded up, but they were cheap and replaceable.

Now the SUV strollers come with airline pilot-type instructions, and we need the coordination of a NASA astronaut to open them, install a child and prepare for takeoff.

When I was telling a friend and fellow grandmother that I was babysitting my grandchildren for a week, she confided that she has been afraid she'd never get her grandchild out of his car seat. I've felt the same about high chairs, double strollers, single strollers, automatic indoor baby swings, and outdoor baby swings. The grandchild had to show me how to stick my finger inside to release the shoulder clasp on the swing's seatbelt mechanism. This newest generation will never conceive of doing anything at all without a seat belt and shoulder harness. My two-year-old granddaughter is able to climb in and out of her stroller herself, and when she climbs in she immediately secures the safety belt herself.

When my daughter gave me my child-minding instructions, she told me the four-month-old drinks when he's thirsty and sleeps when he's tired; no need to follow a schedule. She was right; he smiled his way through the day while sucking his two middle fingers. The challenge was the single stroller in which I had to place his car seat with him buckled in, while remembering the diaper bag, rain cover, sun cover and assorted paraphernalia. And that was only when his sister was at Montessori, and I was just taking him on an outing to No Frills, cramming the groceries into the bottom of the stroller.

Early morning and late afternoon, the transportation of the day was the double stroller, with options for which way each could face. Of course, each child had to be buckled in and adjusted so that kicking each other was not an option. It wasn't easy to maneuver the stroller on city streets and get through traffic lights. I felt like a long-haul truck driver, with the arm muscles to match.

After a week of it, I was getting pretty good, and had a new appreciation for those Strollercize mothers who pack the coffee shops. I salivated outside the Starbucks, but the thought of negotiating the stairs and the lineup with my two-person spaceship had me drinking from a sippy cup outside.

— Louise Rachlis —

Over Superman's Dead Body

I have a warm feeling after playing with my
grandchildren. It's the liniment working.
~Author Unknown

My daughter purchased season tickets to Six Flags St. Louis that included guest passes. All summer long, my grandsons begged me to join them. Since school would be starting in a week, I finally agreed to go, but my husband could tell I wasn't enthused.

"Honey, what's wrong?" he asked.

"It's been almost thirty years since I've been to an amusement park. Don't forget, I just turned sixty."

He chuckled. "Is your life insurance paid up?"

When they pulled in the drive to pick me up, I trudged to the car like a prisoner on death row.

Wiggling with excitement, six-year-old Clayton squealed from the back seat, "Grandma, we're gonna have so much fun!"

Despite my fears, I smiled and said, "I can't wait" — to get back home.

As soon as we arrived at the park the car doors flew open and the boys hit the ground running.

Eleven-year-old Randy said, "Let's ride Mr. Freeze first. It goes the fastest and turns upside-down."

I froze.

When Clayton saw the look on my face, he added, "Unless you're chicken."

Was that a triple-dog-dare? Who couldn't survive twenty-three seconds? Twenty-four seconds later, I had my answer — my stomach. After Mr. Freeze, everything else was uphill. Next we approached the wooden Screamin' Eagle, and I bragged about riding it with their mom when she was a little girl. Oh, my aching back! I didn't remember it being so rickety and rough. But that was nothing compared to the Ninja. My head snapped from side to side as the sharp curves turned into sheer drops. I wobbled off the ride trying to regain my balance.

Randy shouted, "Wasn't that awesome, Grandma?"

"What?" My ears felt like Mike Tyson had used them for a punching bag.

My favorite part of the day was when the boys finally agreed to stop for the picnic lunch we'd packed that morning. They spread a blanket under a large oak tree, and I plopped down, kicking my shoes off my aching feet. What I wouldn't have given for a short nap. Before I could swallow the last bite of my sandwich, my ambitious grandsons jumped up, raring to go. When my daughter said we'd leave after we rode the roller coasters on the other side of the park, my aching body screamed in protest.

We soared through one terrifying ride after another, but the real challenge of the day was our last ride — the Superman Tower of Power. *Great,* I thought, *a new way to be terrorized.* An eternity passed as we waited to be hurled toward the ground. What was I thinking when I'd agreed to spend the entire day at an amusement park? Luckily, we survived the extreme free fall, and the look of admiration in my grandsons' eyes was worth every frightening second.

On the way home, I swallowed an ibuprofen and wondered what time the chiropractor's office opened the next morning.

Clayton beamed. "Grandma, you were super."

Randy chimed in, "Yeah, I can't believe you rode every roller coaster in the park. You're going with us next time."

If I could've moved my head, I would have hung it. Under my breath, I mumbled, "Over Superman's dead body."

—Alice Muschany—

Role Models

71

The Mother Look

A daughter is a mother's gender partner, her closest ally
in the family confederacy, an extension of her self.
~Victoria Secunda

We have all seen it — that look from our mothers that could mean many different things. It could mean, "Don't even think about doing what you are about to do," or "This is your last warning, so you had better be polite, charming and well-behaved, or there will be consequences." Not a word was actually uttered when this look was shared, but the meaning was crystal-clear to the recipient. Ignoring the look did not lead to happy times.

I admit that I have used the Mother Look. It has helped me to have more obedient children in the grocery store, church and family gatherings. When the Mother Look is combined with a Teacher Look, the results are quite impressive.

Now that my daughters are mothers, they have been learning just how helpful this Mother Look is. I have seen them issue silent warnings and marveled at how quickly they have mastered the skill. Their children, as they themselves did when they were young, have tested the Mother Look. But they are learning the wisdom of just obeying if they are on the receiving end of that stare.

I usually don't have to resort to using the Mother Look now that I am a grandmother. I just leave when I see a meltdown approaching. I only go into a store with young children if I am going to purchase something they want. So the Mother Look is not often needed. However, there was a time when one young grandchild did need a little silent reminder, and I used the Mother Look. I knew she had seen it before because she put her hands over her eyes and said, "You look just like my mom when your face is like that."

Yes, I thought to myself, *I have done my job well.*

— Diane St. Laurent —

72

There Was No Plan B

There are two lasting bequests we can give our
children. One is roots. The other is wings.
~Hodding Carter, Jr.

In 2009, my husband and I moved in with my ailing grandmother to care for her in her final days. We celebrated our one-year wedding anniversary by hauling items from our apartment into a storage unit. In this space, we locked up all our belongings except our bedroom set and a crib. One single room would be our private space. There was barely enough room to walk around. In the living room, we set up a small, enclosed area that we could use for the baby during the day.

It was November when we moved in. The doctors told us to make that Christmas extra special; it would most likely be my grandmother's last. During the Christmas season, we decorated her house with lights, put up her first Christmas tree in at least ten years, and hosted the entire family on Christmas morning. In the New Year, some of her siblings came to see her.

It didn't take long for us to realize a few things about my grandmother's health. First, she was not eating properly. If it was up to her, she would hardly put anything on her plate. But if I prepared a plate for her, she would eat everything on it. She was also forgetting to take her medication as scheduled, so we came up with a system to fix that.

These measures improved her health, and we ended up living with her for three years. I learned a lot about her as a result.

My grandmother had graduated high school, entered nursing school, and served as an Army nurse in World War II. She was stationed overseas and part of the first Army hospital unit present at the Battle of the Bulge. Upon returning to the United States, she continued her career as a nurse until the age of seventy-two. Even after retirement, she continued to help several local families with their medical needs.

One morning, I asked my grandmother if she had had a Plan B if she wasn't able to become a nurse. My grandmother chuckled and replied simply, "No." Incredulously, I begged for something. Surely, something else must have interested her as an option to fall back on. Matter of factly, she stated: "There was no Plan B. I made the decision I was going to be a nurse, and that was that. No one was going to tell me otherwise."

Those words stuck with me. I remembered being a high-school student with a dream — one that others felt was foolish and a waste of money. I had allowed those people to push me away from my dream and toward their Plan B for my life.

After stewing on this for several days, I informed my husband that I was going back to school. I was going to pursue my dream even if it meant starting over from scratch. I visited the financial-aid office to apply for scholarships and grants. I did everything I could to get as much of my tuition covered as possible. I even found a great preschool across the street from the school that I could bring my daughter to on the days I had class. I made the decision, and that was that.

After my grandmother passed away, we moved to a new city. Just a few years ago, I made the decision to go to seminary. I knew it didn't make sense to others — the timing and purpose — but I just knew it was to be part of my journey and future. Once again, I found a way, and with the support of my family, I enrolled in classes full-time. Some people would try to talk me out of it, but I had made the decision… and that was that.

My grandmother's tenacity, drive, and determination have motivated me in many ways throughout my life. We don't always need a back-up plan or a safety net. Instead, we can be confident in our ability and go for our dreams.

— Gena B. McCown —

Motorcycle Grandma

Age is an issue of mind over matter.
If you don't mind, it doesn't matter.
~Mark Twain

I popped my head out from underneath my loft bed and called out to my college roommate. "Hey, Grace! Just a head's up. I'm going to give my grandmother a quick call. Should I call her here or in the hall?"

She glanced up from her textbook. "Either is fine. Is this your motorcycle grandma or the other one?"

"Motorcycle grandma," I replied, laughing. "I'll be right back."

I padded out to the hall, my fingers gliding across my phone screen and pressing the familiar digits. Three rings later, I heard my grandma's voice from over 600 miles away.

"Hello, Dana! How are you doing?"

I rubbed my eyes from exhaustion, my body aching from another night of too little sleep.

"It's been fine, Oma. What's the scoop with you?"

"Well…" she began with a devilish lilt in her voice, oblivious to the exhaustion in my tone. And, like the initial shot of a roller coaster, she launched into an intricate tale of her latest and greatest adventure. With her usual dramatic flair, she narrated piece-by-piece the hilarious story of how she decided she wanted to fly a plane, flew up in the air, and then got stuck in the cockpit after she landed.

"Two very handsome men had to help pull me out." I could almost imagine the flirtatious wink on her face. "It was all very exciting."

"Was Bob jealous?" I teased.

She and Bob had met a few years ago, and went from fellow motorcycle enthusiasts to friends and then to something more. Ever the social mover and shaker, she took pride in announcing that she was a cougar — dating a man an entire year younger than her.

In the past year, I had never seen Oma so ridiculously happy. She and Bob spent their days wheeling around on the bike, playing pranks, and pulling crazy stunts.

Last time, it was matching tattoos. The time before that, it was playing golf cart bumper car as they rode in a parade. And now, it was the glider planes.

As she chattered on about her next prank — because "someone has to keep those retirement home residents entertained" — a lump formed in my throat. My grandmother had formed a grand and fabulous life during my months away in Michigan. I missed being a part of that wild life and felt farther away than usual.

I missed the way her eyes lit up after a joke, the way her body dripped from head-to-toe with Chico's jewelry, and the way she mispronounced words with her Dutch accent.

But, most of all, I missed the way she always told me that we were the same, that I was her clone and would have wild adventures just like her.

I didn't feel like her clone at the moment. I felt like a girl who had spent the past week studying hard for a psychology test that didn't go so well.

"So, Dana, when are you coming home?"

"In a month or so, I think. But with finals coming up, I'm not sure I'm ready. I have so much to do before then. I think I'm in a bit over my head."

Her soothing voice caressed me through the phone. "Alright, Dana. Can I tell you a secret?"

"Yeah?" I said, sighing slightly.

"You worry too much. You need to let go and have some more fun. Go skydiving or do something a little crazy!"

"Oma," another heavy breath escaped, "I don't have time…" I was about to recite my long list of to-dos.

She cut me off before I could continue.

"Dana, if I were you, I would be going out and having a blast."

I knew she was right. "Alright, Ohm. I'll try."

"Not just try," she responded with her familiar laugh. "You'll do it." A second later, she added, "You are my clone after all."

I smiled. "True that, 'Cloma.'" She laughed at the familiar nickname.

A knock sounded over the phone. "Oh! That'll be Bob. We're about to go out to happy hour. Call me again soon?"

I promised her I would and hung up.

I walked back into my room, and Grace pulled out her earbuds. "How's the motorcycle grandmother?"

"She's good," I said.

A beat went by. "Hey, Grace?"

"Yeah?"

"How about we don't study tonight. Let's have some fun."

Next month, I decided, I would be the one telling the story of a crazy adventure.

— Dana Drosdick —

74

A Lesson in Equality

Live so that when your children think of fairness,
caring, and integrity, they think of you.
~H. Jackson Brown, Jr.

"Hey, look at that man," I said to my cousins as we critiqued pictures in the directory from the church my grandparents attended. We all scrutinized the picture closely and laughed at the man while we thought up a nickname for him. "How about Rabbit Teeth?" one of us suggested since the man had rather large front teeth. Soon, we had a long list of nicknames for other people, but we were careful not to use these names in front of our grandparents.

Every day, the mocking became a bit more mean-spirited. Then, one day, one of us made the mistake of talking about Rabbit Teeth in front of Grandpa. He looked at us and asked, "Who is Rabbit Teeth?"

There was dead silence as we all looked at each other; none of us wanted to answer this question. Finally, one of us confessed. A look of sorrow crossed Grandpa's face as he processed our answer. We sat in silence as we waited to see what Grandpa would do. He wasn't the type to whip us when we did wrong, but we also knew he didn't let wrong actions slide. There would be a price to pay for what we had done, but nothing prepared us for his response.

Grandpa asked us to sit down so we could talk about what had happened. He started by telling us that he wasn't angry at us for making fun of people, but he was disappointed. Looking back at this incident,

I think Grandpa felt like he had failed us by not sharing the message earlier that he was now preparing to share.

Grandpa made direct eye contact with each of us as he began to speak. He explained kindly, "God has created each person to look different. Some of us have different-shaped teeth or eyes. Some are tall, while others are short. Some are light-skinned, while others are dark-skinned."

Then he made a statement that has rung through my mind for years: "There are no right or wrong groups of people since all are created by God and made in his image." As Grandpa finished speaking, there were tears in his eyes. I realized just how much he had been hurt by the things he had heard us saying. I didn't want to hurt Grandpa. And as I processed what he had said to us, I resolved to learn to value people like he did.

A few years later, when some friends were speaking badly about people who looked different from us, I remembered Grandpa's words and felt empowered to share the message he had told us so many years ago: In God's eyes, we are all equal.

—A E Troyer—

75

A Grandparent's Job

When you look into your mother's eyes, you know that
is the purest love you can find on this earth.
~Mitch Albom

While my daughter did not have any grandfathers, she was blessed with two wonderfully diverse grandmothers. "Nana" and "Momo" each played an important part in my daughter's life. One particular evening when I was busy with the usual chaos in our household, my mother, Nana, offered to give my daughter her bath. While I cleared the dinner dishes, I heard the usual laughter and exclamations that accompanied the bath time of a five-year-old, followed by a period of what seemed to be a serious whispered conversation.

After bath time, my mom came out to the kitchen and joined me in putting away the leftovers. She told me that she and Francesca had had a talk.

"I just want you to know that everything is alright," my mom said.

"What do you mean everything is alright? I didn't know anything was wrong."

"No, it's all good. She just needed to talk," my mom said with a confidence I certainly did not feel.

"Mom, I really need to know what she talked to you about."

"Oh, that's between a granddaughter and her nana."

We had been through a lot in my daughter's first five years of life — with my mother's cancer, my husband's cancer and him losing his job. We worried about how she processed all the stress that had transpired. We were always very open, answering any questions in a way a child her age could understand. So why could she not approach us? I felt a stab in my heart, followed by the immediate sense of fear that someone had hurt her. When I pressed my mom about it, she said not to worry. Not worry? Really?

I turned to my mom and said, "Why couldn't she ask me?"

My mother replied that she had asked Francesca the very same question, to which she had replied, "I know my mom and dad love me, but their job is to decide if I am doing right or wrong. You, Nana, just need to love me."

I never did find out what that whispered conversation was about—my mother has since passed, and Francesca can't remember—but I was grateful that my daughter had a confidante she could trust.

It has been thirty-two years since that conversation, but since I became a "Nana," I totally understand. I hope that I can be the confidante to my grandsons that my mother was to my daughter.

A grandparent's job is not to judge, but to simply love. Oh, how I love my job.

—Loretta Schoen—

76

Fudge and Fathers

*What was silent in the father speaks in the son, and
often I found in the son the unveiled secret of the father.*
~Friedrich Nietzsche

I always felt comfortable with my grandfather, something I couldn't say about my own father. My father was high-strung, demanding and critical, especially of me, the oldest son. His father, Gramps, was the polar opposite. Gramps was hardworking, quiet and patient. In all the years I knew him, I never heard him say a negative word about anyone. I escaped to his house when things got too intense at home. There was always peace at my grandfather's house — peace and fudge.

My grandmother died before I was born, and Gramps never remarried. He lived alone in a red brick bungalow about two miles from my parents' house. Out of necessity, he'd become a good cook. Dinner was always red meat, a starch and a vegetable, but for dessert we had the best fudge in the world.

The fudge Gramps made was heavy, rich and dense. It was studded with walnuts and always tasted to me like the best concoction on the planet. The recipe was a secret he refused to share with anyone. After dinner, I was allowed to take two pieces of fudge into the living room to eat while I watched television. I ate it slowly as *Starsky and Hutch* or *The Carol Burnett Show* played. Gramps joined me after he finished cleaning up the kitchen, and we spent many pleasant evenings together in front of our shows.

As I grew older and spent more time with friends instead of my grandfather, those evenings occurred less often. I still visited Gramps, but other things and people took precedence. By the time I was in my senior year of high school, dinners at my grandfather's house had dwindled down to every other month or so. I had homework, college applications and, the most time-consuming, a serious girlfriend.

"You should visit your grandfather more often." Surprisingly, the person talking was my father. It was a Saturday afternoon, and my dad and I were cleaning out the garage, a chore I was eager to finish since I had a date that night.

"I see Gramps." *More often than you do*, I thought but didn't dare say.

"Not like you used to. You used to spend more time at his house than you did here."

"I'm busier than I used to be."

"And your grandfather is older than he used to be. He's not going to be around forever."

"Then maybe you should visit him," I suggested.

My father shrugged. "He doesn't want me to visit him. He wants to see you. You two have always been like two peas in a pod."

I wasn't sure, but I thought I detected a note of envy in my father's voice. That was a first. Was it possible my dad wanted a better relationship with his dad?

"Well, let's go over there now," I suggested.

"What?"

"The garage can wait. Let's go see Gramps now."

My father paused for a few moments. "No, you go."

"I have a date tonight."

"So go now. He doesn't want to see me."

"How do you know that?" I asked.

"We never got along. Five minutes into the visit, and we'd be all over each other. You go. You're the one he enjoys the most."

I tossed down the broom I was holding. "Didn't you just tell me Gramps is getting older? Don't you want to start getting along with him before it's too late for you, too?"

My father shook his head slowly. "It's already too late for us."

"Only if you say it is," I challenged.

There was a long beat of silence before he responded, "It's always been too late."

"Geez, Dad, I never knew you were a quitter. Gramps told me once that you never gave up on anything."

Angrily, my father opened his mouth and then shut it. After a few moments, he said, "Let's go."

Twenty minutes later, we were walking into the kitchen at my grandfather's house. Gramps seemed surprised to see both of us, but didn't comment. Instead, he got out a plate and loaded it with his famous fudge. "There's a game on. Do you have time to watch?"

In the living room, my father sprawled on the sofa, I sat on the floor, and Gramps relaxed in his recliner. We watched a football game in relative silence as we slowly devoured the entire plate of fudge.

"I forgot how good your fudge is, Dad," my father said after the game was over.

I'd forgotten, too. I'd forgotten a lot of things, like how peaceful my grandfather's living room was and how much I liked being there. I glanced at the clock hanging on the wall over the television set. I needed to pick up my girlfriend soon. Inspiration hit me for the second time that day.

"Gramps, would you mind if I brought my girlfriend over later? She's a big fudge fan, too."

"Then I'd better make another batch. You two finished that one." Gramps got to his feet and headed for the kitchen. My father and I exchanged glances.

"You know something? You're smarter than you look," my father said.

I found myself grinning. Coming from my father, that was about as big a compliment as I'd ever gotten. I got to my feet. "I'm going to help Gramps with the fudge. Maybe he'll show me how he makes it."

It *was* a day of miracles, after all.

— Mark Musolf —

77

What Is Wrong with You People?

If laughter cannot solve your problems, it will definitely dissolve your problems, so that you can think clearly what to do about them.
~Dr. Madan Kataria

My family's sense of humor gets us in trouble. Often. I don't really know what's wrong with us. I certainly didn't know what it was at seven years old when the red-faced man at the top of the dealership stairs yelled, "What is wrong with you people?"

I looked to my mother, thinking maybe she could answer. But no, she—like my grandmother and uncle beside her—stood doubled over, hugging her stomach and wheezing with laughter. I looked to my grandfather, but he, in his dapper suit and shiny shoes, was also too far gone to be of any help.

I hesitate to confess why we were laughing because it reflects poorly on us. We were laughing because an eighty-year-old woman had just fallen—rolled, really—down the dealership stairs and lay at the bottom beside a USED CAR SALE banner. With a bloody nose.

But she was laughing, too. She was one of us, a relative visiting from Germany. We were at my grandfather's car dealership, and this spry, spunky old lady thought one of the salesmen was cute. So, she did what any eighty-year-old woman in a dress would do. She tried to swing her leg over the moped on display at the top of the stairs, lost her balance and rolled down the stairs.

In our defense, we did go over and help her up. She was totally fine, save for the bloody nose and bruised ego. When she was upright, she threw her hands in the air and said, "Ta-da!" See, perfectly fine.

I could go on for days detailing all the times we've found humor in awful things — like the time we got kicked out of a funeral. Or when my grandfather stepped on my grandmother's oxygen tube in the hospital. But I think you've gotten the idea.

For years, I tried to figure out why I found humor in truly unfunny things. It was my grandmother who gave me the answer.

"You laugh, or you cry. Which do you like better?"

These ten words were all I needed to turn on the light bulb. Why cry over things when you can laugh instead? Why see the bad in everything when you can find the good? *Yes,* I thought. *I like this. We're not awful; we're… optimistic.*

How did my grandparents develop this positive attitude? The condensed version: They survived World War II in Germany. My grandfather had been in a concentration camp while my grandmother was sent to live with relatives she barely knew. After the war ended, they emigrated from Germany to the United States with a toddler and an infant, lived in poverty, and worked their way up the economic ladder over years of hard work, sacrifice and struggle. And they did it all with dignity, class and, yes, humor. Laugh when you want to cry.

I am a product of those beautiful, elegant, wickedly funny people. They taught me perseverance. Pride. Resiliency. They taught me — by example — that there was nothing I couldn't bounce back from, and no one could hold me down. They taught me to laugh in the face of fear and adversity. Literally, too. Growing up under the shade of their tree meant loud arguments, constant eating — five times a day — and laughter. So much laughter — at each other usually. I didn't always appreciate that — not when it was directed at me — but if there's anything I've learned, it's that you've got to be able to laugh at yourself and shake it off.

Now that they're gone and just the memories remain, I find myself laughing through the tears. In my mind, I see my grandfather walking into the slider door, my grandmother calling him *dummkopf*, and us laughing, laughing, and laughing. I'm laughing now as I type.

So much has changed since they've passed, but the lessons, just like their faces and the sound of their laughter, are embedded in my DNA. I've passed the gene on to my daughters. Together, we laugh at awful things while people around us ask, "What is wrong with you people?" And we laugh some more.

— Elsa Kurt —

78

Little Lights

The best way to teach children restraint and generosity
is to be a model of those qualities yourself.
~Lawrence Balter

I sat in the waiting room at the DMV with my grandfather as we waited to be called to the counter. We were here to officially get the title for the boat we had just finished building together. We waited patiently, and he told me stories about his time in the Korean War, when he was stationed in the Philippines. I listened intently, grateful for all the time I was lucky enough to spend with him, even if it was at the DMV.

We got called up and met with a nice young man who helped us through the process. He was probably somewhere around my age, in his late twenties or early thirties. He was patient and kind, and made the entire process of being at the dreaded DMV not so terribly painful. As we were getting ready to leave, my grandfather had one last gesture.

"You're a nice young man and have been incredibly helpful. I have something for you," my grandfather told him, as he pulled a mini LED flashlight out of the bag he was carrying his paperwork in. He handed it to the young man, who was very thankful and appreciative. I couldn't help but smile and wonder what was going on in the mind of that young man as my grandfather gave him a flashlight. The smile on his face was genuine, and one of surprise. That was my grandfather's doing. He always surprised those he met with how amazing humanity could be.

My grandfather did this for any individual he met who was kind and helpful. He would go to Harbor Freight Tools weekly, if not daily, with his coupons, and stock up on these mini LED flashlights. Over the years, I watched him give them to waitresses, cashiers at the craft store, and even strangers we would meet while out on walks.

My grandfather passed away a few months after that trip to the DMV, but I was reminded of his kindness and generosity just a few weeks after his passing when I was out shopping at the craft store. I was purchasing some accessories for some wine-bottle lamps we made together, and the cashier looked at me with vague curiosity and recognition.

"Your grandfather used to hand out mini flashlights, didn't he?" the young gal at the check-out register inquired.

"Yeah, that was him. He sure did," I chuckled and reciprocated with a warm smile.

"How is he doing? He was always so sweet and kind when he came in here."

"He actually passed away a few weeks back," I said. My gut wrenched as I gave this response, still not able to fully digest the fact that he was gone. He was never going to tell me another story or help me build another project in his workshop.

"You know, this flashlight he gave me really helped me out that day," the young gal said. She looked at me earnestly as she pulled one of my grandfather's mini flashlights out of her work apron.

"I wasn't doing so great the day he came in," she continued. "I had just been yelled at by the previous customers for our credit-card system being down, and we were only able to accept cash or checks at the time. But your grandfather came in and ended up in my lane for check-out. He witnessed one of these interactions, and he changed my day. He was so kind and even told me a joke that made me smile. I had helped him many times before, and he expressed his gratitude by giving me this flashlight." She looked at the flashlight nostalgically as she told me her story. "That was the last time I saw him, but that simple gesture is something I will never forget." She looked up and smiled at me. "Your grandfather was a great man. I am so sorry for your loss. You were very lucky to have a grandfather like him."

I was beginning to tear up at this point, and I thanked the young girl and gave her a hug before leaving. This got me to thinking about how many flashlights my grandfather had given out over the years, and how many lives he had impacted through this small gesture. Some may roll their eyes or think he was a silly old guy, but to many it meant so much more than just a little trinket given to them by a stranger. It's something I try to remember when I am forced to interact with difficult patients at work or rude people when I am out and about. The smallest gesture of kindness can be just the light that person needs to be guided to happiness. Those little moments of light — be they little flashlights or something else that gives a spark of happiness or hope in life — keep our souls nourished.

— Gwen Cooper —

79

The Duchess of Belmont Shore

Children are great imitators, so give them
something great to imitate.
~Author Unknown

Every moment with the Duchess of Belmont Shore was special, funny, and full of unconventional wisdom. Whenever school was out, my brother and I were shipped off to her beach cottage, where every day was an adventure.

The Duchess, conventionally known as Grandma, wore a heavy steel brace on her leg, which was eight inches shorter than the other. She had walked on crutches since childhood due to polio. To many, this would have been an excuse to sit on the sidelines, but for the Duchess it was an opportunity to lead by love and example.

My grandmother showed us that nothing can keep us from achieving just about anything. She was an accomplished singer who was billed as "Dorothy Green, Girl Baritone" on live radio, wrote a newspaper column, and lived life to the fullest.

Grandma never let her crutches keep her from walking out on the jetty — a bridge made of a pile of rocks going out into the ocean — where she took us fishing. We spent the afternoon catching dinner and enjoying our "nosh bags," as she called the sack lunches she prepared.

She introduced us to what she called her "laughing place," teaching us to use what we have, keep a sense of humor and enjoy being together. Sometimes, we laughed so hard she would say, "I am so happy I could wet my pants."

She also taught us to be resourceful. Can you imagine a lady on crutches hopping a fence to gain access to a neighbor's fruit tree? Today, we might call it trespassing. She called it gleaning, which is when we pick up what has been left behind.

Grandma had a cute little female Fox Terrier whom she lovingly called Terry Poodlums. Back in those days, they only had flea powder, which hardly killed the fleas, so she would put the dog on her lap belly-up and pinch the fleas with tweezers. Terry just loved the attention, and she showed her loyalty by walking unleashed beside Grandma's crutch on many long walks.

Grandma also taught us that good transportation meant using our two feet. She walked 10,000-plus daily steps long before it became popular. From early childhood, we walked all over Long Beach to enjoy the sights and get where we needed to go. Without even realizing it, we learned the value of good exercise.

On occasion, we had a girls' day out when she took me on public transportation to go downtown. I felt so independent as I put my bus token in the slot. She made me feel special when she took me to the second floor of Buffums for lunch and then to See's Candies for a tasty treat. She had a way of making my brother and me each feel like her favorite grandchild. She taught us the importance of spending time and investing in those we love, stressing the importance of family.

Grandma made sure we knew how to be kind, considerate, and polite, teaching us how to socialize with important people while treating all with respect. Despite her silly ideas and sayings, she made sure we spoke English correctly, noting how to use the right verb tense or knowing the proper word for the situation. She reminded us to be grateful and write thank-you notes. We learned when we could just be kids and when we were to behave like adults.

We did a lot of pretending in Grandma's world, which developed our creativity and imagination. We shared dreams of taking a trip in an Airstream trailer. Although we enjoyed many adventures all over the country, they were all from the comfort of her living-room couch.

In my adulthood, someone referred to my grandmother as being handicapped, but it had never occurred to me that she was. She taught me that there are no obstacles, and life is what we make of it. I learned from the Duchess that a handicap is not in your body, but in your mind. Although Grandma has been gone many years, I like to imagine her running through a meadow of flowers on two strong legs, continuing to encourage others along the way.

—Judy Mason—

Don't Rush Off

Tell me a fact, and I'll learn. Tell me a truth,
and I'll believe. But tell me a story,
and it will live in my heart forever.
~Indian Proverb

She was a woman around my own age, and she sounded a little exasperated. "Papaw, just get the small one." She was with a white-haired man and a little girl whom I assume was her daughter. She was no doubt wondering why this nosey, caffeine-deprived stranger was staring at her with tears in her eyes in the middle of a grocery store.

I wanted to tell her she didn't know how lucky she was. I wanted to tell her about my own Pap and Mamaw, and how I hadn't been anyone's granddaughter for six months now. I wanted to tell her that this month would mark the one-year anniversary of my grandmother's passing and how it didn't seem real. I longed to explain that I had a date that evening, and while everyone I knew was excited and supportive, the two people I wanted to tell the most were gone.

But, mostly, I just wanted to say, "Don't rush off."

This was Pap's famous line. I could've been at the house for twenty minutes or several hours, but when I'd go to kiss his cheek and grab his hand, he'd always tell me, "Don't rush off."

He told me that from his recliner, hospital bed, at church, and in the nursing home. He wasn't big on saying, "I love you," but I knew his three words meant the same thing.

Life seems like a rush these days between work, school and extra-curricular activities, but I hope I'm able to heed Pap's advice to linger in the moment before it's gone. I don't want to be so future-oriented that I fail to enjoy the now. I don't want to always be looking for the next best thing because I have all of the best things now. And they are pleading with me to notice and enjoy them before they slip away.

What I wouldn't give for Pap to tell me one last time, "Don't rush off." I'd like to think I'd cancel all my plans, put the keys back in my purse, turn off my cell phone, and sit back down and enjoy our time together.

And to the lady at the grocery store: hug and kiss and laugh and cry and love today. And don't rush off.

—Lindsey Light—

81

My Favorite Age

*You can clutch the past so tightly to your chest that it
leaves your arms too full to embrace the present.*
~Jan Glidewell

She held my baby — just two hours old —
A precious sight that I got to behold.
She ooohed and aaahed and gently stroked his head.
"This is my favorite age," she said.

Her name was Nann — she was a wonderful friend —
An adopted grandma whose love knew no end.
She taught us so much and adored our sweet boy.
Just to be in her presence brought us such joy.

Nann loved playing the role of Grandma-next-door —
As the time would pass, she always wanted more!
And when baby smiles started coming her way,
"This is my favorite age," she always would say.

My boy got bigger, as all babies do;
Crawling and playing, and babbling, too!
Exploring his world and charming us all —
"This is my favorite age!" Nann said, I recall.

Came the toddler time, and walking around—
So many adventures were now to be found!
A toybox appeared at Nann's house just then—
"This is my favorite age," she uttered again.

One day, Nann's son stopped in for a while,
And time with "her boy" just made her smile!
At forty-something years old, she hugged him tight—
"This is my favorite age," she proclaimed outright.

"Miss Nann," I said (for I was very confused),
"Your 'favorite age' seems to be much overused!
Is it a baby? Toddler? Or a son that is grown?
You have more favorite ages than I've ever known!"

"Well, honey…" she said, in her sweet Southern drawl—
"My favorite age just consists of them all!
Isn't that how it should be, as the kids grow?
Each age brings new blessings that you get to know."

I pondered this thought; her advice was so wise…
What an awesome truth that I had not realized!
Every age is special, and fleeting as well;
And then you are left with just memories to tell.

So every time a new phase has begun,
I view this season as my favorite one!
A fresh new perspective is all that it takes,
But—what a difference this little change makes…

Grandma Nann was truly one of a kind;
A more genuine soul would be hard to find.
I am a better mom because of one simple phrase—
And I cling to her words on the craziest days.

Now as my boys grow older, through every stage...
I say to myself, "This is my most favorite age."

—Jennifer "JennyMac" McCarthy—

Modern Grandparenting

82

Wild Card

Talent wins games, but teamwork
and intelligence win championships.
~Michael Jordan

I hurled the pass into the end zone. Boom! Caught! Now I know how Tom Brady feels. Of course, I don't actually play any sport involving balls. But I am a grandma, always vying for number-one ranking among the grandparents. Last week, I nailed a big win against our chief rival. If you share your grandchildren with more than one set of grandparents, you get it. It's a competition.

My husband and I joined the league in 2010. We had the home-field advantage. Our first granddaughter was born in our town hospital and lived a mere three miles from our house. All the firsts — smile, rollover, sit-up, and steps — occurred in our stadium. The local fans supported our team — both sets of great-grandparents, cousins, great aunts and uncles. We understood the rules of possession. When the opposing grandparents visited from Ontario, we kept our distance. After their long weekend, we would resume our status as local resident grandparents.

In 2011, the advantage shifted, like the momentum after a hefty penalty. The parents moved our one-year-old granddaughter to Ontario. Suddenly, we became the underdog. More than simply moving the franchise from one city to another, it involved an international border. I felt the stakes magnify to playoff proportions. This relocation involved honoring a different national anthem, abandoning the Stars and Stripes for a maple leaf, and supplanting football with hockey. Her speech was just developing. The child would surely speak Canadian English, maybe even French, rather than Pittsburgh vernacular. In July 2012, the opposition took over first place. The second granddaughter would be born in their country. It felt as if they sacked our quarterback.

We developed a defensive game plan. For weeks at a time in summers, we rented cottages near the Canadian venue, attempting to level the playing field. Over winter holidays, we traversed white-outs and ice storms to remain competitive. We stayed in rented houses, cottages and hotels over the next five years, investing in our franchise. We brought toys, gifts, our live Labrador mascot and, on several occasions, a set of great-grandparents, all in our effort to regain the number-one slot.

However, in the annual Christmas tournament, we always found ourselves coming from behind. With two small children, the parents were reluctant to travel treacherous roads to Pennsylvania for the holiday. The rival grandparents lived just three hours west, and they had the advantage of a two-holiday Canadian option — Christmas as well as Boxing Day. No matter how hard our son worked to make us feel viable, we recognized our status as second string.

The rivals pulled out their best play last summer when they took the children on a ten-day family trip to Europe. During any other year, that would have put us on the disabled list. However, we had a momentous game plan ready for this year. We moved permanently from northwestern Pennsylvania to northern New York, just twenty-five miles from the granddaughters. Thanks to our gutsy decision, like going for the two-point conversion, we tied the game.

Our new house features a bedroom for the children, and an art studio stocked with paper, markers, paints, modeling clay, and tubs of glitter. Any number of oak trees invites the construction of fairy houses, and we have checked out all the play structures within ten miles. Yet, all of that does not ease the drive, the bridge toll, or the long wait at the border when the parents bring the children to our place.

Coming into the 2016 holidays, we were in a dead heat.

The opponents took the offensive and hosted the grandchildren and their parents for Canadian Thanksgiving, which happens in October.

Of course, we Americans had yet to celebrate that holiday, so we took a bye that weekend. Little or no enthusiasm met us from team Canada for a second Thanksgiving. We lost that challenge and spent Thanksgiving at a hotel buffet.

I rebounded with a quarterback sneak. I had in my possession the American Girl catalog — a book of eighteen-inch dolls designed with exquisite care and detail. Each year, a Girl of the Year was marketed, complete with a personality profile and all the authentic trappings of a well-to-do young lady. I took the catalog with me to share with the granddaughters on my next visit. They loved Lea, that year's doll, and naturally I promised to order one for each of them for Christmas.

Then my doubts surfaced. When would we actually see the little girls? Would it be anticlimactic after the twenty-fifth? Would the dolls seem special amidst all of Santa's surprises? On impulse, I declared that the dolls would be here December first, and that would become American Girl Doll Day. I went online to place a rush delivery. The rivals could take Thanksgiving, and perhaps Christmas, but I would claim December first as my special holiday and win in overtime.

On December first, I drove my car to the border with the dolls gift-wrapped in the back seat. I endured a scolding for exceeding the sixty-dollar limit on importing gifts. Cheerfully, I promised to pay duty next time. At my son's house, I arranged the gift boxes on the coffee table and then drove to the bus stop to meet the granddaughters. Bursting with excitement, they asked if today was the day. Earlier, the older granddaughter had taken a corner of her bedroom and fitted it for the doll with a bed, play area, and work station, even wallpaper. I hoped the younger would love Lea just as much as she adored her baby dolls.

As we entered the house, they dropped their coats and book bags, and dashed for the boxes. The joy as they met their dolls and unpacked the realistic accessories lived up to my wildest hopes. The six-year-old raved about the small passport, complete with photo, so she could present it to the border guard on her next visit to our house. The younger gleefully examined the diminutive camera, compass, and duffle bag. They talked to Lea and tried on her extra outfits.

Of course, each doll was seated at the table for dinner and joined in our play the rest of the evening. We all had pictures taken. The older child used her photo with the doll as wallpaper on her iPad. The younger used my phone to take a portrait of her doll seated in the revered Minnie Mouse chair.

As I donned my coat for the return home, I savored the goodbye hugs and kisses — not just from my granddaughters, but also from the two dolls. "Now you have four granddaughters, Dede," Rayna announced. So this year, no matter what happens between now and January first, I've won the Super Bowl. Of course, a new year means a new championship. Game on.

— Cinda Findlan —

83

Long-Distance Love

*Distance means so little when
someone means so much.*
~Author Unknown

I grew up with my grandma right in our house. She was my best friend until she passed away when I was thirteen. Now, even though my own grandchildren live far away, I want to be just as special to them as my grandmother was to me.

All four of my granddaughters were born in South Africa, so I made ten trips there over seven years just to make sure I built a strong and lasting bond with them. It was expensive, exhausting, and exciting — but worth every minute I spent in cramped airplanes and crowded airports. Thankfully, the family moved to the States a year ago, and although they don't live near me, they are just a few hours away by plane. I make every effort to get together with them regularly.

Recently, I returned from taking care of all four children — ages one, four, six, and seven — for nearly a week while their parents were away. I can't remember ever being so tired. Still, my time with them was full of love and laughter. We made daily outings to special places around their city, and I homeschooled the two oldest in the afternoons while the little ones slept.

We made so many sweet memories that week — like helping the seven-year-old master double-digit subtraction; seeing the six-year-old swim like a dolphin; and watching the four-year-old fearlessly climb to the top of the jungle gym. In turn, the girls taught me how to use Alexa and showed me how to travel on the light rail. And the seventeen-month-old? Her smiles and hugs melted my heart.

Even when I'm not there, I still see our beautiful grandchildren, hear their sweet voices, and watch them grow—through Skype or FaceTime. We learn about their day-to-day activities on Facebook or Instagram, and we get photos through e-mail or Dropbox and see videos over WhatsApp. We can even order them gifts via the Internet, and don't have to worry about how they'll get there.

As a family, we make connecting a priority even though we're all so very busy. We've established weekly Skype traditions that we count on and love. Grandpa often has a milk-and-sweetie party with the girls since he's known to love sweets. And since I am a former teacher, I love to read to them.

The best tradition of all, so far, is our blowing-kisses tradition. We started saying goodbye with the girls blowing a few "girly kisses" my way and me blowing some "Grandma kisses" back. But now simple goodbye kisses have become "hurricane kisses" that blow me off my chair and "baseball kisses" that Grandpa catches in his invisible baseball mitt. What will be next? Maybe it's time to think of some new kind of kisses to blow through cyberspace and right into their hearts.

It still hurts to be so far away from them. I have to admit that I search the Internet for special deals to fly out and see them.

But I'm thankful that we have all this wonderful technology at our fingertips. We have so many ways to connect via our smart phones and the Internet. Yesterday, I watched the toddler sing "Itsy Bitsy Spider" to me on a FaceTime chat. Today, I saw a video of the six-year-old riding a pony. I'm sure my granddaughters are building their own memories of good times with their grandparents, too, and some day they may not even remember which of those good times happened in person and which happened over the Internet.

—Susan G. Mathis—

84

Making a Connection

*Every child comes with the message that God
is not yet discouraged of man.*
~Rabindranath Tagore

Connor was twenty-two months old when he was diagnosed. The doctor told his parents, "Your son is not deaf. His hearing is fine. He has severe, nonverbal autism."

Having worked with special-education students, I had suspected that he was on the autism spectrum.

I am Connor's grandmother, "Bumpy." I wanted to be called Grumpy (because I am so *not* that, unless I haven't had my coffee yet), but our first grandchild couldn't quite manage it. So I became Bumpy.

Even though Connor was very young, I could see a spark in him. His intelligence was in there; we just had to figure out how to get it to come out. I made it my job to make sure Connor had the best chance at being as successful in life as he could be.

We got him into the local Easter Seals program right away. They started teaching him sign language. The first word he learned was "more." Anytime he would fuss for more to eat or drink, we would take his hands, make the sign and say, "More." Then we'd give it to him.

The first time I had an insight into how his brain worked was when he wanted more of something and I told him to show me "more." He took *my* hands, squished the fingers into the proper position, and tapped them together. *Oh, my goodness. He thought the "more" sign was made by doing it to the other person! Why? Because that was what we were doing to him. He's brilliant!* Apparently, he was also very literal, but that was an eye-opening insight.

When he turned three, he aged out of the Easter Seals program and lost three months of learning as his parents went through the process of getting him into public early education. In this program, they wanted to teach him to communicate using picture exchange, so he had a huge binder of pictures that were attached to the pages with Velcro. When he wanted something, he was supposed to pull a picture card from the binder and present it to another person. That didn't work so well. The binder was cumbersome, so his parents didn't take it anywhere. It just wasn't a good fit for their family.

During this time, my husband, Gramps, had a job change, and we had to move. We had moved many times, but never without our children. Our younger son was in the Army, deployed to Afghanistan. Connor and his sister needed to stay where they were, as their father and mother shared custody. Moving out of state was one of the hardest things I've ever had to do. Thankfully, we are only four hours away from our grandchildren, and I make it a point to get up there once a month. Sometimes, weather or illness causes us to miss a month, but I get back up there as soon as I can. My biggest fear was that Connor would forget who I was.

Connor spent two years in the public-school program. I didn't believe he was getting all the help he needed, so I started researching Applied Behavior Analysis (ABA) therapy for him. Tuition at an ABA therapy school was about the cost of a new car. Even with insurance, the co-pay was impossible for a young family to cover. I've heard stories of families mortgaging their homes and living in poverty to afford to send their child to an ABA program. Then our son lost his job, which turned out to be a blessing in disguise. Connor then qualified for Medicaid and was able to receive ABA therapy.

At his new school, they concentrated on having him verbalize. He loves Disney/Pixar movies, so the first word they taught him was "movie." They combined it with the sign, and he learned to make the "M" sound. It was a start.

At five, he was still in diapers. I told them they had to get him potty-trained. Cute as he is, no one wants to be changing adult diapers. It took ten days of very strict training, but he did it. Now, when he has to go to the bathroom, he goes. If someone wants him to go to the bathroom before going out or to bed, they make the "toilet" sign and tell him to "go potty." He does. Big milestone!

Connor also started mimicking at this time. If we told him to say something, he gave it his best shot. It may not have been perfect, but it was close enough to understand. I cried the first time his daddy told him to "Say 'Bumpy,'" and Connor said, "Bumpa."

On one visit, after Connor had been learning about making eye contact, he turned my face to his and looked into my eyes. When I turned my head, he turned my face back to his again and looked into my eyes. We have a picture of Connor with his hand on my cheek, gazing into my eyes. It is one of my favorite moments and one of my favorite pictures.

Connor recently turned nine years old. He continues to make slow verbal progress. Last month, his daddy held up random *Scrabble* tiles, and Connor named the letters. I was so proud!

Years ago, I made Connor a photo book that I call Connor's Face Book. It has pictures of family members' faces and a little statement about how each person loves him. On our last visit, I took it out and started going through it with him. I named each person. When my picture came up, I named myself and held the picture of me next to my face. I did the same thing for the picture of Gramps, trying to help Connor make the connection that we are the people in the book.

That night, after we had returned home, our son texted me a picture of Connor sleeping… with his face book open to my picture. Yup, I melted. Connor was missing me. He knows who I am and that Bumpy and Gramps love him.

We have five grandchildren now, and we love each of them for the unique person God created them to be. I have to admit, though, those "connecting moments" with Connor are the best!

— Pam Horton —

The Perfect Recipe for Grandparenting

*I think togetherness is a very important
ingredient to family life.*
~Barbara Bush

I was married for ten years before I had kids. "Your dog might be the only grandchild I'll ever have," my mother would lament. She even carried a picture of my Miniature Schnauzer in her purse to show to friends.

When I gave birth to the first of my two boys, my parents showed up at the hospital with a cake and a bouquet of balloons, wearing hats proclaiming, "I'm the grandma" and "I'm the grandpa."

They took to their new roles with gusto, just as they had to parenting my brother and me when they adopted us as babies. My parents lived close by and never missed a birthday party or sporting match. When we visited them, my mother would ply the boys with slices of homemade apple pie or cinnamon cookies. My father loved whipping up chocolate-chip pancakes made to order.

Once or twice a year, my mother would invite us over to make donuts, a tradition my grandmother had started. My mom would carefully prepare her kitchen ahead of time, with a rolling station, frying station, and sugaring station. My kids always gravitated to the frying station, where they would plop the cut-out dough into sizzling oil. Eventually, they would tire of the process, and we would be relieved that no one had gotten burned. Several hours later, my mom and I would finish baking and collapse on the couch.

Whether it was playing board games or picking blackberries to make jam, the kids loved their time with their grandparents. Kids don't stay little forever, though. As they grew, my mom began to worry. "I'm afraid they might not want to visit me anymore," she would tell me over and over.

She was right. "I just want to hang out with my friends" became a common refrain. Eventually, they no longer wanted to make the half-hour trek to see their grandparents.

At the same time, my parents were slowing down a bit. One day, my dad took the kids to the local basketball court. He fell and cut his head badly. We realized Dad had lost his balance and decided that going to basketball with Grandpa was off the table from that day forward.

My boys' preteen years were the toughest for my parents. On a trip abroad to Spain, my son Miguel, who had become a foodie, argued nonstop with my father over what restaurant we'd go to on my birthday. We walked from restaurant to restaurant perusing menus that featured everything from paella to cheese and ham croquettes, but neither of them could agree. By the time we picked one, I was in tears.

That wasn't the only aggravating incident. One summer day, my mom took my boys and their two cousins to the beach. Later, in the car driving home, the kids delivered a litany of complaints. My niece was upset that her brother had thrown sand in her face. He claimed it was an accident. My sons argued about whose turn it was to play on the Game Boy. Everyone clamored for a snack, but there was no food left in the basket their grandmother had lovingly packed that morning. After the incessant whining, my mom was so fed up that she pulled over about a mile away from the house at the bottom of a steep hill.

"I'm tired of your complaints. You'll have to walk the rest of the way," she announced.

Getting out and having to walk up the hill, under her watchful eye, worked to subdue the kids for the rest of the day.

"I can't handle this," my mother told me that evening. "This isn't what I signed up for as a grandma." She just wished to be "Fun Grandma" at this stage of her life, so I figured I could give it to her.

From that moment forward, I kept my parents' time with the boys limited to fun family traditions — like baking together and making jam. The boys started to value their carefree time with their grandparents.

Before my older son left for college last fall, we joined my parents for our annual donut-making day.

"Now don't make them too thick," my mom reminded us as my son rolled out the dough. "They won't cook well. And don't touch the dough too much, or they'll be tough."

Eventually, she took a seat at the kitchen table and let the boys take over. What a difference a few years had made in our family tradition. This time, the boys got so caught up in the creativity of experimenting with new shapes and cooking times that they stuck through until the end. Mid-baking, they took a break and posted their donut designs on Instagram.

"Come on, Grammy," my son said, "pose with us." She grinned as my son held up his iPhone.

Later, as we recovered from our sugar high on the couch, my parents engaged my boys on a topic they love — technology. Pretty soon, my boys were teaching my parents how to send a voice-activated text.

"This will save me so much time," my mom gasped.

Now, my parents stay in touch with my older son while he's at college as much as I do — maybe even more — with the help of FaceTime and texting. Sometimes, they exchange food photos and recipes.

They are so close that my mom learned before I did that my son had broken up with his girlfriend.

"If you ever want to reach him, call on a Friday," my mom texted me recently. "He doesn't have class, and he has the whole weekend ahead."

When my son came home from college recently, my dad brought steaks to grill.

Afterward, the boys passed around a new dessert they have been perfecting — truffles made with Oreo cookies.

"Where did you find this recipe? It's so creative," my dad said.

"We found it on Reddit," my son said with a laugh. "I'll have to show you what that is later. They aren't quite as good as Grammy's donuts, but we'll keep trying."

Then we took turns trying out my younger son's new virtual-reality system.

"Oh, this is the most incredible thing I've ever seen," my mom said as she adjusted her 3D goggles and floated rapidly down a virtual river. She really felt like she was on that river.

My son held her hand so she wouldn't fall down.

— Allison A. de Laveaga —

86

Building Bonds

Everything good, everything magical happens between
the months of June and August.
~Jenny Han, The Summer I Turned Pretty

This will no doubt be my last summer at the beach cottage I've been renting for the last twelve years. Each summer, I see less of my grandsons as the world widens for the two kids who once played so steadfastly in the sand with their buckets and shovels.

Despite the distance between New York and Boston that separated us most of the year, I dreamed of building a lasting relationship with the boys. By the time they were four and six, I felt time slipping away and sent my daughter on a mission to find a summer place I could rent nearby. When she discovered this small cottage one house back from the ocean and thirty minutes from where she lived, it felt like a perfect fit. None of us imagined the run we would have here — twelve years of early-evening dips in the ocean after work, kids and grownups playing on the beach, and backyard cookouts followed by games around the kitchen table.

I loved it when the boys spent the night and I was their sole caregiver. After long days at the beach and trips to Baskin-Robbins, we'd barbecue hot dogs or hamburgers on the grill. Evening activities varied from settling down with a book, to watching television, to releasing pent-up energy. During our time together, four Harry Potter volumes were released, read and reread. Together, we watched three summer Olympics, annual Shark Weeks and countless Red Sox games. Jumping contests were conducted across the upper level of two sets of bunk beds. Airborne objects of varying sizes and shapes whizzed back and forth when we least expected them.

"Grandma, come quick!" On a clear night with a full moon, the younger boy called from the back yard where he was tinkering with an old telescope. Stepping aside so I could take a look, he whispered, "This is a life-changing moment, Grandma." At eight years, it seemed a big order, filled with mystery and promise.

Today, at sixteen and eighteen, the boys put me to shame discussing politics or world events. Both are talented musicians, polite and thoughtful. Don't let anyone tell you that the modern youth are a bad lot; I know better.

During my first years renting the cottage, I considered one of its charms the absence of a phone. To use the payphone or scavenge enough bars for a cell-phone call required a two-mile drive to the CVS parking lot. But over the years, despite technological deficits, I grew dependent on its devices. This year, arriving at the cottage with a malfunctioning laptop as well as a new cell phone, I was desperate for help. And who better than two millennials to rescue me?

I set up a date and offered to pick up the boys. "Have you forgotten I have a driver's license now, Grandma?" the eighteen-year-old replied. As little tots, arriving at the cottage, they'd burst right in. This day they knocked and, after I opened the door, they moved like first responders toward my dormant devices. "This computer is ancient, Grandma. But if all you need is e-mail and word processing, we'll get you back in business." The instructions for my new cell phone were rejected out of hand. "Just ignore the manual, Grandma. Trust us, trial and error works much better." In an hour, my laptop was up and running, and I'd mastered basic skills for my cell phone, including a good introduction to texting. I knew this was the way to keep in touch with today's youth, and I vowed to use it.

Afraid I might not see them after this house call, I invited the boys to hang around, have some lunch, and go down to the beach for a swim. But they were already pummeling a ball back and forth, itching to get on with their day. I gave them each a hug and some money. "I love you, guys."

"We love you, too, Grandma. Maybe we'll come down again for a cookout and a game of *Rummikub*."

"That would be wonderful. But you can't leave without helping yourselves to a fudge bar—for old time's sake." They were sucking on their popsicles when they left, a tender flashback to earlier years.

It was a life-changing moment. For the first time, I knew our bonds would be permanent, even without the cottage.

—Ann Barnett—

87

Making Magic with Sidney

Never, ever doubt in magic. The purest, honest
thoughts come from children. Ask any child if they
believe in magic, and they will tell you the truth.
~Scott Dixon

Whenever anyone told me how amazing it was to be a grand-parent, I'd offer an oh-so-patient smile and say, "I'm sure it is...." Good heavens, they all said the same things: "You're gonna love being a grandma...," or "It's the best thing you'll ever do...," or "If I'd known how great it was to be a grandparent, I'd have done that first!" Blah-blah-blah.

Then Sidney Anne was born. She was the sweetest, softest, most loveable bundle of joy I'd ever beheld. When the nurse placed her in my arms, my heart did more than melt. It filled in the part I didn't even know was empty.

The first time I left Sidney to drive the six hours home, I cried for fifty miles. Leaving her was so painful; it was like I'd snagged my heart on a nail as I left, leaving a jagged hole. My comfort came from knowing I'd soon return.

Since I didn't live close, I worried my little sweetheart might forget me between visits. By the time she was three, I'd invented a way to make sure she'd remember.

Enter the Magic Suitcase.

My plan? To tuck a gift in a zipped pocket located on the front of my suitcase. Other items were hidden under my packed clothes, to be retrieved as needed. I'd bring one item for each day of my visit and pretend it materialized by magic.

At home, I shopped for small toys or books to delight Sidney, acquiring a stash sufficient for my next stay. Then, when I arrived, I introduced the Magic Suitcase with a whopper of a tale. "That pesky suitcase of mine was up to something strange on the trip," I said. "It rumbled around on the back seat, shook like crazy, and made the silliest squeaks. I can't figure out why. Should we check inside and see?"

Eyes wide, Sidney nodded, took my hand, and walked with me as I dragged the suitcase into the guest room. We inspected it together, examining the sides and back. Everything looked okay. Then, I caught my breath, turning to her. Had she just seen that jerky movement in the front pocket? What if something was hiding in there? Shouldn't we take a look?

Sidney gave a brave unzip and gazed up at me as if to ask permission to proceed. At my go-ahead gesture, she reached into the compartment and carefully drew out the first surprise — a Littlest Pet Shop Pal. Her mouth formed a happy O.

"Tell Gramsey thank you," my daughter said, standing behind us.

I turned and waved away her request. "It wasn't me. It was magic!"

My daughter rolled her eyes. And off we went on a new adventure that continued over the next year-and-a-half. Arriving at their house, I'd roll in the mysterious Magic Suitcase and tell my tale of the backseat disturbances. Sidney couldn't wait to unzip the pocket and see what was inside. Together, we'd play with the new toy or read the book and make our own magical memories. Then we'd repeat the search the next day. And the next. That little suitcase kept us busy.

When my daughter became pregnant again, I envisioned the need to double my shopping output. Now I'd need surprises for two. Finding fresh treasures for Sidney had gotten trickier and trickier. How could I possibly keep up the suitcase-toy production when I had twice the magic to make?

In my absence, Sidney began to wonder when Gramsey was coming again with the Magic Suitcase. My daughter, worried that Sidney had become greedy, determined it was time to shut down our story. "The

Magic Suitcase is broken," she announced. The end. Though relieved to let it go, I worried Sidney would be disappointed.

But she accepted her mama's verdict without fuss. Perhaps she'd raked in enough tiny toys to last a while. Or her attentions were diverted by the excitement of welcoming a baby brother into the family.

On my next visit, Sidney didn't mention the suitcase and ran to greet me with her usual big hug. "Hi, Gramsey! Let's play."

Wow. She remembered me! Even without the magic.

Maybe I was memorable enough on my own.

— Cathy Elliott —

21st Century Grandparents

Everyone needs to have access both to grandparents
and grandchildren in order to be a full human being.
~Margaret Mead

Our grandson has just turned three, and he's the sweetest, funniest child. He likes to show us his new toys or shoes. He tells us what he did at daycare. He goes into the garden to show us the birds or the fish, and we watch him get better and better at riding his bike. We talk to him at bath time and bedtime. He gives us kisses and hugs, shows us pictures he's drawn, and offers us pieces of his candy.

It's very important that we have this interaction and bonding with him, and the only thing that hinders us at all is that all this quality time has to take place via Skype and WhatsApp, because we live in Europe and our grandson lives in Australia.

When my husband and I learned we were going to be grandparents, we were excited but concerned. While we waited eagerly for the baby's safe arrival, we wondered how we would be able to bond with a grandchild whom we might see only once a year, or perhaps even less. How would we make an emotional connection when our contact would have to be largely via the Internet?

The months went by. At home, we made our own preparations for the baby. We searched for cute clothes and gifts and sent them out to Australia so that we felt involved in the preparations. Finally, our beautiful grandson arrived safe and sound. Thanks to the power of modern technology, we were immediately included. Just minutes after he was born, we received photos of him and his mum in the delivery room. The next day, we spoke to them on Skype for the first time, and saw his little wrinkly face and sleeping smiles.

We watched him grow from new baby to chubby cheeks and fists, to the crawling stage and then a toddler. In all that time, his mum sent photos to update us on his progress, and we tried to speak to him at least once a week. We spoke to him as if he were there in the room, even though he had to watch us on a screen. Perhaps he thinks we live in outer space! We told him we loved him and said "Well done" every time he showed us something he could do. We blew kisses to him and received them in return. He didn't always understand, of course. One time, he tried to give us a crayon so we could colour his picture with him. Another time, he wanted me to try on his hat.

Three Christmases came and went, along with his first and second birthdays, before we finally put enough money by to visit our grandson and the rest of the family in Australia. We were going to spend two whole weeks of "real time" with him, and we couldn't wait. As we flew halfway around the world, I wondered how he would react to meeting us in his own real world instead of on a screen.

The plane touched down in Perth, and we waited in the Immigration queue. I had butterflies in my stomach! We passed through Immigration, collected our bags and headed for the door marked "ARRIVALS." When we reached the doors and they slid open, our Australian family was waiting for us. We waved, they waved back, and my grandson let go of his mum's hand and ran toward us. I bent down to meet him, and he jumped up into my arms. He threw his little arms round my neck, and we showered each other with kisses.

It was a magical moment. My grandson ran toward me with such love and enthusiasm that it proved all the long-distance efforts had been worth it. All the times we'd spoken on the screen had helped us to bond with him. Despite all my concerns, we made a loving connection with him, all thanks to 21st century technology!

— Brenda Evans —

A Grandma by Any Other Name

*Nicknames stick to people, and the most ridiculous
are the most adhesive.*
~Thomas Chandler Haliburton

I knew when our first grandchild was born that she wouldn't be calling me "Grandma." Bailey is my stepson's daughter, so there were two biological grandmothers ahead of me when it came to choosing a grandmother name.

"What would you like to be called?" my husband, newly dubbed "Grandpa," asked.

"How about 'Joanypony'?"

"Why not? It's a little unconventional," he said with a fond smile, "but then, so are you."

Joanypony was my childhood nickname, and close friends still called me that. It was chosen, I was told, because I was frolicsome and playful, like a pony. A free spirit, they said.

The fact that my husband and I were the third set of grandparents invited to visit newborn Bailey did not diminish my joy when I first held my granddaughter. She was even more beautiful in person than in her photo. After she learned to talk, hearing her giggle and say "Joanypony" for the first time was thrilling.

We didn't see Bailey as often as I would have liked, but I was determined to make our time together special. We particularly enjoyed going for walks, exploring her beautifully landscaped suburban neighborhood. One day, seeing a tree with a lush, green branch close to the ground, I reached for the branch and sang, "Oh, beautiful tree, won't you dance with me," swinging my arm back and forth.

"Come, dance with us," I beckoned to Bailey. The two of us dancing with the tree brought me such joy that I started to sing,

"Zip-a-dee-doo-dah, zip-a-dee-ay

"My, oh, my, what a wonderful day."

After that, we always looked for trees to sing and dance with, and good hills to roll down.

I'm a writer and have always loved journaling, so when Bailey was five, I gave her a yellow journal with butterflies on the cover. I encouraged her to write about her family and pets, and all the things we did together. Bailey's younger sister Peyton had watched her journal. At age three, even though she could only scribble, Peyton asked for her own journal.

When it was time for Peyton to visit us on her own, at age six, she phoned me. "I can't wait to write in my journal," she said. "Now that I'm in first grade, I can finally write words!"

When she arrived at our house and saw the 237 journals that lined my bookshelves, she asked, "When I get older, will you read me your journals?"

"I'll read you something right now," I said, pulling one from the shelf. She snuggled next to me on the sofa.

"Peyton came to visit," I read, "and wanted me to keep her company while she used the potty. As she was sitting there, I started to laugh. She asked, 'Why are you laughing?'

"'Because I love you so much and am so glad you're visiting.'

"She smiled up at me. 'Want me to come again?'"

I shut the journal and said, "That was a fun day."

Peyton gave me a hug. "I love you, Joanypony."

Though there were lots of things I did with both granddaughters, there were also special things I did with each. With Peyton, one special project was making an outfit for Rae, the little white bear I had bought for myself twenty years earlier on my way to meet Peyton's grandpa for the very first time. Our date was to take place at a hotel restaurant. On the way, I stopped at the hotel gift shop, and the little bear caught my eye. At the time, I was fifty, divorced and childless. I'd gone on a lot of disappointing dates and hoped the little white bear would bring me luck.

Peyton loved the story about Rae being as old as my relationship with her grandpa. We even took the little bear on our honeymoon.

As we sewed a hat for Rae, Peyton held the little bear close and asked me, "Why didn't you have children?"

"I wanted to, except they took a part out of my body you need to make a baby. But that's okay. You and Bailey are the little girls I never had."

Now, eleven years after I was first asked to choose a name for myself, the girls have outgrown their delight in calling me Joanypony. On a recent visit, we were watching a movie about a teenage girl who yearned to be a champion ice skater. She befriended a young man who operated the Zamboni at the rink where she practiced.

"What's a Zamboni?" the girls asked me.

"A Zamboni smooths out the ice for the skaters."

Toward the end of the movie, upset about the challenges she'd encountered, the skater went to a pond to practice, but it was too rough and bumpy for skating. Suddenly, the young man from the rink appeared with his Zamboni to save the day.

Immediately, I had an idea.

"My new name is JoanyZamboni!" I announced. "But you can just call me Zamboni."

They loved it.

On their next visit, Bailey said, "You're my Zamboni. You help smooth out my life."

I wonder if Zamboni will stick, or if I'll have to find another name to capture their changing needs and my evolving awareness of what my spirit can offer them.

For now, the others are welcome to "Grandma" and "Grammy." I'm happy to be Zamboni.

—Joan Leof—

Nanny Granny

A grandmother is a babysitter who watches the kids
instead of the television.
~Author Unknown

"I quit teaching in order to write, not become Nanny Granny!" My daughter stared at me, crestfallen. She was the single mother of two girls, the older one with autism. She worked long hours as a nurse manager at a local hospital to support them. I knew she needed help, but I had already put in my time raising five children, and I had worked with hundreds of students in my teaching career. I was done with the responsibility of kids.

However, that small voice inside me was not done. Before the first two weeks of school had been completed, I began feeling the pull. I hated the idea of my two youngest grandchildren sitting in before- and after-care programs at school, the first to arrive and the last to leave. After all, my internal voice argued, who was going to love those children more than family? Who else would have the patience and understanding to help my grandchild with autism?

Much to my daughter's delight, I gave in and altered my plans.

Thus began the routine. My daughter brought the children over at six, clad in pajamas and still rubbing their eyes. I got them ready and drove them to school, picked them up, and helped with homework in the afternoon. I stepped in for class projects and special events. I went to teacher conferences, and I worked out a discipline system for the granddaughter with autism, as she had been disrupting her class.

Things improved at school, and we became a smooth running machine.

Much to my surprise, I loved it. I had officially become Nanny Granny.

My husband got into the act, too. He came home from work to two little girls wrapping themselves around his waist. He played cards and board games, and read books complete with the full cast of characters' voices. He even took the younger granddaughter out and taught her how to change a tire, check the oil in the car, and catch a baseball. I will never forget the look on my daughter's face when she pulled into the driveway and saw her eight-year-old with a tool bag tied around her waist, using a power drill as she helped Grampie build a new front deck.

The next summer, my daughter took her girls on a vacation to the Oregon coast. I was determined to enjoy my week off and take full advantage of the time to myself. I was working on my writing one day, and it was going well. I was on a roll. Then the phone interrupted me. I answered and heard sniffling.

"Grammie?" came the tiny, strangled voice of my granddaughter, Aidan.

"Hi, baby," I replied. "How are you doing?"

To my surprise, she burst into sobs. I struggled to understand all her words, but the message was clear: She missed her grandmother. I soothed and comforted her until she managed to calm down. Her mother got on the phone to tell me that they were on the beach near Haystack Rock in Cannon Beach, Oregon. She told me that as they strolled from one tidal pool to the next, Aidan had dragged her feet until she plunked herself down on the sand, lost in distress and tears. She missed me!

That sweet little girl had refused to be consoled until she could hear my voice. I think my heart swelled to twice its size. Every day of their vacation, I received at least one phone call so that she could talk to me and share her adventures.

At summer's end, she presented me with a glass container filled with Hershey's Hugs & Kisses. She said she knew I would need them since she would be at school all day, and I would miss her. She was right. I did.

The girls aren't quite so small anymore, but they are still part of our daily routine. I know that my daughter is grateful for the blessing of a grandmother to love and care for her children while she is away. I think, however, that I am the recipient of the greater blessing.

— Marcia L. Wells —

Every Grandparent Counts

A grandmother is a safe haven.
~Suzette Haden Elgin

lthough my marriage to your son failed, and he walked away from me and our daughter, you continued to spend time with your granddaughter. You made sure she knew just how much both sides of her family loved her even though her parents were no longer together. You kept in touch on a weekly basis to build a bridge so that one day, when her father was ready, it would be easier for them to have a relationship — having you as a common ground.

I agreed with you about this. I wanted them to know each other. Were we crazy for even trying to mend a relationship between a father and daughter that never started in the first place? Regardless of how other people felt, we were somehow on the same page. We knew what was best for our little girl. You were a big part of her life. She grew attached to you.

The years passed, and I remarried and created a new life with another family. They viewed my daughter as their own grandchild. She now has so many grandparents to love her and nurture her as she grows up.

As life was going well for us in our new family, it took a tragic turn for your family. An auto accident flipped your world inside out, and your attention had to turn to your own daughter and her long recovery process. Visits with your granddaughter took place less often until they eventually stopped completely. She asked about you daily.

She deeply missed you and your time together. My daughter often asked difficult questions, such as, "Mommy, where is Grammy, and why hasn't she come to see me?" "Do you think Grammy forgot about me or doesn't love me anymore?" And, "Did I do something wrong? Is that why Grammy doesn't want to come see me?"

I explained to my daughter that her aunt had been in an accident, and Grammy was very busy taking good care of her. "She loves you and will not forget about you," I assured her. I encouraged her to keep praying for Grammy to be brought back to us, but said it would take time. I was not just saying that to convince my daughter; I believed it.

One afternoon, I went to a laundromat that I usually do not visit. I had always gone to the same place to do our laundry, but for some reason, I chose a different place this time. It was one of the best decisions of my life. As I turned down an aisle of dryer machines, there you were folding clothes!

My first impulse was to walk away without saying a word. After all, what could I say after all this time? How could I control my emotions enough to have a civil conversation for the benefit of my daughter? Maybe I was better off leaving well enough alone. But I could hear my daughter asking, "Mommy, did I do something wrong that made Grammy mad at me? Is that why she doesn't come to see me anymore?" That thought brought tears to my eyes and the inner strength I needed to walk over to you and say hello.

First, we made a lot of small talk, but suddenly I just came out and asked you, "What happened? Where have you been, and why haven't you come to see her?" I couldn't believe the words came out of my mouth, but I needed answers not only for me but for my daughter. Before you could answer, I began to explain. "She misses the time you spent together, and she asks about you daily."

She replied, "But you remarried, and I thought that meant I would no longer be welcomed in her life. I thought your new husband's parents would take over the role of grandparents."

I said, "Yes, I got remarried, and his parents are also her grandparents, but no one could ever replace her Grammy! She loves you and misses you deeply! No one can take the place of Grammy, not now and not ever."

We continued to talk and catch up on the years that had passed. After some time, our laundry was finished, and we exchanged numbers so we could make plans for you to get reacquainted with your granddaughter. Then we said goodbye and went our separate ways.

Things started off slowly after our first phone call. But over the years, trust has been rebuilt, and your relationship has grown stronger. That was thirteen years ago, and that little girl is now a twenty-two-year-old college senior. Over the years, not only has a strong, wonderful relationship been rebuilt between the two of you, but that has led to an amazing relationship with her biological father. I could not have hoped for my prayers to be answered so fully!

— Autumn Alexander —

Chapter

10

Legacies through the Generations

Easter Ham Pie

If God had intended us to follow recipes,
He wouldn't have given us grandmothers.
~Linda Henley

M y mother always wanted a daughter. She never actually came right out and said it, but certain comments she made over the years left little doubt in my mind. Four of mom's sisters had been blessed with daughters. One sister in particular, my Aunt Eva, lived a few miles away in Hammonton, New Jersey, and she had two nearly perfect girls. So, whenever my mother needed a daughter fix, Joan and Sandy were there to fill the prescription.

They didn't take all the heat off me, though. Mom still expected me to learn how to cook and help her with the chores around the house. She would often point out that even my father cooked the spaghetti on Sundays, prepared with our own homegrown and fresh-canned tomato sauce, and topped with Italian sausage, meatballs and hand-grated Parmesan cheese.

So that's how I ended up being the chosen one who was to carry on the Capoferri family tradition of making Easter Ham Pie. This secret recipe was only supposed to be handed down to a Capoferri daughter or granddaughter. And tradition required that it had to be a direct descendant, too, which daughter-in-laws were definitely not. Although my Uncle Tony had three daughters, they were from Aunt Stella's previous marriage, so they were out.

The real reason behind all the intrigue was that my mother collected recipes and she wanted this one badly. So, eventually, she convinced my grandmom that, since there weren't any daughters or granddaughters in the family, and as I was her first grandson, I was her last best hope if she didn't want the secret recipe to die with her.

I was about eight years old when Mom told me I had been deemed worthy to receive the knowledge of the ages. And she couldn't understand why I wasn't very excited about it.

"Aw, Mom," I cried, "only girls bake pies. Why can't she teach you?"

"Because Grandmom chose you to know the secret. It's an honor! You'll break her heart if you turn her down."

Even at the tender age of eight, I knew there wasn't any glue strong enough to mend a grandmother's broken heart. So, I reluctantly agreed to do it.

Bright and early on Saturday, the day before Easter, I trudged next door at the appointed time. But before I could even knock, Grandmom swung open the door. After one look at her beaming face, my entire attitude changed.

"So, you ready to learn how to make-a the Easter Ham-a Pie?" she asked.

"I think so, Grandmom," I nodded. "Is it hard?"

"Nah." She shook her head. "Joost-a always remember: When you only put good-a tings in, even better tings-a come out!"

She slid a plate to the corner of the kitchen table, pointed at the chunks of imported ham and cheese she had already prepared, and said, "First-a, you smell."

I took a deep sniff, and the pungent aroma made my mouth water immediately.

"Now, you taste-a," she commanded.

After I popped a few pieces of ham and cheese into my mouth, she nodded and asked, "Good-a, no?"

"Mmm." I nodded, smiling as the savory chunks of ham and cheese literally melted in my mouth.

"Now, you listen to me," she said, as she began unrolling a long, wax-paper-covered sheet of dough. "You mama, she ting she's gonna get all-a my secrets troo you. But I only teach-a you if you promise you don-a tell-a nobody else. *Capisce*?"

Confused, I asked, "But why, Grandmom?"

"Because," she said, as she sprinkled on some flour and began using the rolling pin to flatten the dough, "that's what-a my mama said-a to me… an-a that's what-a my mama's mama said-a to her."

Then, with a serious look on her face, she added, "Joost-a the daughter suppose to learn. But, you mama, she's-a right… there's no gales in-a the family this time. So, what am I suppose to do?" She shrugged, and then smiled and said, "I teach-a you, that's what. So, raise-a you right hand to God and make-a me you promise… okay?"

"Yes, Grandmom," I said, raising my right hand. "I promise." And I meant it, too.

All in all, it took about two-and-a-half hours to prepare and bake that Easter Ham Pie, and I got to eat the very first slice of mine on Easter morning, right after seeing what the Easter Bunny had left for me in my basket. I can't say I've ever eaten a piece of Easter Ham Pie since that tasted even half as good.

To the question of whether I ever divulged my grandmom's secret recipe to my mother, the answer is no. Truth is, I didn't have to because she already knew Grandmom's top-secret ingredient: love.

— Bruce Capoferri —

The Absent Grandmother

What we have once enjoyed we can never lose; all that
we deeply love becomes a part of us.
~Helen Keller

My grandson had just turned one. I was lucky to be with him to celebrate his birthday. His other grandmother, Wendy, was not.

Wendy was the first person, after my son and daughter-in-law, to hold Benji after he was born.

Did I envy her? Of course!

She and her husband Richard lived near Tom and Amy in California, and I live on the East Coast. She was in their lives on a daily basis, in and out of their house all the time. When Benjamin was born, our roles were clear. She was destined to be the grandma on the ground. I would be the fly-in grandma.

Wendy was a smart, funny person with a generous spirit. She had everything it takes to be a terrific grandma. I knew she would be a loving, fun presence in Benji's life, and she and I would always support each other as fellow grandmas.

Still, I couldn't help but envy her. Whenever she or Amy posted a photo of Wendy holding the baby on Facebook, some small part of me wished it could be me.

Then one Thursday morning, I got a phone call from my son, Tom. "Wendy died unexpectedly last night," he told me. "We need you to come out and help us with the baby."

Although she was consistently positive and upbeat about it, Wendy had Crohn's disease. Crohn's is a serious illness, but not ordinarily fatal. Nobody had expected it to kill her.

I was stunned. The kids were devastated.

A day later, I was in California helping take care of Benji while the kids and Richard mourned Wendy and planned her funeral.

I welcomed the chance to take a more active role in Benji's life, but not under these circumstances! Yes, I'm a wonderful grandmother. And I'm great with babies. Keeping a baby happy is one of my superpowers.

But Benji, who deserves two terrific grandmothers, was left with just one.

It was an unspeakable loss.

Although Benji was just seven months old when Wendy died, Amy has always been determined to keep her memory alive for him. She talks about her mother often. She's filled the walls of their home with her photos. She often shares videos of her mother with Benji.

When we celebrated Benji's first birthday, she played him a video of Wendy singing "Happy Birthday" to him.

Some grieving people are unable to talk about their loved one. Amy is taking the opposite approach. Wendy is not going to fade from the memory of anyone in this family if my daughter-in-law has anything to do with it!

Amy's efforts to honor her mother have made me aware of how present my own mother was in my son's life, even though Mom died many years before he was born.

Wendy was just sixty when we lost her. Mom, too, died far too young at fifty-seven. We were very close. A day doesn't go by that I don't miss her.

Because she stays in my heart and is so often in my thoughts, I spoke of her frequently as Tom was growing up. I'd quote her opinions or comment on whether she'd like or dislike something. "Mom would be proud," I'd tell my son when he excelled in school. Or "Mom would plotz," I'd say when he did something — like rock-climbing or scuba-diving — that would have made my overly protective mom very anxious.

As a result, my son has a good sense of who his maternal grandma was and what she meant to me. Her value system. Her likes and dislikes. Her quirks and foibles. Her favorite sayings and catch phrases. He knows what she'd do in many situations, both big and small.

Without ever having met Rahl Warren, Tom grew up knowing how wonderful she was and how much I love her. I hope that being aware of this is consoling to Amy as she strives to raise Benji to know and love Wendy.

Keeping Mom's memory alive, of course, isn't the same thing as being with her.

So what does the surviving grandmother owe the absent one?

I do what I can to keep Wendy's spirit alive in Benji's life. When I'm with my grandson, I try to channel his "Grammy," to include her in the time he and I spend together. I mention her often to Benji, in the same way that I spoke about my own mother to my son.

One of my biggest regrets is that my mom never got to meet her own grandchildren, who were born many years after she died. She would have adored them.

Nothing would have made her happier than being a grandma. And nobody would have been a more loving, supportive person in my son's life.

All of Wendy's loved ones are comforted by the fact that she got to hold Benji, to care for him, to share the first seven months of his life. And there are plenty of photos and videos of the two of them that we can share with Benji as he grows.

He may not remember her, but he'll always know that he was loved by her.

It's more than my own mother got.

Wendy was with us for far too brief a time and will always be missed. But she died a beloved grandma, and her family is committed to keeping her memory alive.

It isn't enough, of course, but it's what we have.

— Roz Warren —

A Visit with Grandma

94

Fill your paper with the breathings of your heart.
~William Wordsworth

handful of years ago, I was visiting with my grandma at her apartment. Her new home was located within an assisted-living retirement community. It had been a few years since Grandpa had passed away, and Grandma decided it was time to downsize her home of forty years.

It was a good move for my grandma. She always loved being around people. Being alone in a large house was more than she could handle, both practically and emotionally. At her new home, she saw mealtime as a chance to have dinner with her neighbors. She took every opportunity to participate in the recreational activities and the classes that were offered.

On this particular visit, Grandma told me about a life-story writing class that she was taking. Each week, the participants were given a writing prompt that would help them recall stories from their past. Grandma had this strong desire to write down her stories, but she was overwhelmed with where to begin and what to include. There was so much that she didn't want to miss.

I happened to know that both of my grandparents had already written quite a bit of family history. Several years prior, my kids and I had given them a gift we called "Journal in a Jar." A decorated mason jar was filled with strips of paper with a question on each one. The questions ranged from "What is your favorite food?" to "What has been your greatest life lesson?" The gift included a journal for each of my grandparents with instructions to draw a slip of paper from the jar, write or paste the question at the top of a blank journal page, and jot down their responses.

When I reminded Grandma of this, a light bulb went off. She did remember completing this journal as well as writing down some of the research she had done on her family history. I helped search through her storage unit until we found an entire box that included these journals as well as several other family-history gift books, newspaper clippings, photos, cards and other notes she had collected.

We sat together, thumbing through each of the items and reading the stories. Grandma would laugh until she cried as she relived some of her favorite memories that came to life again through her journals.

Before I left that day, Grandma asked if I would help her compile these stories and some of the records she kept into one document that she could give to each of her children, grandchildren, and great-grandchildren. I agreed, and we worked on this project together.

Something very special happened while I was helping Grandma gather and create her stories. I got to know my ninety-year-old grand-mother as a child. I was introduced to her as a teenager. I caught a glimpse of what life was like for my grandma as a young adult and newlywed. She had written stories about life as a young mom, and about the biggest struggles she had faced in her life. In some cases, she actually addressed the reader, saying: "Kids, you won't remember this, but when I was young, the milkman actually delivered bottles of milk to our doorstep," and she continued with a story about that time.

Reading her stories was like sitting across the table from a friend. I learned who my grandma was outside of just being my grandma.

Each time I would visit, Grandma would send me home with multiple items and the stories behind them. These things ranged from wedding gifts that she and Grandpa had received, to platters, dishes, and decorations that had been passed down from her ancestors.

During this time of gathering and compiling, Grandma faced some health issues. But she never stopped wanting visitors, and she never slowed down on sharing her stories. It took over a year, but I finally had a draft of her manuscript, with a photo of her on the front and her name listed as the "author." I was excited to see the look on her face when she flipped through the pages of her life, laughing and crying and proud to have authored her first book. I called my dad to see if he would like to go along with me to present the manuscript to her.

When Dad returned my call, he told me that Grandma had passed away in her sleep.

I didn't get to see her laugh and cry and enjoy the memories she had written down. I didn't get to present to her what she had worked hard to preserve.

But I did get to see tears of joy on the faces of my family members as I read some of my grandma's thoughts at her funeral. In her own words, Grandma was able to share how she wanted to be known and remembered. Her book became an instant "bestseller" for the people on her family tree.

Personally, I have a better understanding of who I am because I have a better understanding of where I came from. My grandma's stories created that connection. It is a gift that continues to live on.

Grandma's life was her story. And her story was her legacy. Each time I open her journals or the book she created, it's like having one more visit with Grandma.

— Robin Grunder —

95

Me and My Shadow

You've gotta dance like there's nobody watching.
~William W. Purkey

There we were posing with our matching pink leotards in the living room — my four-year-old granddaughter Carolyn and me. As I looked down, I noticed Carolyn had her toes pointed, arms extended, and a smile from ear to ear. Never would I have guessed at seventy that I would be dancing with my granddaughter beside me, and that I would be called "Dancin' Grammie."

Carolyn is one of my twenty-two grandchildren who are scattered all over the map. I became Dancin' Grammie a few years earlier when I lived in California and took up tap dancing with a group called the Hot Flashes. (That's another story!) I usually saw my grandchildren at holidays or when another sibling was born. After birthing seven children myself, I was considered somewhat of an expert — always in demand. When I did visit, the children loved to have me tap dance and show them a few steps. I can still see them twirling around in circles until they got dizzy and staggered to the couch. They would wear homemade costumes to do a "show" for their mommies and daddies. We would perform many times during my visit.

It wasn't until Grandpa and I moved to Indiana and lived close to Carolyn that I acquired my own full-time student. She wanted to learn new steps all the time and caught on quickly. She tried to teach me, too. I always wanted to do splits, and Carolyn, who could literally jump into them both ways, worked very hard to help me to do just that. It quickly became apparent, though, that splits were hazardous to my health.

For our first performance, Carolyn and I decided to do something simple. We chose a slow tap dance with lots of shuffles and flap ball changes to the song "Me and My Shadow." We wore matching costumes — black velvet leotards with little skirts, lots of bling, feathered hats, and shimmery dance hose. We took center stage — the middle of a beach house — at a family reunion later in the year, and we were quite a hit.

That was just the beginning. Soon after, I started a volunteer senior entertainment group where I taught others to tap dance, and we performed at local nursing homes to bring joy to residents. Carolyn continued dancing, and I happily attended all her performances during her younger years and through her high-school musicals. When she started college, Carolyn began learning "silks," a new genre that involved aerial dancing with gymnastic tricks. My heart would leap to my mouth as she twisted her body into positions that looked physically impossible, still smiling from ear to ear. What started with a little girl tap dancing in the basement ended with a teenager spinning high in the air.

Now she is teaching and performing aerial silks while awaiting a call from a school on the East Coast that prepares dancers for companies such as Cirque du Soleil. All this recognition couldn't have happened to a more deserving young lady. Not only does Carolyn have talent, but she has the biggest, kindest, most loving heart.

Those early days of Carolyn being my shadow started something that I will treasure forever. It led us down an unexpected path — we're both dancers! Break a leg!

— Queen Lori —

96

Grandma's Ring

Carve your name on hearts, not tombstones.
A legacy is etched into the minds of others
and the stories they share about you.
~Shannon L. Alder

I t consists of two round, flat onyx stones and a row of tiny diamonds snaking between them. It sounds glamorous, but it's actually quite ordinary. The stones are scratched, and the diamonds are small and dull, probably damaged from years of scrubbing her house with Lysol and bleach. But it's the most precious jewelry I own because it was hers.

Grandma never removed it, as seen in all the family photos. It's clearly visible on her hand throughout my parents' wedding album. As she stands lined up next to her daughter and new son-in-law, she gently touches the ring with her thumb on the same hand, as if making sure it's still there. She does it in every photo.

When we were little and admired it on her finger, Grandma held it out and informed us it was her wedding ring, which seemed odd because it didn't resemble the solitaire diamond our mother wore. She said the snaking diamonds formed an "S" for Simmons, her last name. But that seemed like a stretch, even to our young eyes. Either way, it was a gorgeous piece of art — because it was on Grandma's finger.

The ring was present when Grandma wrapped her arms around us in a big hug after we walked through the side door of her tiny home. She'd kiss our cheeks while we inhaled her lovely scent of Sweetheart soap and Emeraude perfume. She wore it when she pressed her hands deep in a bowl of Christmas cookie dough, mixing up her famous recipe while we waited patiently at her dining-room table with our rolling pins and Santa cookie cutters.

She wore it on our special birthday weekends, when each of us got to spend the night with her, then wake the next morning and venture to the Woolworth five-and-dime store or Southgate Shopping Center to pick out a birthday treasure. The ring was present later that day when we'd grab a bite at the Sears lunch counter, and then purchase a bag of Swedish Fish candy for the bus ride home. As she tucked us in that night, her hand wore the ring that scratched our backs as we lay horizontally across her big bed, singing "Jesus Loves Me" until we fell asleep.

She was wearing it the day I dropped my precious Tubsy doll and cried buckets of tears as her leg broke off in the process. She wore it for the dozens of months following, when she attempted every version of adhesive, construction, duct, and first-aid tape trying to repair her. The ring was witness to the day she tried and failed at one last trick: applying chewing gum to Tubsy's leg socket, resulting in a pink, sticky mess. Then Grandma's ring was drowned in soapy water as she softly bathed my poor little maimed doll, then handed her (and her leg) gently back to me and declared that Tubsy's broken leg "just made her more special." Grandma said it, so I believed it, too.

One unbearably sad day after Grandma died, my siblings and I went through her house, dividing up her useless, priceless treasures. When we got to this ring, of course, we all wanted it. So, we decided that each of us would wear it for a few months, and then pass it on. I took my turn a few times, and then dutifully released it when required. About the third time around, I reluctantly produced the ring when my time was up. My kind, loving sisters informed me that the ring didn't really fit their fingers anyway, and that I should just keep it. I accepted tearfully.

Now, I save the ring for special occasions when I want Grandma with me. I place it on my finger for fun trips or fancy dinners — events I know she'd enjoy. I also slip it on when I need support, like on job interviews or, more recently, chemo appointments. As I wear it, I gently touch it with my thumb, making sure she's still there....

—Joan Donnelly-Emery—

97

A Legacy 100 Years in the Making

That is your legacy on this Earth when you leave this Earth: how many hearts you touched.
~Patti Davis

When I was about twelve years old, I was having a casual conversation with my mom when she mentioned "my grandma Cora." I stopped her abruptly and said, "What was her name? Your grandma?"

"Cora," my mom repeated. "It's an old-fashioned name. C-O-R-A."

My twelve-year-old self announced, "Well, I like that name. And when I have a daughter someday, I'm going to name her Cora. Only, I think I'll spell it with a K... something different. Maybe Khoura."

And then, at age thirty-two, I was blessed with the news that I was expecting a baby. As my husband and I were on our way out to dinner one evening, we had our first discussion about baby names. It was very early in the pregnancy, and we threw around some possibilities for both boys and girls. We discussed what we liked and what we didn't. I assumed this to be the first of many conversations on the topic, and I looked forward to perusing lists online, buying baby-name books, and crossing names off a huge list until we finally came to the perfect one that we both agreed upon.

And then I remembered Cora — my mom's grandmother's name that I first fell in love with twenty years earlier. I had never met my great-grandmother, but she had been an important figure in my mother's life. I hadn't thought about that name in so long. I wondered if I would even consider it now that it was no longer just a childish dream of the future.

"I always liked the name Cora for a girl," I said to my husband. He thought about it for just a moment before saying, "I do, too. Cora — I like it." I said it again, over and over, picturing my unborn child with this name (only now I preferred the traditional spelling) and said, "I really do like Cora." I went on to explain how I came to know this name. My husband said, "So, if it's a girl, she's Cora." And that settled it. One conversation in the car decided it before we had even arrived at the restaurant. Was it supposed to be that easy?

The remaining months of my pregnancy passed, and we never changed our minds about the baby's' name. On May eighteenth, Cora was born eight days past her predicted due date. She was perfect in every way.

My parents came to the hospital to meet their new grandchild. My mother held the baby lovingly in her arms, forming an instant bond that has remained unbreakable to this day, six years later. At one point, she said, "You know, my grandma Cora was born in May, too. As a matter of fact, I think it very well might have been May eighteenth, but I don't know for sure."

A few weeks later, it crossed my mind to search online for details about my great-grandmother, especially to see if I could find out what day she was born. A quick Google search proved that she was, of course, born on May eighteenth — more than 100 years earlier. I'm still amazed at the irony of my daughter being born on the same exact date as her great-great-grandmother with the same name. And I absolutely love how my mother has bridged the gap between five generations: She cherishes the memory of her own grandmother, while making new memories with her granddaughter.

— Kristen Yankovitz —

98

Sight Unseen

Families are like branches on a tree. We grow in
different directions, yet our roots remain as one.
~Author Unknown

It took a moment for the news to sink in. I had a grandmother. My cousin, sitting at my dining-room table, laid out pictures one at a time. "This is your aunt. This is your grandmother." My what?

A few weeks prior to this visit, I had shared my birth mother's name with my cousin. For fifty-three years, I didn't know anything about my birth family. Then the state offered adoptees their original birth certificates for a small fee. There were no promises that names of birth parents would be on them, but it was worth the chance. I had forgotten I had even sent for it when, six months later, a piece of mail with the official state logo arrived in my mailbox. It didn't jump out at me as I opened the day's mail, and I thought it was probably just a notice to renew my car registration or something like that.

Then I opened it, and goose bumps pushed the hair on my neck straight up as I pulled my birth certificate from the envelope. There it was, my mother's name. There was no father's name, but this was enough — I had my birth mother's name.

My cousin has a genealogy business. She had looked for my birth mother before with no luck. But now she had a name. It didn't take her long to find her. "I have news. I'll come to your house at four." And there we were, looking at pictures of people who looked like me. "Unfortunately, your mother has passed away. But I spoke to your aunt.

She told me the whole story and is very interested in meeting you." She set another picture on the table. "And this is your grandmother." *I have a grandmother.* I couldn't believe it.

After two days of processing the pictures and information, I decided to call my aunt. With shaky hands, I dialed her number. She answered, and my mouth went dry. I introduced myself. Her voice quivered, "Oh, honey, I've thought about you and wondered where you were for fifty-three years."

She shared my mother's story with me. My mother was not married and had a four-year-old daughter. There was no way she could afford another child. The decision was made to give me up for adoption, and they never discussed it again. My aunt and my grandmother retired to Florida. Not fond of cold weather, I told her, "I am not opposed to visiting Florida this winter." She was thrilled. We made plans to meet.

I was excited and nervous at the same time. Would they accept me? It's one thing to talk on the phone and exchange e-mails, yet another to meet face to face.

After checking into a hotel and getting some lunch, it was time for Meeting #1: with my aunt and uncle. My cousin Joan and my son Jason were with me. As soon as we pulled into their driveway, my uncle appeared on the porch with a big smile on his face. I thought they surely could see my heart pounding. As I approached him, he welcomed me and opened the door. My aunt stood just inside. With tears in her eyes, she gave me a big hug. I heard my uncle say, "When she got out of the car, it could have been Jeannie." That was my birth mother's name.

We had a delightful time looking at pictures and telling stories. Laughter punctuated the conversation. It was a great start to our visit. After supper, we went to the assisted-living facility where my grandmother lives. She was excited to meet me. As she turned in her chair to see me, she shook her head and said, "Oh, my." For a few seconds, she just stared at me. Then she took my hands in hers and said, "It's my Jeannie." She looked so happy. She echoed my aunt, "I always wondered what happened to that baby. Where was she? Was she alright?" We hugged and then talked about her life and stories of my mother growing up.

The next day, we all went to visit my great-aunt, who was ninety-nine. She stared at me for a few seconds, too, before saying to my grandmother, "That's your Jeannie." We had an amazing time with the two of them — more stories, more laughter. So many times, when I laughed or gestured, they would say, "That's Jeannie."

As I said goodbye to my grandmother that night, she hugged me tight and said, "I love you." At first, I wondered how she could love me — she didn't really know me. But in an instant, I understood why she could say that: I'm her granddaughter. It's the same way I love my grandchildren from the moment I see them. Even before they were born, I loved them. This visit was the meeting most of us have at the hospital, peering into the nursery, figuring out whose nose she has. My grandmother didn't have that experience, but she often wondered about me, and she loved me. It was easy for her to say "I love you" because she has for fifty-three years, sight unseen.

The nerves have been replaced with a sense of overwhelming blessing. What a gift to have a grandmother and other new family members who love me. Who knows? Maybe there is more blessing to come — they gave me the name of my birth father.

— Lisa J. Radcliff —

99

Where It All Began

Finding the path our ancestors walked is not
always easy, but the reward of the journey
makes the effort worthwhile.
~Author Unknown

I t all started with a leaky bathroom, and it ended in a trip to a different continent. Two unrelated events — one mundane and one
extraordinary — drew me closer to my grandmother.

My husband and I had hired a handyman to fix our bathroom.
He had brought two young helpers along. Being the trusting sort of
people who had the good fortune not to have to think otherwise, we
left this little work crew alone in our home. Every afternoon when I
returned home from a day's teaching, the two young men, who were
often there alone, proudly showed me the work they had completed. We
would chat and sometimes share a cup of coffee as they headed out the
door. I didn't know then that, on one of those days, my grandmother's
ring was in one of the young men's pockets.

My nona was a busy woman with silver-gray hair who always wore
a housecoat or apron. She crossed the ocean from Italy as a nineteen-
year-old who was engaged to marry a man in America. She raised six
children in this country and was fiercely proud of each one of them.
For my whole life, it seemed that my grandmother was busy, stirring a
pot on the stove, rolling dough for her famous white-frosted cookies,
sewing, crocheting, and praying the rosary every day.

On the occasion of her seventieth birthday, my aunts and uncles pooled together a tidy sum of money to buy my grandmother a stately ring. They chose a ring with a large marquise-cut ruby set in a wide band of filigreed gold. The only time her hands were still was when she wore her big ruby ring.

To me, the ring was like an invitation to grab one of her hands while she finally let others toil in the kitchen. I would rush to sit beside her, searching for a passageway into her heart. "Tell me about when you were a girl, Nona," I would plead. It was so hard to imagine that my grandmother had an entire family I did not know, a landscape that was different, a culture unlike my own. She would wave her hand and say that was in the past. My mother would soothe me by telling me that it was hard to talk about the people, places, and customs she left behind.

In her ninety-second year, Nona's busy hands slowed down. She began to take long naps in the afternoon. I remember going to visit one day. The aroma of her cooking was no longer in the air, and her apron hung on a hook. I knew she was close to saying goodbye, and it saddened me to think she would take all of her stories with her.

When Nona passed, each one of her children selected some items to remember her by. I gasped when my mother handed me her large ruby ring. My grandmother had three daughters, and I had twelve first cousins. How could this have filtered all the way down to her last granddaughter? "Everyone knew you loved Nona's ring," my mother said as she passed it to me. How strange it was to see it in a box and not on Nona's hand.

When I slipped that ring onto my own finger, it did not look right. I felt as if I was playing dress-up, wearing something from someone I admired but had not grown into being just yet. I was now a young mother, and it was my turn to have busy hands. I put the ring back in its box and put it in a drawer away from any other jewelry I owned. Sometimes, I would take it out, place it on my finger and think of her, and then return it to the drawer.

One morning, a week after our bathroom project was complete, I went to retrieve the ring. It was Valentine's Day, and for some reason I wanted to gaze at that beautiful red stone before I left for work. When I opened the box, it was empty! My husband reported the incident to the police, and when they heard we had an unsupervised work crew in the house, we were lectured about our foolishness. To our great surprise, one of the young men confessed to taking the ring. As a mother, I felt a great sense of compassion for him when I learned he had an addiction problem and was truly sorry for his offense. As part of his probation sentence, he was ordered to pay back the value of the ring.

Upon questioning, he revealed that the ring was not brought to a pawnshop but melted down for the gold. A monthly check would arrive in the mail from the court as his restitution, but the ring was lost forever, and the checks brought little solace. I did not want to deposit them in our regular bank account even though the money would have been helpful. Somehow, using the money to pay bills seemed disrespectful. My husband suggested we buy a new ring and begin our own tradition, but just like Nona herself, the ring could not be replaced.

After many, many months, the amount was paid in full. The money sat in a separate bank account, and we went on with our busy lives raising three girls, one of them named for her great-grandmother. One day when she asked me about my grandmother, a new idea began to take root. Perhaps the way to honor my grandmother was to go to the place where her story started.

Over the years, I added to my special bank account. Extra tutoring jobs, rebate checks, and even garage-sale funds made their way into my account. Eventually, there was enough money to cover the costs for our whole family to travel to Italy.

I felt the presence of my grandmother walk with me when I strolled down the streets of her city. I finally gazed at her landscape and heard her first language spill from the mouths of the people in all the places we visited. I breathed in the smells from bread baking in the pastry shops and prayed in the church where her family worshiped. We soaked her in as we met people who revealed a hint of her smile, too. Finally, I saw where her journey had started.

The ring was gone forever, but in its place was the story of a woman whom I longed to know. She showed me it was never about a ring; it was always about her heart and mine.

— Elizabeth Rose Reardon-Farella —

100

The Writing Bureau

The love in our family flows long and deep,
leaving us memories to treasure and keep.
~Author Unknown

I've tried to declutter. I've even thrown out pieces of furniture that I no longer used but had kept "just in case." I threw out school projects and exercise books that my mum had kept lovingly for years. I threw out knickknacks, odds and ends, and birthday cards received from friends and family. I took bags and bags of clothes to the thrift store and gave books and DVDs to anyone who would have them. The more I threw away, the lighter I felt. Letting go of all of this unnecessary stuff felt great.

I developed this throw-it-out mentality about five years ago and, up until recently, had stuck with it. However, in the last month or so, I may have changed my throw-it-out ways. In fact, I may have stepped onto the path of hoarding.

What led me to this path? The answer: a writing bureau.

I went to my grandparents' house to collect it. It had fascinated me as a child. I'd spent hours rooting through the drawers that were packed full of photographs and papers. A "secret" drawer inside housed an array of broken watches and odds and ends. Next to the secret drawer, my grandfather kept his paperwork, and in amongst the paperwork were wooden rulers that folded in and out, envelope openers shaped like swords, and dozens of pairs of scissors. Every time I looked in that bureau (which was a lot), I discovered something new. I think I half expected to open it one day and step into Narnia.

Just before my grandfather passed away ten years ago, he reminded my grandmother that he'd promised me that I could have the bureau when I grew up. When my grandmother passed away at the end of last year, my mum reminded me that the bureau belonged to me if I still wanted it. After rearranging my furniture and contemplating an extension to my kitchen to house the bureau, I made space and arranged to collect it.

Three weeks prior, my mum and uncle had invited my sister, my cousin and me to my grandparents' house to spend one last evening there. We were getting takeout and had the opportunity to look around the house and choose some keepsakes. I was the first to arrive.

It was strange being in the house without my grandmother there. At first, I was hesitant to look through her belongings. It didn't feel right. Eventually, I began to look, starting downstairs. In the living room, I noticed my grandmother's chair. I remembered how we'd squeeze onto the one seat together even though there were three other chairs available. I looked in the kitchen and saw the patterned crockery that my grandparents used when we came for dinner. Upstairs, I looked through my grandmother's wardrobe and discovered the fur coat I used to dress up in as a little girl — the same fur coat that my grandmother would wrap my sister and me in when we were unwell. I looked inside the medicine cabinet; it still had the same smell that it had all these years (and possibly some of the same lotions and potions).

Memories flooded back to me. Being among my grandparents' belongings felt safe and familiar. I wanted to hold onto that feeling. The only way I could think to do that was to take some of their belongings home with me. That night, I went home with the fur coat and a fruit bowl. *That's enough*, I thought. *Remember the mantra. No more clutter.*

I gave in, though. Last Monday, I went to collect the bureau. The house had been sold, and it was almost empty. Most of the big items of furniture were gone. All that remained was the bureau, a few items that a charity was coming to collect, and bags and boxes of stuff that was not useful or beautiful. "Take anything you want," my mom had said. "It'll all be gone tomorrow."

I'd only come for the bureau. I couldn't take anything else. *I've got my mantra,* I thought. That is, until I started to look.

To the untrained eye, this clutter was all worthless. But to the trained eye of a granddaughter, it was priceless. I found the wooden salad servers that my grandparents used when we went to their house for dinner. I discovered the knitting needles and patterns that my grandmother used to make clothes for us. I found a bag of greeting cards sent by various family members to my grandparents over many decades. I couldn't believe they'd kept it all.

I was being taken on another trip down Memory Lane and back again. My search continued. I went into the sheds in the garden and noticed a toilet-roll holder in one of them. Growing up, I used my grandparents' outdoor toilet as quickly as I could to avoid the spiders. I uncovered tins of paint from when my grandfather asked my sister and me to help him paint his garden gnomes. I also found a box of cotton reels and hundreds and hundreds of buttons. I discovered photos of my sister and me as children with handwritten notes to my grandparents on the back.

They had kept everything. They had no mantra; they had a house full of stuff and memories.

I wanted to keep those memories alive. The only way to do so was to take more stuff. That day, I left my mantra behind and took the salad servers, a big bag of knitting needles even though I don't knit, a chicken-shaped egg holder, an assortment of plates and kitchen utensils, several books and a giant bag full of birthday cards.

Mantra shmantra. Clutter is the way forward.

— Katie Nash —

What They Learn

One person caring about another
represents life's greatest value.
~Jim Rohn

He was holding his grandfather's hand, guiding him toward the cruise ship's jet pool. They stopped at the edge, and Andrew gently helped his grandfather into the pool. Then he got in and sat next to him. I watched them spend the next half-hour together, deep in conversation — a young man and his elderly grandfather enjoying talking together while soaking in the pool.

My thoughts drifted back to my son's younger years and all the trips we made from Canada to Scotland in an attempt to make certain our children had a good relationship with their grandparents. Between trips, we encouraged our children to keep in touch with their grandparents. As our children matured, they would visit their grandparents on their own during school breaks.

Years later, long after his grandmother had passed away, Andrew accepted a contract to work and live in Egypt for a few years. He was a young man by then, with a busy life. About a year into his contract, we asked Andrew if he would consider joining us on a Mediterranean cruise; he would share a cabin with his grandfather. We were delighted when he arranged to meet us in Rome to join the ship.

It was a difficult cruise. Papa was far more feeble than we realized and wasn't able to partake in many of the excursions we had planned for each port. We took turns staying with him on the ship. Allan and

I observed the care and consideration our son demonstrated toward his grandfather. At times, it seemed he had more patience than we had; we were proud and grateful for his kindness.

Papa died sixteen months after that cruise. Some of the family traveled to Scotland for his funeral. Afterwards, we stood at the top of Dumbarton Rock, overlooking a view of the River Clyde, and I watched Andrew tip the urn to gently tap out the last granules of his grandfather's ashes.

We spent a week after the funeral cleaning out Papa's flat. I watched our son gently unclasp the bowling pins from his grandfather's lawn-bowling club blazer and place them in a small wooden box. Andrew had been a spectator at many of his grandfather's tournaments.

I thought about all the lessons his grandfather had taught him while attending these tournaments together. There was the value of friendship, team spirit, winning with grace and losing with dignity, as well as the merits of exercise, no matter your age. Papa had been an important role model throughout Andrew's childhood. The bond between a child and a grandparent leaves a lasting and lifelong imprint, and my children have benefited mightily from that.

— Kathy Dickie —

Meet Our Contributors

Autumn Alexander is a mother of five daughters. She enjoys spending time with her family, photography, traveling and writing about her life experiences.

Elizabeth Alonzo is a student of the creative arts, dabbling in writing, crochet, knitting, cardmaking, quilting, and stamp carving.

Anne Bardsley's favorite title is Gigi! She is the author of *How I Earned My Wrinkles* and newly released, *Angel Bumps Hello from Heaven*. She lives with her "Wrinkle Maker" of a husband in St. Pete, FL. Learn more at www.annebardsley.com or e-mail her at annekbardsley@yahoo.com.

Ann Barnett grew up in a factory town in Pennsylvania. Moving to New York she raised two daughters, taught school, and lived on the Hudson River in an old wooden boat. Now retired, she surrounds herself with good books, sharp pencils, and an up-to-date passport.

Sarah Barnum is a freelance editor with a passion for writing and riding. After a career managing a therapeutic riding program for children with special needs, she started TrailBlaze Writing & Editing. Sarah enjoys ranch life in Northern California with her husband and Appaloosa horse. Learn more at www.trail-blazes.com.

Greg Beatty writes poetry, short stories, children's books, and a range of nonfiction. He's published hundreds of things — everything from poems about stars to essays on cooking disasters. When he's not writing, he walks with his dog, dabbles in martial arts, plays with his grandchildren, and teaches college.

Jill Burns lives in the mountains of West Virginia with her wonderful family. She's a retired piano teacher and performer. Jill enjoys writing, music, gardening, nature, and spending time with her grandchildren.

Jack Byron lives in Southern California and is trained as an illustrator. He worked extensively with Alzheimer's patients while attending art school. This experience remains among the most positive and rewarding episodes in his life, and something that he draws upon for both his illustration work and his writing.

Bruce Capoferri recently retired from auto sales and lives with Barbara, his wife of forty-seven years, and a cat named KriKat. A member of South Jersey Writers' Group, his story "The Malocchio" appears in the anthology *Reading Glasses*. Bruce is also a singer-songwriter and a member of Nashville Songwriters Association International.

Sharon Carpenter lives outside Memphis, TN in a little town known for BBQ and fried chicken. Sharon's biggest fans are her husband Jesse, three incredible kids who morphed into six amazing adults, and three grandkids who call her Sassy.

Lorna Cassie-Bywater resides in Huntsville, Ontario but she and her husband winter in Florida. Lorna taught elementary school, English as a second language, and for twenty years did television interviews. She enjoys kayaking, travel, reading, writing and playing the ukulele.

JoAnne Check graduated from Kutztown University and lives in North Carolina. She's authored six books of historical fiction as well as contributed to the *Chicken Soup for the Soul* series. Currently, she is working on a novel titled *Mad Mattie*. She also loves art, travel, gardening, and camping in the great outdoors. Learn more at joannecheck.com.

Linda Carol Cobb taught English electives at the same Virginia Beach, VA, high school for thirty-seven years. She sponsored award-winning forensic teams and newspapers. Unwilling to retire, she teaches seminars, copyedits and coaches public speaking. She writes true stories about her Tennessee family and personal experiences.

Courtney Conover is a mom, writer, and yoga teacher who never met a candy she didn't like. No, wait: black licorice! But she eats her peas daily, because… balance. She lives in Michigan with her husband and young children and she's very grateful her mother lives nearby. Learn more at courtneyconover.com and on Facebook.

Gwen Cooper received her B.A. in English and Secondary Education in 2007, and completed the Publishing Institute at Denver University in 2009. In her free time she enjoys krav maga, traveling, and spending time with her husband and Bloodhound in the beautiful Rocky Mountains. Follow her on Twitter @Gwen_Cooper10.

Kala F. Cota lives in a small Oregon logging community. She recently retired after thirty years of teaching preschool in her home. She enjoys spending time with her husband, their two grown children and their three granddaughters. E-mail her at kccota@frontier.com.

Allison A. de Laveaga is a spiritual director, writer and mom living in Berkeley, CA. She writes a blog on parenting, spirituality and other topics. She enjoys long walks, reading, listening to podcasts, traveling and speaking Spanish. She is writing a book on spiritual journeys.

Kathy Dickie lives in South Surrey, British Columbia. She recently retired and is enjoying extensive travel around the world with her husband. In between their trips, Kathy devotes her time to family visits, quilting, documenting ancestry research and writing short stories.

Born in Cleveland, OH, **Joan Donnelly-Emery** received a Bachelor of Fine Arts in Musical Theater from Syracuse University. She performed in shows regionally and on tour, and enjoyed a long stint appearing in Orlando theme parks. She now lives in Tennessee with her husband, Alan, and their Terrier, Dottie. She is a rabid Cleveland Browns fan.

Dana Drosdick is a senior at Calvin College, studying Digital Communications and Spanish. In her spare time, she enjoys writing, traveling, and setting new goals of faith, creativity, wellness, and stewardship.

Thalia Dunn currently resides in New Jersey with her family and an assortment of cats. She teaches Spanish in a local high school, which keeps her busy. During her free time she writes poetry and essays and also loves trekking through local parks for early morning runs where she gets new ideas for writing.

Cathy Elliott's cozy mysteries reflect her interests from quilting and antiques to playing fiddle with friends and sweet grandgem time. Her books include: *A Vase of Mistaken Identity*, *Medals in the Attic*, and *A Stitch in Crime*. She is also a contributing author to Guidepost's *Every Day with Jesus* and *All God's Creatures*.

Brenda Evans has written as a hobby since she was a child. An all-around creative person, she studied Creative Arts at university and then gained an M.Ed in educational drama. She has worked as a teacher since 1982 and is now taking time off to develop her writing more seriously.

Melissa Face lives in Prince George County with her husband and two young children. She is an English instructor at the Appomattox Regional Governor's School. Her essays have been published in local and national magazines, as well as in twenty *Chicken Soup for the Soul* books. Learn more at www.melissaface.com.

Betty Farkas-Hart was born and raised in France and has been living in the United States for the last fifteen years. She lives in Florida with her husband, children and cats. She enjoys taking her family to Honeymoon Island whenever she can! They relax and enjoy the water and the beautiful scenery that Florida offers.

Cinda Findlan, a retired professor of Education, lives with her husband on Wellesley Island, NY. She dedicates her time to writing, painting, and enjoying her two granddaughters. Cinda looks for humor and meaning in life as a senior, recounting weekly experiences in her blog at PowerAgers.com.

Kristi Cocchiarella FitzGerald has a degree in English and is a Willamette Writer's member and NaNoWriMo finisher. She has had articles on costumes published in *Renaissance* magazine and three stories published in the *Chicken Soup for the Soul* series. She is published in and an editor for *Fine Lines*, a creative journal out of Omaha, NE.

Marianne Fosnow lives in Fort Mill, SC. She loves to read and enjoys writing as a way to preserve memories. She is proud to be a contributor to the *Chicken Soup for the Soul* series.

Joyce Carol Gibson has kept a journal since she was a teenager. Her first book release was in 2016 when she published *Salvage Yard of Souls*. Without the journal, the book would have been impossible to write twenty years later.

When **Kam Giegel** was little, she would sit on a large rock by her backyard creek with pencil and paper, dreaming of being a writer. Today she is living that dream, loving the adventure writing e-books, articles, newsletters and copy for the Alternative, Holistic, Integrative and Functional Medicine community.

Susan J. Gordon writes for many publications. She and her husband have two wonderful sons, two amazing daughters-in-law, and six spectacular grandchildren. Her memoir, *Because of Eva*, was published in

2016. Her book, *Wedding Days: When and How Great Marriages Began*, will be re-published in 2019. Learn more at susanjgordon.com.

David A. Grant is a freelance writer from southern New Hampshire. His work has been published in two prior *Chicken Soup for the Soul* books. He enjoys being "Papa" to his grandchildren. David's first full-length work of fiction was released in late 2018. David can often be found cycling the back roads of New Hampshire.

Robin Grunder is a journalist and ghostwriter specializing in the area of life-story and memoir, but most of her time is spent answering to the name of "mom," and "grandma." Robin teaches at writers' conferences and is currently working on a book series about leaving a legacy in writing. Learn more at robingrunder.org.

Dana Hinders received her Bachelor of Arts in Journalism from the University of Iowa in 2003. She is a full-time freelance writer and editor, living in rural Iowa with her husband and son. Growing up, her grandparents always encouraged her love of reading and storytelling. E-mail her at danahinders@gmail.com.

Pam Horton is a special education substitute teacher, life coach, and author. Whether she is writing an article, blog, newsletter, fiction, nonfiction, or children's book, Pam encourages others to move positively forward. She enjoys spending time with her husband and their family, especially their five grandchildren.

Del Howison, along with his wife Sue, is the creator and owner of Dark Delicacies in Burbank, CA. He is an award-winning editor and author having won the Bram Stoker Award for which he was nominated four times. He has also been nominated for the Shirley Jackson Award and the Black Quill Award.

Jeanie Jacobson is on the Wordsowers Christian Writers leadership team. She's been published in *Focus on the Family* and *Live* magazines, the *Chicken Soup for the Soul* series, and other anthologies. Jeanie loves visiting family, reading, hiking, and dancing. Grab her book, *Fast Fixes for the Christian Pack-Rat* online. Learn more at JeanieJacobson.com.

As a child, before she could even read, **Nancy Johnson** dictated stories to her mother, who wrote them down and encouraged her to continue writing. Taking her mom's advice, Nancy has written for a variety of national and regional publications. In 2015, The Press Club of Cleveland named her Best Essay Writer in Ohio.

MJ Keenan is a retired elementary school teacher, having taught kindergarten through third grade for many years. MJ enjoys writing, reading, walking, and spending time with her husband Ken and their children, grandchildren, and four dogs.

Elsa Kurt is a multi-genre author and speaker. She currently has eight novels published, as well as three novellas through Crave Publishing. She is a lifelong New England resident and married mother of two grown daughters. E-mail her at authorelsakurt@gmail.com.

Sharon Landeen, a retired elementary teacher, keeps young by volunteering at local schools through Literacy Connects, and by making blankets for Project Linus. She is a graduate of the University of Oregon and enjoys traveling and spending time with her children, grandchildren and great-grandchildren.

Andi Lehman holds a degree in communications from the University of Memphis and freelances in multiple markets. She enjoys writing devotionals, children's books, and nonfiction stories about amazing animals or ordinary people doing extraordinary things. Her story "Pussy-Willow Wisdom" is for Reyn in memory of her beloved Pop-pop.

Joan Leof has written a memoir titled *Fatal If Swallowed: Reclaiming Creativity and Hope Along the Uncharted Path*. A collection of twenty of her published personal essays appears in her book, *Matryoshka:*

Uncovering Your Many Selves Through Writing. As creator of Write to Heal, she facilitates journal workshops for groups and individuals.

Ina Massler Levin was a middle school teacher and later, the editor-in-chief at an educational publishing house. In retirement, she has been indulging her love of travel and ballroom dancing with her husband Michael. Ina also loves spending time with her family, especially her new granddaughter, Elianna Mae.

Lindsey Light received her Bachelor of Arts in English from Wright State University and her Masters of Arts in English from the University of Dayton. She is currently pursuing a Ph.D. in Educational Leadership while raising her two redheaded babies, Deacon and Nora, and her fur baby, Larkin.

Barbara LoMonaco received her BS from the University of Southern California and has an elementary teaching credential. Barbara has worked for Chicken Soup for the Soul since February 1998. She wears many hats there, including Senior Editor. She is a co-author of *Chicken Soup for the Mother and Son Soul*, released in 2006, and *Chicken Soup for the Soul: My Resolution*, released in 2008.

Queen Lori (age ninety) is mother of seven, grandmother of twenty-two, and a first-time contributor to the *Chicken Soup for the Soul* series. She began writing after being crowned queen of the 2016 Erma Bombeck Writers' Workshop. Lori leads and tap dances with the Prime Life Follies. Follow her at ErmaQueen.com.

Judy Mason received her MSN at Azusa Pacific University in 1991. She teaches in a Registered Nursing program as an Adjunct Professor in Southern California and serves on the Board of Directors for two nonprofits. Judy enjoys running for charity, working toward making a positive impact on the world, and spending time with her grandchildren.

Susan G. Mathis is a grandma of four and multi-published author of historical fiction: *The Fabric of Hope: An Irish Family Legacy, Christmas Charity*, and *Katelyn's Choice*. She has five books coming out soon and is also a published author of two premarital books and two children's picture books. Learn more at www.SusanGMathis.com.

Jeremy Mays currently resides in Mt. Vernon, IL where he is an English teacher at the local high school. In his free time, Jeremy enjoys writing (typically horror stories), ghost hunting, collecting horror movie memorabilia, and spending time with his wife, Courtney, and his nine children.

Nicole Ann Rook McAlister has studied journalism and pursues an avid interest in world religion and mythology. Nicole enjoys adventures in camping, sunrises on the beach, painting, crafting and all manner of such things. Several of her pieces have been on exhibit at the Whitesbog Historic Village in Browns Mills, NJ.

Jennifer "JennyMac" McCarthy uses her gift of poetry to capture memorable moments. When not homeschooling her three sons and taking care of the household, she spends time writing, reading, and enjoying family and friends. A graduate of Stetson University and USF, she is delighted to be included in the *Chicken Soup for the Soul* series.

Gena B. McCown is a native of South Florida and has been married for twenty years to husband Justin. They have three daughters (Casey, Shelby, and Naomi). Gena is an author, speaker, teacher, and ministry leader.

Robin K. Melvin is married to an Army veteran. She has three children and five grandbabies. She enjoys coffee and hiking. She writes the faith column for her hometown newspaper and plans to publish an inspirational book. Robin writes to inspire others to live large and love well. E-mail her at Robinkmelvin@gmail.com.

Catherine (Cat) Moise lives in rural Ontario where she is in awe of the trees and the secrets they whisper. Working with and raising children inspired her regular contributions to a parenting column. Her work has been published in *Today's Grandparent*. She is Grammie to five, soon to be six, inspirational grandchildren.

Marya Morin is a freelance writer. Her stories have appeared in publications such as *Woman's World* and Hallmark. Marya also penned a weekly humorous column for an online newsletter, and writes custom poetry on request. She lives in the country with her husband. E-mail her at Akushla514@hotmail.com.

Diane Morrow-Kondos loves writing about her grandparenting experiences at tulsakids.com/Grand-Life/. Her first book, *The Long Road to Happy: A Sister's Struggle Through Her Brother's Disabilities* will be published in 2019. For updates visit www.dianemorrowkondos.com. Diane enjoys competing in triathlons and open water swims.

Teresa Murphy lives in New Jersey and holds a Bachelor's degree in Journalism. In addition to writing, she enjoys hiking, painting, biking, and visiting the beach with her husband and three children.

Alice Muschany lives in Flint Hill, MO. She loves being retired and spending time with her grandchildren. Her hobbies include hiking, photography and writing. E-mail her at aliceandroland@gmail.com.

Mark Musolf lives in Minnesota with his wife. Mark enjoys football, house projects, and reading historical nonfiction.

Katie Nash completed her law degree at the University of Southampton, United Kingdom in 2008 and qualified as a lawyer in 2012. Katie lives in London with her husband James, their two children George and Eleanor, and their dog Hudson. Katie enjoys traveling, running, and writing about everything and anything.

Herchel E. Newman has always been a storyteller. His writing and photography go hand in hand. He loves romancing his wife and they are marriage mentors. His five grandchildren give him joy and lots of material. As an Air Force and professional firefighter veteran he says every day is an adventure to write about.

Diane Page is the pen name of a proud mother, daughter, and wife who has also been a nonfiction writer for over twenty years. Her essays have been published in seven anthologies and national magazines. She hopes her story opens hearts and builds compassion for transgender people.

Laura Niebauer Palmer received her graduate degree in English from DePaul University in 2013. She lives in Austin, TX with her husband and son. Laura enjoys traveling, volunteering and writing about her parenting adventures.

Ashlee Petrucci is an English teacher and creative writer living in Alberta. A wanderlust for travel has inspired worldwide explorations; one of which resulted in her first publication, a nonfiction vignette, "Marriage?" in the anthology, *Emails from India*. She is currently finishing her first novel.

Julie Phayer wrote and edited at a newspaper and a public affairs office before trading in her pumps for slippers — fitting footwear for a freelance writer with a home office. Julie enjoys reading and spending time with her family. She is a Court Appointed Special Advocate for children who are victims of abuse or neglect.

Connie Kaseweter Pullen lives in rural Sandy, OR, near her five children and several grandchildren. She earned a B.A., with honors, at the University of Portland in 2006, with a double major in Psychology and Sociology. Connie enjoys writing, photography and exploring nature. E-mail her at MyGrandmaPullen@aol.com.

Evan Purcell is an English teacher who has taught children in Bhutan, Zanzibar, China, and Russia. Right now, he's living in the beautiful mountains of Kazakhstan. He also writes romance novels for various publishers.

A resident of Ottawa, Ontario, **Louise Rachlis** is a perpetual writer, acrylic artist and runner with her fellow "Antiques of Steel." To her grandchildren, she is "BabaLou."

Lisa J. Radcliff is an author and speaker in the Philadelphia area. Her book, *Hidden with Christ: Breaking Free from the Grip of Your Past*, reveals her personal story of childhood sexual abuse and the freedom she found in Christ. Lisa is married and has three sons and five grandchildren.

Elizabeth Rose Reardon-Farella received her Bachelor's degree in Elementary Education from Molloy College and her Masters of Science degree in Literacy from Adelphi University. She is a first grade teacher at St. Edward the Confessor School in Syosset, NY. She enjoys traveling, yoga and writing inspirational stories.

An award-winning author, **Heather Rae Rodin** has a passion for writing stories. As a mother of six grown and married children, family time, writing, and speaking keep her life full. She and her husband, Gord, live on acreage near Peterborough, Ontario. Learn more at heatherraerodin.ca or e-mail her at hrodin@hopegrows.ca.

Linda Saslow was a contributing reporter for *The New York Times* on Long Island for more than twenty years. She is also the author of three published nonfiction books and her articles have appeared in many national and local magazines. When not writing, she spends as much time as possible with her grandchildren.

Melanie A. Savidis received her Bachelor of Arts from Allegheny College and her Masters of Education from the University of Rochester. She teaches in the Rochester City School District. Melanie and her husband Mike have three sons. She enjoys writing, playing music and traveling.

Loretta Schoen grew up in Brazil and Italy and now resides in Florida. She loves traveling and spending time with her grandsons. She conducts workshops on how to survive medical adversity and has just published her debut book, *Surviving Medical Mayhem: Laughing When It Hurts*.

Vicki Schoen is a retired ESL teacher, custodial grandmother, and author. She wrote, and her granddaughter Aveena illustrated, *Dary Dragon Can't Go Home* — for the youngest victims of the opioid epidemic. Her second novel, *Mommy Sang Him to Sleep*, will be available this spring. Learn more at vickischoen.com.

Yvonne Curry Smallwood has been writing inspirational stories for more than twenty years but her absolute favorite pastime is vacationing with family and friends. When she is not writing, you can find Yvonne in a craft store purchasing yarn for the many crochet items she creates and donates to local charities.

Michael T. Smith was thrown into the role of a grandfather in 2005, when his stepdaughter and her three boys moved in with him and his wife. It was a shock to him. His quiet world was gone. However, the year they were with him proved to be life-changing for the better.

Sheryl Smith-Rodgers of Blanco, TX is a writer and photographer who's been published in many state and national publications. Sheryl, who has a journalism degree from Trinity University, gives spider presentations and blogs about the native gardens she and her husband, James Hearn, tend at their home. E-mail her at sherylsr@ymail.com.

Diane St. Laurent is a wife, mother to three and grandmother to seven. Good times for her include swimming, reading, writing, and planning adventures with her family and friends.

Suzette Martinez Standring's syndicated spirituality column for GateHouse Media has run since 2008. She wrote *The Art of Column Writing* and *The Art of Opinion Writing*. Her family is her crowning achievement. Learn more at www.readsuzette.com.

Kathleen Steele is a retired educator living with her husband in St. Clair Shores, MI. She finds retirement to be a gift of time allowing her to pursue her dream of writing. Kathleen treasures time spent with her family and also enjoys traveling, photography, boating, and almost every sport except running.

A E Troyer enjoys spending time with God, her family and friends. She has worked in volunteer services in Haiti for fourteen months and at a Bible Institute in Pennsylvania for eight years. Currently, she is living in northern Pennsylvania and working on strengthening her relationship with Jesus and finding healing from past drama.

The most important thing in **John Volpe's** world is his family. He is the father of four and grandfather of eleven. He loves writing and has done rhymes and stories for all of them over the years. John and his wife live just north of Toronto. E-mail him at johnavolpe@rogers.com.

Pat Wahler is a proud contributor to fifteen *Chicken Soup for the Soul* books. She is the author of *I am Mrs. Jesse James*, *Let Your Heart Be Light: A Celebration of Christmas*, and *Midnight the One-Eyed Cat*; written under the supervision of one bossy cat and a lively Pekingese-mix. Learn more at www.PatWahler.com.

Roz Warren writes for everyone from the *Funny Times* to *The New York Times* and has been featured on both *Morning Edition* and the *Today Show*. This is the seventh time her work has appeared in a *Chicken Soup for the Soul* book. E-mail her at roswarren@gmail.com or visit www.rosalindwarren.com to learn more.

Rebecca Waters is an educator turned author. She has penned two novels, *Breathing on Her Own* and *Libby's Cuppa Joe*. Both fall in the category of Contemporary Women's Fiction. Rebecca enjoys her eight grandchildren, who all still call her "Doll."

Rita Renee Lange Weatherbee lives in the Black Hills of South Dakota, perfect surroundings for the writer she is becoming. She is the mother of three daughters and grandmother of thirteen grandchildren. Her hobbies include reading, hiking, scenic drives and pursuing her goal of traveling to all fifty states.

Marcia L. Wells received her Bachelor's degree with a major in English and minor in history, and a Master's degree in secondary education. After teaching secondary students for many years, she left education to pursue her other interests. She has written two fantasy books under the name M.L. Wells and is working on a third.

Kathy Whirity is a syndicated newspaper columnist who shares her musings on family life. She and her husband, Bill, are the proud grandparents of seven grandchildren who keep them on their toes, filling up their empty nest with the joys of grandparenthood. E-mail her at kathywhirity@yahoo.com.

Ernie Witham writes the humor column "Ernie's World," which appears in the *Montecito Journal* in Santa Barbara, CA. He is the author of three humor books, including his latest travel humor book: *Where are Pat and Ernie Now?* E-mail him at erniesworld.humor@gmail.com.

Sherri Woodbridge writes about her experience with Parkinson's disease weekly at *Parkinson's News Today*. She lives in Oregon with her husband, has three great children and three beautiful grandkids. She enjoys gardening, writing, and birding. She is currently working on a book about living with Parkinson's without fear.

Kristen Yankovitz resides in Cleveland, OH with her husband and six-year-old daughter. She enjoys writing and spending time with her family. Kristen is the Director of Sales & Marketing at a commercial janitorial firm, as well as a contributing blogger for *Northeast Ohio Parent* magazine.

Meet Amy Newmark

Amy Newmark is the bestselling author, editor-in-chief, and publisher of the *Chicken Soup for the Soul* book series. Since 2008, she has published more than 150 new books, most of them national bestsellers in the U.S. and Canada, more than doubling the number of Chicken Soup for the Soul titles in print today. She is also the author of *Simply Happy*, a crash course in Chicken Soup for the Soul advice and wisdom that is filled with easy-to-implement, practical tips for enjoying a better life.

Amy is credited with revitalizing the Chicken Soup for the Soul brand, which has been a publishing industry phenomenon since the first book came out in 1993. By compiling inspirational and aspirational true stories curated from ordinary people who have had extraordinary experiences, Amy has kept the twenty-six-year-old Chicken Soup for the Soul brand fresh and relevant.

Amy graduated *magna cum laude* from Harvard University where she majored in Portuguese and minored in French. She then embarked on a three-decade career as a Wall Street analyst, a hedge fund manager, and a corporate executive in the technology field. She is a Chartered Financial Analyst.

Her return to literary pursuits was inevitable, as her honors thesis in college involved traveling throughout Brazil's impoverished northeast region, collecting stories from regular people. She is delighted to have come full circle in her writing career — from collecting stories "from the people" in Brazil as a twenty-year-old to, three decades later, collecting stories "from the people" for Chicken Soup for the Soul.

When Amy and her husband Bill, the CEO of Chicken Soup for the Soul, are not working, they are visiting their four grown children and their first grandchild.

Follow Amy on Twitter @amynewmark. Listen to her free podcast — "Chicken Soup for the Soul with Amy Newmark" — on Apple Podcasts, Google Play, the Podcasts app on iPhone, or by using your favorite podcast app on other devices.

Thank You

We owe huge thanks to all of our contributors and fans. We were overwhelmed by the thousands of stories and poems you submitted about your experiences as a grandparent or a grandchild. Our Associate Publisher D'ette Corona, our Senior Editor Barbara LoMonaco, and our editors Susan Heim, Laura Dean, and Crescent LoMonaco made sure they read every single one.

Susan Heim did the first round of editing, D'ette Corona chose the perfect quotations to put at the beginning of each story, and editor-in-chief Amy Newmark edited the stories and shaped the final manuscript.

As we finished our work, D'ette Corona continued to be Amy's right-hand woman in creating the final manuscript and working with all our wonderful writers. Barbara LoMonaco and Kristiana Pastir, along with Elaine Kimbler, jumped in at the end to proof, proof, proof. And, yes, there will always be typos anyway, so feel free to let us know about them at webmaster@chickensoupforthesoul.com, and we will correct them in future printings.

The whole publishing team deserves a hand, including Executive Assistant Mary Fisher, Senior Director of Marketing Maureen Peltier, Senior Director of Production Victor Cataldo, and our graphic designer Daniel Zaccari, who turned our manuscript into this beautiful book.

Sharing Happiness, Inspiration, and Hope

Real people sharing real stories, every day, all over the world. In 2007, *USA Today* named *Chicken Soup for the Soul* one of the five most memorable books in the last quarter-century. With over 100 million books sold to date in the U.S. and Canada alone, more than 250 titles in print, and translations into nearly fifty languages, "chicken soup for the soul®" is one of the world's best-known phrases.

Today, twenty-six years after we first began sharing happiness, inspiration and hope through our books, we continue to delight our readers with new titles, but have also evolved beyond the bookstore with super premium pet food, television shows, a podcast, video journalism from aplus.com, movies and TV shows on the Popcornflix app, and licensed products, all revolving around true stories, as we continue "changing the world one story at a time®." Thanks for reading!

Share with Us

We all have had Chicken Soup for the Soul moments in our lives. If you would like to share your story or poem with millions of people around the world, go to chickensoup. com and click on "Submit Your Story." You may be able to help another reader and become a published author at the same time. Some of our past contributors have launched writing and speaking careers from the publication of their stories in our books!

We only accept story submissions via our website. They are no longer accepted via mail or fax. Visit our website, www.chickensoup. com, and click on Submit Your Story for our writing guidelines and a list of topics we are working on.

To contact us regarding other matters, please send us an e-mail through webmaster@chickensoupforthesoul.com, or fax or write us at:

Chicken Soup for the Soul
P.O. Box 700
Cos Cob, CT 06807-0700
Fax: 203-861-7194

One more note from your friends at Chicken Soup for the Soul: Occasionally, we receive an unsolicited book manuscript from one of our readers, and we would like to respectfully inform you that we do not accept unsolicited manuscripts, and we must discard the ones that appear.

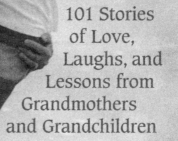

Chicken Soup for the Soul.

Grandmothers

101 Stories
of Love,
Laughs, and
Lessons from
Grandmothers
and Grandchildren

Jack Canfield,
Mark Victor Hansen
& Amy Newmark

Paperback: 978-1-935096-64-1
eBook: 978-1-61159-187-3

More heartwarming

Chicken Soup for the Soul

MOM KNOWS BEST

101 Stories of Love, Gratitude & Wisdom

Amy Newmark

Paperback: 978-1-61159-987-9
eBook: 978-1-61159-287-0

stories about love and wisdom

Chicken Soup for the Soul®

Grand and Great

Our **101** BEST STORIES

Grandparents
and Grandchildren
Share Their Stories of
Love and Wisdom

LARGE
PRINT

Jack Canfield
& Mark Victor Hansen
edited by Amy Newmark

Paperback: 978-1-935096-09-2
eBook: 978-1-61159-170-5

Classic tales of love,

Our
101
BEST
STORIES

Chicken Soup
for the Soul

Older &
Wiser

Stories of
Inspiration,
Humor, and
Wisdom about
Life at a
Certain Age

LARGE PRINT

Jack Canfield
& Mark Victor Hansen

edited by Amy Newmark

Paperback: 978-1-935096-17-7
eBook: 978-1-61159-177-4

wisdom and the young at heart

Chicken Soup *for the* Soul

Changing your world one story at a time®
www.chickensoup.com